Extra Class

FCC License Preparation for Element 4 Extra Class Theory

by
Gordon West
WB6NOA

Fifth Edition

Master Publishing, Inc.

This book was developed and published by:
Master Publishing, Inc.
Niles, Illinois

Editing by:
Pete Trotter, KB9SMG

Thanks to Suzy West, N6GLF; Chip, K7JA; Janet, KL7MF; Robert, K2RM;
Bob, W6LOG; Ken, W6IEZ; Bryon, N6IFU; Clint, K6LCS; Peter, AF6DS;
George, WD6EJO; Jim, N6JF; Steve, K4CJX; Jim, KS4O; Carl, AF6HE; John,
K6JFG; Bill, K6ACJ; Tom, W6ORG; Bernie, K2YA; Ron, N1ABB; Don,
W6GPS; Jim and family, N3UZ; Tom, W6WC; Jerry Black; Alan, KB3HIP;
George and Rosie, WA6RIK; and Neil, KC2KY.

Julian Frost, N3JF photography
Mr. Elmer and cartoons by Carson Haring, AC0BU
CD masters by Mike Koegel, N6PTO

Printing by:
Arby Graphic Service
Niles, Illinois

Photograph Credit:
All photographs that do not have a source identification are either courtesy of
RadioShack, the author, or Master Publishing, Inc. originals.
Cover photo by Larry Mulvehill, WB2ZPI, *CQ Magazine*

Fifth Edition
9 8 7 6 5 4 3 2 1

Table of Contents

QUESTION POOL NOMENCLATURE
The latest nomenclature changes recommended by the Volunteer Examiner Coordinator's Question Pool Committee (QPC) for the Element 4 question pool effective July 1, 2008 and valid to June 30, 2012 have been incorporated in this book.

FCC RULES, REGULATIONS AND POLICIES
The NCVEC QPC releases revised question pools on a regular cycle, and deletions as necessary. The FCC releases changes to FCC rules, regulations and policies as they are implemented. This book includes the most recent information released by the FCC when this copy was printed.

Preface

Amateur Extra Class is the highest-level Federal Communications Commission license you can hold in the amateur radio service. Achieving the Extra Class license immediately opens up additional sub-bands for voice operation on worldwide frequencies, along with additional, exclusive Extra Class sub-bands for Morse code and data. Your Extra Class license gives you full operating privileges across the complete spectrum of every ham radio band!

The Morse code test has been totally eliminated for all classes of amateur radio license. Prior to 2000, Extra Class applicants were required to pass a 20 word-per-minute Morse code test. From 2000 through 2006, the code test for General Class was reduced to 5 words-per-minute, which also satisfied the Extra Class code requirement. On February 23, 2007, all Morse code testing was completely eliminated by the FCC. And guess what? More hams than ever are learning the code and practicing CW over the worldwide airwaves, with no fear of a code "stress test!" So if you haven't already done so, I encourage you to learn the code. It's fun!

Achieving the Extra Class license allows you to administer all amateur radio exams. As an Extra Class licensee, you may be accredited as a Volunteer Examiner to prepare and administer ham exams as a member of a 3-person VE team. You also could qualify to become a contact volunteer examiner to help coordinate ham exam teams in your area. This is a great way to help our hobby and service grow!

The new Element 4 Extra Class question pool included in this book is valid for written examinations from July 1, 2008 through June 30, 2012. The total number of questions in the new pool are about the same as in years past – 738, with 50 of these multiple choice questions appearing on your upcoming Extra Class exam. No additional math complexity has been added to this new fresh pool, but there are many new questions on newer operating modes and techniques. My book explains everything about the Extra Class:

- *Chapter 1* reviews the operating privileges you'll earn when you pass your Extra Class exam.
- *Chapter 2* is a brief review of the history of ham radio licensing and explains the exam requirements for all of the current FCC Amateur Radio licenses.
- *Chapter 3* contains all 738 Element 4 questions and answers, along with my full description of the correct answer, followed by the correct answer key.
- *Chapter 4* tells you what to expect on examination day, and reviews the latest FCC e-filing requirements.

Welcome Advanced and General Class operators to Extra Class exam preparation! Get set for new privileges and increased VE opportunities. I hope to hear you on our top bands very soon!

Gordon West

73

Extra Class Privileges

The Extra Class amateur operator/primary station license permits you to use all segments of every worldwide band for long-distance voice, data, and video amateur communications, expanding your General Class or grandfathered Advanced Class operating privileges. Of course, you also keep all of the privileges you earned as a Technician Class operator.

Extra Class has always been recognized as the "top" amateur radio license because of the unlimited skywave privileges it provides on each of the worldwide ham bands. Earning the Extra Class privileges requires passing written exams for Element 2, Technician Class, and Element 3, General Class, prior to taking your Element 4 exam.

Never in the history of amateur radio has it been easier than now to achieve the Extra Class license. There no longer is a Morse code test required. Certainly, the old 20 wpm code requirement was a huge obstacle for many accomplished ham radio operators who wanted to achieve Extra Class but just couldn't get past that tough, tough CW test. In February, 2007, the Federal Communications Commission ended code test requirements for all amateur radio licenses, concluding that "...this change eliminates an unnecessary burden that may discourage current amateur radio operators from advancing their skills and participating more fully in the benefits of amateur radio." Most other nations had already dropped their Morse code test requirements, too.

Just because the code test has been eliminated, it doesn't mean earning your Extra Class license will be a snap. For most of us, it requires having spent time developing our operating skills, and means spending some serious time diligently studying the advanced electronic theory and operating techniques asked in the question pool. Once you pass your exam, becoming an Extra Class means you've reached the top of our hobby and service.

The Extra Class license allows you to give something back to the amateur service as a volunteer conducting examinations. As an Extra Class amateur operator, you may become a lead Volunteer Examiner. You are qualified to prepare and administer all levels of amateur radio testing as a member of a 3-person accredited VE team. You also can help recruit and organize other hams to serve on your VE team. This is a great opportunity to help our hobby grow and prosper!

When you pass your Extra Class examination, you will gain a 25-kHz "window" of exclusive CW privileges at the bottom end of each of the 80-, 40-, 20-, and 15-meter bands. You also gain a total of 150 kHz of additional "windows" of exclusive Extra Class phone privileges on 75-, 20-, and 15-meters. If you are a General Class operator upgrading to Extra, you will gain valuable DX operating privileges on the Advanced and Extra Class bands. Remember, grandfathered Advanced Class operators continue to enjoy their own sub-band privileges indefinitely.

WORLDWIDE SPECTRUM

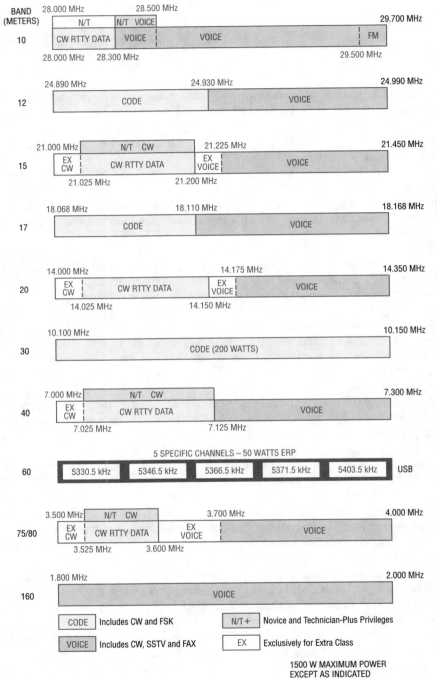

Figure 1-1. Extra Class Privileges

And, as an Extra Class operator, you will be eligible for the AA-ALx2 or 2x1 short-block call signs that are reserved exclusively for those amateurs who have made it to the very highest level of license in the amateur service. You may wish to take advantage of the Vanity Call Sign program, too, to select specific, available call letters of your choice (see Chapter 4 for details on this).

And probably best of all, when you reach Extra Class you do not have to prepare for anymore license upgrades. You're the top!

Now, let's take a look at privileges of the Extra Class license.

THE EXTRA CLASS LICENSE

Let's begin by taking a look at *Figure 1-1*, which graphically illustrates your overall Extra Class privileges on the 160-meter medium-frequency (MF) band from 1.8 to 2.0 MHz, and on the 80-, 40-, 30-, 20-, 17-, 15-, 12-, and 10-meter high frequency (HF) bands from 3.0 to 30 MHz.

Morse code privileges – where only CW and data are allowed – are shown in the designated area on the left side of each band edge. The areas that include voice privileges are shown in the designated areas on the right. In the 80-, 20-, and 15-meter bands, we illustrate areas exclusively for Extra class that are not shared with grandfathered Advanced Class operators. If you are upgrading from Advanced Class, passing the Extra Class exam immediately gives you access to these Extra Class sub-bands.

If you're upgrading from General Class, you not only gain all Extra Class sub-bands, but you also gain all grandfathered Advanced Class sub-band privileges, too. In other words, as an Extra Class operator, *you get everything!*

Take a look at *Figure 1-1* for Extra Class HF license privileges and see the "EX" – this is where you have *exclusive* voice operating privileges and CW privileges shared with no one other than Extra Class operators.

EXTRA CLASS LICENSE PRIVILEGES

160 METERS: 1.8 MHZ - 2.0 MHZ.

Your Extra Class privileges are the same as grandfathered Advanced and General on this band. You may operate voice and code from one end of the band to the other. The 160-meter band is great for long-distance nighttime communications. It is located just above the AM broadcast radio frequencies. At night, 160 meters lets you work the world.

75/80 METERS: 3.5 MHZ - 4.0 MHZ.

As an Extra Class operator, your exclusive voice privileges have recently been expanded to include 3.600 to 3.700 MHz, not shared with any other class of ham license. This is a huge increase for night time DX voice contacts, well over 6000 miles away. You also gain exclusive CW privileges at the bottom of the band.

40 METERS: 7 MHZ - 7.3 MHZ.

Extra Class operators have an exclusive 25 kHz of CW operating at the bottom of the band. Voice privileges now begin at 7.125, a recent increase in "elbow room" on the 40 meter band. At nighttime, it's possible to operate both code as well as voice throughout the world on 40 meters. However, 40 meters is shared with worldwide AM shortwave broadcast stations, so at night be prepared to dodge megawatt carriers playing everything from rock and roll to political broadcasts. During daylight hours, the range on 40 meters is limited to approximately 500 miles.

30 METERS: 10.1 MHZ - 10.15 MHZ.

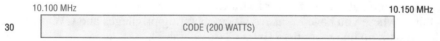

This is a shared band for code only between General, grandfathered Advanced, and Extra Class operators. 30 meters is located just above the 10-MHz WWV time broadcasts on shortwave radio. Voice is not allowed on this band by any class of amateur operator. Maximum PEP power level is limited to 200 watts.

20 METERS: 14 MHZ - 14.350 MHZ.

Extra Class operators have 2 band segments of exclusive frequency privileges. For CW, you gain the bottom 25 kHz of the band. For voice, you have exclusive use of 14.150 to 14.175 MHz, not shared with any other class of license! Happy DX! Of course, since the Extra Class license offers all band privileges, you can operate on those shared frequencies for Advanced and General Class, too.

20 meters is where the real DX activity takes place. Almost 24 hours a day, you should be able to work stations in excess of 5,000 miles with a modest antenna set up. If you are a mariner, most maritime mobile operations take place on the 20-meter band. If you are into recreational vehicles (RVs), there are nets all over the country especially for you. And if you enjoy DXing the world and collecting rare QSL cards, 20 meters is where the action is!

17 METERS: 18.068 MHZ - 18.168 MHZ.

18.068 MHz	18.110 MHz	18.168 MHz
17	CODE	VOICE

There is plenty of elbow room here with a lot of foreign DX coming in during the day and evenings. While the Extra Class operator does not have any exclusive portions on 17 meters, Extra Class licensees have the entire band from 18.068 MHz all the way up to 18.168 MHz. Voice begins at 18.110 MHz, and is shared with General and grandfathered Advanced operators.

15 METERS: 21.0 MHZ - 21.450 MHZ.

The Extra Class operator has 2 exclusive operating segments on the 15 meter band. The bottom 25 kHz is reserved for the Extra Class operator. 21.200 to 21.225 MHz is also reserved for Extra Class operators, along with full privileges all the way up to the top of the band, 21.450 MHz.

The 15-meter band is loved by hams throughout the world because it has extremely low noise, and strong signal levels. There is little power line noise on 15 meters, and almost no atmospheric static. Band conditions on 15 meters usually favor daytime and evening contacts in the direction of the sun. Late at night, 15 meters begins to fade away, and you won't get skywave coverage until the next morning. 15 meters is a popular band for mobile operators because antennas are smaller.

12 METERS: 24.890 MHZ - 24.990 MHZ.

24.890 MHz	24.930 MHz	24.990 MHz
12	CODE	VOICE

The 12-meter band is a daytime band for the best long-range DX, and the Extra Class operator shares this entire band with General Class and grandfathered Advanced Class operators. CW starts at the bottom of the band at 24.890 MHz, and voice begins in the middle of the band at 24.930 MHz. There is plenty of excitement on the 12-meter band, and antenna requirements are smaller.

10 METERS: 28.0 MHZ - 29.7 MHZ.

BAND (METERS)	28.000 MHz		28.500 MHz		29.700 MHz
	N/T	N/T VOICE			
10	CW RTTY DATA	VOICE	VOICE		FM

28.000 MHz   28.300 MHz   29.500 MHz

There is plenty of excitement shared by all classes of amateur operators on the 10-meter band. Worldwide and continental band openings may pop up anytime there are extra amounts of solar activity. And during the summertime, Sporadic-E ionospheric conditions make 1,500-mile band openings exciting for all operators on "10." The Extra Class operator has the entire 10-meter band from top to bottom, with plenty of CW activity at 28.1 MHz, propagation beacons at 28.2 MHz, phone excitement between 28.3 MHz to 29.0 MHz, and all sorts of elbow room, including FM operation, way up there between 29.5 and 29.7 MHz.

VOICE BAND EXPANSION

The Federal Communications Commission's WT Docket 04-140 Report and Order, issued in late 2006, amends Part 97 Rules to provide expanded voice privileges on the worldwide bands for General, Advanced and Extra Class operators. Novice and Technician licensees also were given additional CW privileges on the 80-, 40-, 15-, and 10-meter bands. This Report and Order is the FCC's response to "grossly underused... waste in spectrum..." within the CW portion of these bands. The Report and Order also removed the 200 watt power limitation for General, Advanced, and Extra Class operators in the CW portion of these bands.

On 75 meters, Generals may now operate voice from 3800 to 4000 kHz, an increase of 50 kHz. Advanced Class licensees are able to operate voice from 3700 to 4000 kHz, a 75 kHz increase. Extra Class operators gain 150 kHz of voice elbow room from 3600 to 4000 kHz.

On 40 meters, Advanced and Extra Class operators are able to use voice from 7125 to 7300 kHz, an increase of 25 kHz. General Class may now use from 7175 to 7300 kHz, a 50 kHz increase.

On 15 meters, Generals gain an additional 25 kHz of voice from 21.275 to 21.450 MHz.

Novice and Technician operators gain Morse code only privileges in an expanded portion of the lower half of 10-, 15-, 40-, and 80-meters.

Technician Class operators, who have never passed a code test, are now permitted 10 meter SSB voice communications from 28.300 MHz to 28.500 MHz, giving brand new ham operators a taste of skywave SSB voice communications on a portion of one worldwide band. As a new Extra, spend some time on "10" and encourage these new hams to upgrade!

6 Meters and Up. Your Extra Class license allows you unlimited band privileges and unlimited emission privileges shared with all classes of license from Technician Class on up on the following bands:

Meters	Frequency
6 meters	50-54 MHz
2 meters	144-148 MHz
1.25 meters	222-225 MHz (219-220 MHz Digital)
70 centimeters	420-450 MHz
35 centimeters	902-928 MHz
23 centimeters	1240-1300 MHz

Microwave Bands. Many Extra Class operators are employed by companies that specialize in microwave electronics. The Extra Class license allows for unlimited privileges and unlimited emission privileges on the following microwave bands:

Frequency	Frequency
2300-2310 MHz	47.0-47.2 GHz
2390-2450 MHz	75.5-81.0 GHz
3.3-3.5 GHz	119.98-120.02 GHz
5.65-5.925 GHz	142-149 GHz
10.0-10.5 GHz (popular X band)	241-250 GHz
24.0-24.25 GHz	All above 300 GHz

Look for plenty of Extra Class excitement on the 10-GHz band. This may soon become the new frontier for those amateur operators establishing records on microwave frequencies.

BECOME A VOLUNTEER EXAMINER

Here's some additional information to further encourage you to become a Volunteer Examiner once you upgrade to Extra Class.

The Telecommunications Act of 1996 removed many of the burdensome conflict-of-interest, record keeping, and financial-certification requirements previously imposed on VEs and VECs (Volunteer Examiner Coordinators). As a result of these rule changes, there no longer are any regulatory prohibitions preventing VEs or VECs from distributing license preparation (study) materials (with or without profit) to anyone, or from being employed by a company that manufactures or sells amateur radio station equipment or license study materials. Amateurs who serve as ham class instructors may now distribute license preparation materials to their students and also serve as Volunteer Examiners for the course examinations. Serving as a VE is a great way to help our hobby grow!

BE AN EXTRA CLASS ELMER – TEACH A CLASS

When you pass your upcoming Extra Class exam, you will have arrived at the TOP! You can share your enthusiasm for our amateur radio service by becoming a Ham Instructor. The W5YI Ham Instructor program is designed to help spread the word – and training – to hobby radio enthusiasts to encourage them to earn their entry-level ham radio license.

Ham Instructors may find kids and scouting as a great place to introduce ham radio and develop amateur radio training classes. Boaters, flyers, and RVers are *all* interested in what amateur radio can do to make their traveling safer and more enjoyable. You might become an Elmer and help them locate club or local weekend classes to earn their entry-level Technician Class license.

The new Technician Class license is the ideal starting point for everyone wanting to learn about ham radio. No Morse code test involved! The Technician exam trains would-be hams on techniques of going on the air for the first time, and learning about all

Become a Ham Ambassador and help our hobby grow!

the excitement ham radio has to offer, including repeaters and satellites.

As a W5YI Ham Instructor, the industry will support you with free band plan charts, frequency guides, and other training materials. Extra Class Ham Instructors help our service continually grow. To learn more about the W5YI Ham Instructor program, call 800-669-9594, and join the outreach program to bring more kids and radio enthusiasts into our hobby and public service.

SUMMARY

Whether you are upgrading to Extra Class from the grandfathered Advance Class license or the General Class license, you will gain some exciting new privileges on shared and Extra-only voice and CW portions of the bands for worldwide communications. This is where all the rare DX happens, and you will be operating in an area of the lower portion of the sub-bands where General Class operators can only listen in with envy!

But your biggest privilege as an Extra Class operator is the ability for you to work closely with a Volunteer Examination Coordinator and serve as a VE team leader. Now that General Class operators, along with grandfathered Advanced Class operators, may also assist Extra Class operators in administering license exams, your roll as a contact Volunteer Examiner will be an important one for the growth of the testing teams – and the growth of our hobby – throughout the country.

2

A Little Ham History!

Ham radio has changed a lot in the 100+ years since radio's inception. In the past 15 years, we've seen some monumental changes! So, before we go any further, I'd like to give you a brief history of ham radio licensing in the U.S. After all, as an Extra Class operator administering exams, you should be able to answer those "rookie" questions about the history of our hobby.

In this chapter you'll learn all of the licensing requirements under the FCC rules that became effective April 15, 2000. And you'll learn about the six classes of license that were in effect *prior* to those rules changes. That way, when you run into a Novice, Technician Plus or Advanced class operator on the air, you'll have some understanding of their skill level, experience, and frequency privileges.

WHAT IS THE AMATEUR SERVICE?

There are more than 650,000 licensed amateur radio operators in the U.S. today. The Federal Communications Commission, the Federal agency responsible for licensing amateur operators, defines our radio service this way:

"The amateur service is for qualified persons of all ages who are interested in radio technique solely with a personal aim and without pecuniary interest."

Ham radio is first and foremost a fun hobby! In addition, it is a service. And note the word "qualified" in the FCC's definition – that's the reason why you're studying for an exam; so you can pass the exam, prove you are qualified, and get on the Extra Class bands.

Millions of operators around the world exchange ham radio greetings and messages by voice, teleprinting, telegraphy, facsimile, and television worldwide. Japan, alone, has more than a million hams! It is very commonplace for U.S. amateurs to communicate with Russian amateurs, while China is just getting started with its amateur service. Being a ham operator is a great way to promote international good will.

The benefits of ham radio are countless! Ham operators are probably known best for their contributions during times of disaster. In recent years, many recreational sailors in the Caribbean who have been attacked by modern-day pirates have had their lives saved by hams directing rescue efforts. Following the 9/11 terrorist attacks on the World Trade Center and the Pentagon, literally thousands of local hams assisted with emergency communications. In addition, over the years, amateurs have contributed much to electronic technology. They have even designed and built their own orbiting communications satellites.

If you study hard and make the effort, you are going to the top echelon of our service – Extra Class! Follow the suggestions in my book and your chances of passing the written exam are excellent.

A BRIEF HISTORY OF AMATEUR RADIO LICENSING

Government licensing of radio stations and amateur operators began with The Radio Act of 1912, which mandated the first Federal licensing of all radio stations and assigned amateurs to the short wavelengths of less than 200 meters. These "new" requirements didn't deter them, and within a few years there were thousands of licensed ham operators in the United States.

Since electromagnetic signals do not respect national boundaries, radio is international in scope. National governments enact and enforce radio laws within a framework of international agreements, which are overseen by the International Telecommunications Union. The ITU is a worldwide United Nations agency headquartered in Geneva, Switzerland. The ITU divides the radio spectrum into a number of frequency bands, with each band reserved for a particular use. Amateur radio is fortunate to have many bands allocated to it all across the radio spectrum.

In the U.S., the Federal Communications Commission is the government agency responsible for the regulation of wire and radio communications. The FCC further allocates frequency bands to the various services in accordance with the ITU plan – including the Amateur Service – and regulates stations and operators.

In the early years of amateur radio licensing in the U.S., the classes of licenses were designated by the letters "A," "B," and "C." The highest license class with the most privileges was "A." In 1951, the FCC dropped the letter designations and gave the license classes names. They also added a new Novice class. In 1967, the Advanced class was added to the Novice, Technician, General and Extra classes. The General exam required 13-wpm code speed, and Extra required 20-wpm. Each of the five written exams were progressively more comprehensive and formed what came to be known as the *Incentive Licensing System.*

In 1979, the international Amateur Service regulations were changed to permit all countries to waive the manual Morse code proficiency requirement for "...stations making use exclusively of frequencies above 30 MHz." This set the stage for the creation of the Technician "no-code" license, which occurred in 1991, when the 5-wpm Morse code requirement for the Technician class was the eliminated.

By this time, there were a total of six Amateur Service license classes – Novice, Technician, Technician-Plus, General, Advanced, and Extra – along with five written exams and three Morse code tests used to qualify hams for their various licenses.

The Amateur Service Is Restructured

Following an extensive review begun in 1998, the FCC implemented a complete restructuring of the U.S. amateur service that became effective April 15, 2000. Today, applicants can only be examined for three amateur license classes:

- Technician class – the VHF/UHF entry level license;
- General class – the HF entry level license, and
- Amateur Extra class – a technically-oriented senior license.

Most recently, the FCC updated its amateur radio rules by eliminating the Morse code test requirement. The new rule went into effect in February, 2007, and it means that you can earn any class of license – Technician, General, and Extra class – simply by passing written exams.

Individuals with licenses issued before April 15, 2000, have been "grandfathered" under the new rules. This means that Novice and Advanced class amateurs are able to modify and renew their licenses indefinitely. Technician-Plus amateur licenses will be renewed as Technician class, and these licensees will retain their HF operating privileges indefinitely. The FCC elected not to change the operating privileges of any class, so you may hear some of these "grandfathered" hams when you get on the air. And, all Technicians gained HF CW sub-bands.

Self-Testing In The Amateur Service

Prior to 1984, all amateur radio exams were administered by FCC personnel at FCC Field Offices around the country. In 1984, the VEC (Volunteer Examiner Coordinator) System was formed after Congress passed laws that allowed the FCC to accept the services of Volunteer Examiners (or VEs) to prepare and administer amateur service license examinations. The testing activity of VEs is managed by Volunteer Examiner Coordinators (or VECs). A VEC acts as the administrative liaison between the VEs who administer the various ham examinations and the FCC, which grants the license.

A team of three VEs, who must be approved by a VEC, is required to conduct amateur radio examinations.

In 1986, the FCC turned over responsibility for maintenance of the exam questions to the National Conference of VECs, which appointed a Question Pool Committee (QPC) to develop and revise the various question pools according to a schedule.

That completes your history lesson. If you'd like to learn more, visit The Ham Radio History forum at www.YahooGroups.com/list/Ham-Radio-History.

OPERATOR LICENSE CLASSES AND EXAM REQUIREMENTS

To qualify for an amateur operator/primary station license, a person must pass an examination according to FCC guidelines. The degree of skill and knowledge that the candidate demonstrates to the examiners determines the class of operator license for which the person is qualified.

Anyone is eligible to become a U.S. licensed amateur operator (including foreign nationals, if they are not a representative of a foreign government). There is no age limitation – if you can pass the examinations, you can become a ham!

Today, there are three amateur operator licenses issued by the FCC – Technician, General, and Extra. Each license requires progressively higher levels of learning and proficiency, and each gives you additional operating privileges. This is known as *incentive licensing* – a method of strengthening the amateur service by offering more radio spectrum privileges in exchange for more operating and electronic knowledge.

There is no waiting time required to upgrade from one amateur license class to another, nor any required waiting time to retake a failed exam. You can even take all three examinations at one sitting if you're really brave! *Table 3-1* details the amateur service license structure and required examinations.

Table 3-1: Current Amateur License Classes and Exam Requirements
(Effective April 15, 2000)

License Class	Exam Element	Type of Examination
Technician Class	2	35-question, multiple-choice written examination. Minimum passing score is 26 questions answered correctly (74%).
General Class	3	35-question, multiple-choice written examination. Minimum passing score is 26 questions answered correctly (74%).
Extra Class	4	50-question, multiple-choice written examination. Minimum passing score is 37 questions answered correctly (74%).

ABOUT THE WRITTEN EXAMS

What is the focus of each of the written examinations, and how does it relate to gaining expanding amateur radio privileges as you move up the ladder toward your Extra class license? *Table 3-2* summarizes the subjects covered in each written examination element.

Table 3-2. Question Element Subjects

Exam Element	License Class	Subjects
Element 2	Technician	Elementary operating procedures, radio regulations, and a smattering of beginning electronics. Emphasis is on VHF and UHF operating.
Element 3	General	HF (high-frequency) operating privileges, amateur practices, radio regulations, and a little more electronics. Emphasis is on HF bands.
Element 4	Extra	Basically a technical examination. Covers specialized operating procedures, more radio regulations, formulas and heavy math. Also covers the specifics on amateur testing procedures.

No Jumping Allowed

All written examinations for an amateur radio license are additive. You *cannot* skip over a license class or by-pass a required examination as you upgrade from Technician to General to Extra. For example, to obtain a General class license, you must first take and pass the Element 2 written examination for the Technician class license, plus the Element 3 written examination. To obtain the Extra class license, you must first pass the Element 2 (Technician) and Element 3 (General) written examinations, and then successfully pass the Element 4 (Extra) written examination.

TAKING THE ELEMENT 4 EXAM

Here's a summary of what you can expect when you go to the session to take the Element 4 written examination for your Extra class license. Detailed information about how to find an exam session, what to expect at the session, what to bring to the session, and more, is included in Chapter 4.

All amateur radio examinations are administered by a team of at least three Volunteer Examiners (VEs) who have been accredited by a Volunteer Examiner Coordinator (VEC). The VEs are licensed hams who volunteer their time to help our hobby grow.

Examination sessions are organized under the auspices of an approved VEC. A list of VECs is located in the Appendix on page 273. The W5YI-VEC and the ARRL-VEC are the 2 largest examination groups in the country, and they test in all 50 states. Their 3-member, accredited examination teams are just about everywhere. So when you call the VEC, you can be assured they probably have an examination team only a few miles from where you are reading this book right now!

The Element 4 written exam is a multiple-choice format. The VEs will give you a test paper that contains the 50 questions and multiple choice answers, and an answer sheet for you to complete. Take your time! Make sure you read each question carefully and select the correct answer. Once you're finished, double check your work before handing in your test papers.

The VEs will score your test immediately, and you'll know before you leave the exam site whether you've passed. Chances are very good that, if you've studied hard, you'll get that passing grade!

Want to find a test site fast?
Visit the W5YI-VEC website at **www.w5yi.org**, or call 800-669-9594.

GETTING/KEEPING YOUR CALL SIGN

Once the VE team scores your exam and you've passed, the process of getting your upgrade FCC Amateur Radio Licenses begins – usually the same day.

At the exam site, you will complete NCVEC Form 605, which is your application to the FCC for your license upgrade. If you pass the exam, the VE team will send the required paperwork on to their VEC. The VEC reviews the paperwork submitted by your exam team and then files your application with the FCC. This filing is done electronically, and your upgrade license will be granted and posted on the FCC's website within a few days. As soon as you pass your exam, you are permitted to go on the air as a licensed Extra Class operator.

Should you keep your old call sign, or ask for a new one? If you check the box on the Form 605 asking for a new call sign, the FCC's computer will assign one to you. But you might not like what you get. So I suggest you stick with your old call sign, and if you want a new, specific call file an application for a Vanity Call Sign. See Chapter 4 for more details.

IT'S EASY!

Probably the primary pre-requisite for passing any amateur radio operator license exam is the will to do it. If you follow my suggestions in this book, your chances of passing the Extra Class exam are excellent.

Yes, indeed, the year 2000 brought some big changes to ham radio, and everyone comes out a winner! There has never been a better time to join the top ranks of ham radio hobbyists. So study hard! We hope to hear you on the Extra Class bands very soon.

3

Getting Ready for the Exam

This chapter includes the entire, new Element 4 Question Pool questions and answers that can be used to make-up your 50-question Extra Class Element 4 written theory examination *exactly as they will appear on your exam.* Your exam will have 50 questions, and a score of 37 or more correctly-answered questions (74%) will earn you a passing grade – which means you cannot have more than 13 wrong. Answer at least 37 questions correctly, and you pass the Extra Class examination!

> THIS EXTRA CLASS QUESTION POOL IS VALID FROM
> JULY 1, 2008, THROUGH JUNE 30, 2012.

The Element 4 question pool contains a total of 738 active questions and multiple-choice answers and distracters (the false answers are called *distracters.*) 50 of these questions will appear on your upcoming Element 4 written examination. All of these examination questions, plus the precise multiple-choice answers – one of which is the correct answer – *are identical to those included in this book.*

The Volunteer Examiners are not permitted to reword the questions, nor are they permitted to change any of the right or wrong answers (but they can change the A B C D *order* of the answers). *Every question in this book, letter for letter, word for word, number for number, and every right and wrong answer, will be exactly the same on your upcoming 50-question Extra Class Element 4 exam.*

In this new 5th edition of my book, my emphasis is to educate you about Extra Class operating techniques, rules and regs, propagation, electrical theory and practical circuits, antennas, and more. I do this by placing the correct answer key at the very end of my explanation of the correct answer that appears after each question and 4 possible answers. In addition to some memory tricks to help you remember the correct answer, I also provide hints on how to identify wrong answers that often look very much like the correct one. Of course, my explanations will not appear on your test papers when you take your Element 4 written exam.

The new Element 4 Extra Class question pool was developed by the Question Pool Committee of the National Conference of Volunteer Exam Coordinators. They began by carefully reviewing the most recent Extra Class question pool, editing out more than 100 obsolete or duplicate questions, and then adding in about 100 brand new questions designed to keep the pool up-to-date with newer technology and current FCC rules and regulations. This new 2008-12 question pool was carefully developed by the QPC under the leadership of chairman Jim Wiley, KL7CC, Anchorage Amateur Radio Club VEC; and committee members Roland Anders, K3RA, Laurel Amateur Radio Club VEC; Perry Green, WY1O, ARRL VEC; Larry Pollock, NB5X, W5YI VEC, and Editor Tom Fuszard, KF9PU, Milwaukee Radio Amateurs Club VEC.

Three dozen additional volunteers (including me!) also contributed potential test questions to the Question Pool Committee. We all want to thank the members of the Question Pool Committee and their Editor for their dedication and the hundreds of hours spent updating a very old Extra Class pool that contained some Q&As dating back to the '60s. Thanks, Team, for a fresh, new Extra Class question pool!

WHAT THE EXAM CONTAINS

Again, your exam will be comprised of 50 questions taken from the Element 4 question pool. The new pool is divided into 10 sub-elements. *Table 2-1* shows you the subelement topics, the total number of questions for each sub-element, and the number of questions from each subelement that will appear on your exam. Carefully study *Table 2-1* – it will help you understand how the questions are distributed among the 9 sub-elements and how your exam will be constructed.

Table 2-1. Question Distribution for the Extra Class Element 4 Exam

Subelement Number	Subelement Topic	No. of Questions in Pool	No. of Questions on Exam
E1	Commission's Rules (FCC rules for the Amateur Radio services)	85	6
E2	Operating Practices & Procedures (Amateur station operating procedures)	69	5
E3	Radio Wave Propagation (Radio wave propagation characteristics)	36	3
E4	Amateur Radio Technology & Measurements (Amateur Radio practices)	72	5
E5	Electrical Principles (Electrical principles as applied to amateur station equipment)	72	4
E6	Circuit Components (Amateur station equipment circuit components)	89	6
E7	Practical Circuits (Practical circuits employed in amateur station equipment)	129	8
E8	Signals and Emissions (Signals and emissions transmitted by amateur stations)	61	4
E9	Antennas and Transmission Lines (Amateur station antennas and feed lines)	114	8
E0	Safety	11	1
Total		738	50

(Titles in parentheses are the subelement titles on which you will be examined.)

NOTE: *The Element 4 Question Pool originally contained 741 questions. Three questions were deleted by the QPC prior to publication of this book, resulting in a pool with 738 active questions. The deleted questions do not appear in this book*

QUESTION POOL VALID THROUGH JUNE 30, 2012

The Element 4 question pool in this book is valid from July 1, 2008, until June 30, 2012. During this period, the questions and answers are frozen. The exact numerical values found in each Extra Class question and answer will remain precisely the same. If FCC rules change or advancements in technology cause any question to become obsolete, that question will be eliminated from your test and there will be no surprises in the exam room.

The new 2008-12 Extra Class Element 4 pool covers many new subject areas designed to keep the Extra Class questions fresh:

- *Ham Rules and Regulations on band edge SSB operation*
- *Satellite operation and modes*
- *ATV and SSTV technicalities*
- *Contest operating*
- *Contest log files*
- *PSK and QPSK*
- *Antenna takeoff patterns*
- *Antenna analyzer versus SWR bridge*
- *NPN transistors*
- *Impedance calculations*
- *Q for a series tuned circuit*
- *dBm noise floor calculations*
- *Roofing filter topics*

- *Receiver blocking dynamic range*
- *Intermodulation Interference*
- *Third order intercept levels*
- *Noise blankers*
- *RF attenuators*
- *Schottky Barrier diodes*
- *Emitter amplifier bias*
- *Third order intermodulation distortion*
- *Parametric amplifiers*
- *High voltage power supply filters*
- *Frequency counters*
- *Antenna modeling*
- *Safety practices, RF radiation hazards, Hazardous materials*

QUESTION CODING

Each question in the Element 4 Extra Class pool is assigned a coded number using a system of numbers and letters. *Figure 2-1* explains the coding for question E5G09. "E" stands for Extra Class Element 4 question pool. "5" indicates subelement 5, Electrical Principles. "G" indicates the sub-element group on Circuit Q; Reactive Power; Power Factor. "09" indicates the ninth question dealing with this topic.

Indicates Extra Class Element 4

Indicates the actual question number from this group's topic

E 5 G 0 9

Indicates the question is taken from subelement 5 — Electrical Principles

Indicates a specific topic — Circuit Q; Reactive Power; Power Factor

Figure 2-1. Examination Question Coding

If you carefully study the numbering scheme, you will find that each subelement is divided into topic groups, and there will be one question on your examination taken from each topic group. If there is a specific group of questions which are giving you a hard time, study them later. Only one question will be taken from any one group.

To facilitate in identifying subelement groups, we describe the subelement contents by individual groups of questions. This is good news for those of you who may be a bit rusty on a specific topic, knowing ahead of time that your upcoming Extra Class examination will only have one question out of each topic group.

STUDY HINTS

You're probably saying: "738 questions and answers is an overwhelming number of questions and answers to memorize for the new Extra Class exam!" But good news – almost every question is asked at least twice with just slightly different phrasing. Many of the math questions are based on single-formulas; and once you know the formula, you can easily answer the 4 or 5 questions based on that formula.

The mathematical formulas that you will need for the upcoming Extra class test are noted with an ▶ in the question pool that follows, and they are summarized in the Appendix on pages 278 to 282. Memorize the formulas, understand how to use them, and make sure you know the correct units to use. Many times you may have to convert kilohertz (kHz) to megahertz (MHz), or vice versa.

Work your book! Put a check mark beside questions you have down cold, and circle those that may need a little bit more study. Highlight those that appear to be brain-busters, and figure out ways to memorize the correct answers. Begin to memorize the formulas, and learn how to apply them to arrive at a correct answer. In many cases, there are handy shortcuts to help you through the longer formulas, and a little humor now and then should keep you on track.

If you study the questions and answers for a half hour in the morning, and a half hour in the evening, it should take you approximately 30 days to prepare for the Extra Class exam. If you are a grandfathered Advanced Class operator, it may take you only 15 days to prepare for your upgrade. One week before the exam, highlight each question's correct answer and spend that week only looking at the question and highlighted correct answer.

QUESTIONS REARRANGED FOR SMARTER LEARNING

The first thing you'll notice when you look at how the Element 4 question pool is presented in my Extra Class book is that I have completely rearranged the entire question pool into logical topic groups for easier learning. This rearrangement is the same presentation I use when I teach my 4-day Extra Class seminars. Rather than having to jump back and forth between subelement topic areas to study similar-topic questions, I take you LOGICALLY through the entire question pool with all of the Q&A arranged into 16 topic areas. For example, in the numerically-ordered question pool as issued by the QPC, antenna questions are sprinkled throughout various subelements. The same thing is true of questions about transmit bandwidth and many other topics. Here is a list of the topic areas and the page numbers on which each begins in this book:

We provide a numerical cross-reference of all of the Element 4 questions in the Appendix, on page 274, so if you need to look up a specific question by its number, we tell you precisely the page that it is on. This logical re-arrangement of questions is an absolute exclusive training method with all Gordon West ham radio test preparation books.

Just as in my Technician Class and General Class books, I have taken every single question in the Element 4 pool and placed it within the proper topic area for logical learning as a group. My classroom students love this approach to learning, and you will, too! Key words are also highlighted in *blue* in the explanations.

ADDITIONAL STUDY MATERIALS

Passing your Extra Class exam will require plenty of Q&A study. You can back-up the material in my book with some additional resources that will help you learn – and understand – the material.

First, there is my 6 CD audio course for Extra Class that is an excellent addition to this book. If you spend a lot of time in your car or pickup, or if you just learn better by listening, my audio CD course is for you. It follows the same outline as this book, and I include many sounds of Extra Class operation to help bring the material to life.

Next, if you like learning at your PC, study software is available that accompanies my book. This W5YI program includes the answer explanations from my book. When you take a practice exam, the software shows you the correct answer, scores your work, and tells you where you need to focus your study efforts.

You can back up all of this material presented in my book, audio course, and software program the well-illustrated "basic" books we offer on electronics – *Basic Electronics, Basic Communications Electronics,* and *Basic Digital Electronics* – all of which are available where you purchased this book, or from The W5YI Group. If you are extra technical, we also have 4 Engineer's Mini Notebooks written by Forrest M. Mims III, which parallel great electronic projects with step by step instructions. Check out these additional study materials in the back of this book.

Of course, the real learning of the material covered in these questions happens after you pass your exam and get on the air as an Amateur Extra Class operator!

EXAMINATION QUESTIONS

Let's get started reviewing the 738 Q&As, 50 of which will be chosen for your upcoming Extra Class exam. Read over the question and see if you already know the answer. Next, spot the likely answer and then read my explanation of the correct answer. Finally, at the end of the explanation, I give you the correct A, B, C, or D answer. These Q&As are exactly the same as those found on your upcoming Extra Class exam – verbatim. Use a small card to cover up the explanations and then slowly reveal the 4 possible answers, the explanation, and then the correct answer. Put a check mark beside the question number if you answered it correctly. Put an X if you need more study with a specific question.

Work the book! In our classes, I can usually tell who will pass the exam the first time by looking at their marked up textbooks.

Ready to get started? Here we go with the first series of questions.

E1A01 When using a transceiver that displays the carrier frequency of phone signals, which of the following displayed frequencies will result in a normal USB emission being within the band?
A. The exact upper band edge
B. 300 Hz below the upper band edge
C. 1 kHz below the upper band edge
D. 3 kHz below the upper band edge

Worldwide high frequency transceivers may automatically select the correct upper sideband or lower sideband when you start jumping around the bands. (Newer sideband transceivers also include the upper sideband requirement for the 60 meter band.) Let's say you are on 20 meters and dialed in to the maritime mobile net frequency of 14.300 MHz. This is the CARRIER frequency, and on 20 meters, our 14.300 MHz voice emission will modulate UP approximately 2.8 kHz. Your transmitted voice will then occupy just under 3 kHz of bandwidth, spanning from 14.300- to 14.303-MHz. The test question and correct answer illustrate the requirement that any upper sideband signal must have the displayed carrier dial frequency at least *3 kHz below the upper band edge*. 14.347 MHz would be the closest we would want to dial our carrier frequency to stay within the upper limit of the 20 meter band. [97.301, 97.305] **ANSWER D**

E1A03 With your transceiver displaying the carrier frequency of phone signals, you hear a DX station's CQ on 14.349 MHz USB. Is it legal to return the call using upper sideband on the same frequency?
A. Yes, because the DX station initiated the contact
B. Yes, because the displayed frequency is within the 20 meter band
C. No, my sidebands will extend beyond the band edge
D. No, USA stations are not permitted to use phone emissions above 14.340 MHz

No! Every so often you may hear a DX station calling CQ too close to a band edge. Don't be tempted to operate out of band by telling them that they are too close to the band edge! *Band edge operation may result in sidebands extending beyond the US band edge limits*, which is a rule violation for us. [97.301, 97.305] **ANSWER C**

E1A02 When using a transceiver that displays the carrier frequency of phone signals, which of the following displayed frequencies will result in a normal LSB emission being within the band?
A. The exact lower band edge
B. 300 Hz above the lower band edge
C. 1 kHz above the lower band edge
D. 3 kHz above the lower band edge
This question now has us on lower sideband, maybe 40 meters, so we need to *stay 3 kHz ABOVE the lower band edge* to stay within the band. It would be considered poor operating practice to intentionally hug a band edge, and switch to the non-conforming sideband. [97.301, 97.305] **ANSWER D**

E1A04 With your transceiver displaying the carrier frequency of phone signals, you hear a DX station's CQ on 3.601 MHz LSB. Is it legal to return the call using lower sideband on the same frequency?
A. Yes, because the DX station initiated the contact
B. Yes, because the displayed frequency is within the 75 meter phone band segment
C. No, my sidebands will extend beyond the edge of the phone band segment
D. No, USA stations are not permitted to use phone emissions below 3.610 MHz
On 80 meters, we use lower sideband, and the lowest frequency near the voice band edge that we would select as our dial carrier frequency would be 3.603 MHz. *US operators on 3.601 MHz are extending illegally beyond the USA band edge* of the phone segment. [97.301, 97.305] **ANSWER C** www.iaru-r2.org/bandplan

E1A09 Which frequency bands contain at least one segment authorized only to control operators holding an Amateur Extra Class operator license?
A. 80/75, 40, 20 and 15 meters
B. 80/75, 40, 20, and 10 meters
C. 80/75, 40, 30 and 10 meters
D. 160, 80/75, 40 and 20 meters
When you pass your Extra Class examination, you will gain *exclusive* voice sub-bands on 15-, 20-, and 80/75-meters. You also gain *exclusive* CW sub-bands on 15-, 20-, 80/75-, and 40-meters. NO band charts are permitted for the exam, so be sure to review the multiple band charts in this book, and *spot your sub-band privileges on 80/75-, 40-, 20-, and 15- meters*. [97.301] **ANSWER A**

E1A06 What is the maximum power output permitted on the 60 meter band?
A. 50 watts PEP effective radiated power relative to an isotropic radiator
B. 50 watts PEP effective radiated power relative to a dipole
C. 100 watts PEP effective radiated power relative to an isotropic radiator
D. 100 watts PEP effective radiated power relative to a dipole
Now we are studying the relatively new channelized 60 meter band. We are permitted 5 upper-sideband channels, and here are your dial carrier frequencies:

5330.5 kHz USB
5346.5 kHz USB
5366.5 kHz USB
5371.5 kHz USB
5403.5 kHz USB

Effective radiated power, relative to a dipole, is limited to 50 watts. The dipole would be considered unity gain, dBd, so, theoretically, you could likely run 90 watts into a minus 3dB loaded mobile antenna and be within the rules. Keep a record of your calculations, and don't exceed effective radiated power limits! Also, keep your mic gain low, so not to exceed the 60 meter band 2.8 kHz upper sideband frequency excursion limit. The frequencies listed are what your radio's dial will show in upper sideband. [97.303] **ANSWER B**

E1A07 What is the only amateur band where transmission on specific channels rather than a range of frequencies is permitted?
  A. 12 meter band   C. 30 meter band
  B. 17 meter band   D. 60 meter band

It is only on our *60 meter band* where our ham radio transmissions, upper sideband only, are limited to *5 specific channels.* [97.303] **ANSWER D**

60 METERS	5 SPECIFIC CHANNELS – 50 WATTS ERP					VOICE SIDEBAND
	5330.5 kHz	5346.5 kHz	5366.5 kHz	5371.5 kHz	5403.5 kHz	USB

E1A08 What is the only emission type permitted to be transmitted on the 60 meter band by an amateur station?
  A. CW
  B. RTTY Frequency shift keying
  C. Single sideband, upper sideband only
  D. Single sideband, lower sideband only

On *60 meters*, only single sideband, upper sideband only, is permitted. 2.8 kHz maximum USB bandwidth, so keep your mic gain low. Not even CW is allowed on 60 meters – *just SSB upper sideband.* [97.303] **ANSWER C**

E1A13 When a US-registered vessel is in international waters, what type of FCC-issued license or permit is required to transmit amateur communications from an on-board amateur transmitter?
  A. Any amateur license with an FCC Marine or Aircraft endorsement
  B. Any amateur license or reciprocal permit for alien amateur licensee
  C. Only General class or higher amateur licenses
  D. An unrestricted Radiotelephone Operator Permit

This is a great question dealing with maritime mobile operation when out on the high seas. If the vessel is flying the American flag, registered in the United States, *any ham radio transmissions MUST be from an FCC-licensed amateur operator or reciprocal permit for alien amateur license.* Years ago there was the false belief that once someone was in international waters, ANYONE could transmit over ham radio without a license. Not so – your ham license is required, and is separate from the ship's marine radio license or the captain's radio operator permit. [97.5] **ANSWER B**
www.arrl.org/regulations

E1A12 If an amateur station is installed on board a ship or aircraft, what condition must be met before the station is operated?
- A. Its operation must be approved by the master of the ship or the pilot in command of the aircraft
- B. The amateur station operator must agree to not transmit when the main ship or aircraft radios are in use
- C. It must have a power supply that is completely independent of the main ship or aircraft power supply
- D. Its operator must have an FCC Marine or Aircraft endorsement on his or her amateur license

If you are planning a long cruise on your pal's boat, or taking a ride in his airplane, make sure you have received *approval by the captain (master of the ship) or aircraft pilot* before you begin to transmit. Look at the other 3 incorrect answers – they sound logical, but only the answer we just gave you is correct. [97.11] **ANSWER A**

E1A05 Which is the only amateur band that does not permit the transmission of phone or image emissions?
- A. 160 meters
- B. 60 meters
- C. 30 meters
- D. 17 meters

Our 30 meter ham band extends from 10.100 to 10.150 MHz, just above the 10 MHz WWV time broadcasts. *No phone or image emissions are allowed on 30 meters!* But don't get disappointed – 30 meters is the perfect band for CW, radio teleprinter (RTTY), and data emissions, up to 300 baud; and for FSK, the frequency shift of mark and space must not exceed 1,000 Hz. Power output on the 30 meter band is 200 watts maximum, and we must be careful not to cause harmful interference to non-ham US and international operations on this band. [97.305] **ANSWER C**

30 METERS — 10.100 MHz — CODE + DATA (200 WATTS) — 10.150 MHz

---

E1B03 Within what distance must an amateur station protect an FCC monitoring facility from harmful interference?
- A. 1 mile
- B. 3 miles
- C. 10 miles
- D. 30 miles

The Federal Communications Commission recently automated its monitoring stations. Now there are remote-controlled, unmanned monitoring stations, and all amateur *operators within one mile of those stations must contact the local FCC engineer in charge* to ensure they do not cause harmful interference to that remote-controlled monitoring unit. [97.13] **ANSWER A**

E1F08 What is the National Radio Quiet Zone?
- A. An area in Puerto Rico surrounding the Aricebo Radio Telescope
- B. An area in New Mexico surrounding the White Sands Test Area
- C. An area surrounding the National Radio Astronomy Observatory
- D. An area in Florida surrounding Cape Canaveral

A national *radio quiet zone* has been established in Maryland, West Virginia, and Virginia near the *National Radio Astronomy Observatory*. The quiet zone restriction applies to "constant-on" stations like beacons and repeaters. Operation from your home or vehicle would not be affected unless you actually enter the property of the National Radio Astronomy Observatory in Greenbank, West Virginia. [97.3] **ANSWER C**

E1B02 Which of the following factors might cause the physical location of an amateur station apparatus or antenna structure to be restricted?
   A. The location is in or near an area of political conflict, military maneuvers or major construction
   B. The location's geographical or horticultural importance
   C. The location is in an ITU zone designated for coordination with one or more foreign governments
   D. The location is significant to our environment, American history, architecture, or culture

The environmental impact of a proposed installation is now a big consideration on anything that may have *significant impact on American history, architecture, or culture*. For instance, you would not want to place a station on an Indian burial ground. [97.13] **ANSWER D** www.fcc.gov/mb/facts/otaro.html

---

E1B04 What must be done before placing an amateur station within an officially designated wilderness area or wildlife preserve, or an area listed in the National Register of Historical Places?
   A. A proposal must be submitted to the National Park Service
   B. A letter of intent must be filed with the National Audubon Society
   C. An Environmental Assessment must be submitted to the FCC
   D. A form FSD-15 must be submitted to the Department of the Interior

If you plan to install your station on a wildlife preserve, or an area listed as a historical place, you will need to *submit an environmental assessment to the FCC* for its review and approval. Be prepared for an extremely long wait before your permit is granted! [97.13, 1.1305-1.1319] **ANSWER C**

E1F02 Which of the following operating arrangements allows an FCC-licensed US citizen to operate in many European countries, and alien amateurs from many European countries to operate in the US?
   A. CEPT agreement   C. ITU reciprocal license
   B. IARP agreement   D. All of these choices are correct

The *CEPT agreement* (European Conference of Postal & Telecommunications Administrations – CEPT) is great news for all U.S. Advanced and Extra Class amateur operators *when visiting many countries in Europe* – NO MORE RECIPROCAL PAPERWORK! Before leaving for Europe, obtain a copy of FCC Public Notice DA99-1098, released June 7, 1999, along with the original and copies of your U.S. ham license. This paperwork is necessary in case you are asked about the equipment you are bringing into that country at customs. Have fun in Europe with ham radio! Don't forget your paperwork and the required FCC Public Notice. [97.5] **ANSWER A**

Participating CEPT countries, as of January, 2003, are:

Austria	Finland	Lithuania	Spain
Belgium	France & its	Luxembourg	Sweden
Bosnia &	possessions	Monaco	Switzerland
Herzegovina	Germany	Netherlands	Turkey
Bulgaria	Hungary	Netherland Antilles	Ukraine
Croatia	Iceland	Norway	United Kingdom &
Cyprus	Ireland	Portugal	its possessions
Czech Republic	Italy	Romania	
Denmark	Latvia	Slovak Republic	
Estonia	Liechtenstein	Slovenia	

Good To Know: *European Reciprocal Licenses Now Limited to Advanced & Extra Class Licensees*

The European Conference of Postal and Telecommunications Administrations (CEPT) has revised its table of equivalence between FCC amateur licenses and the CEPT license. Effective February 4, 2008, Recommendation T/R 61-01 (as amended) now grants full CEPT privileges only to those U.S. citizens who hold an FCC-issued Advanced or Amateur Extra Class license. This means that those US licensees who hold an FCC-issued General or Technician license are no longer eligible for full operating privileges in countries where CEPT-reciprocal operation had previously been permitted. U.S. Novice class licensees have had no reciprocal operating privileges under the CEPT provisions.

E1F03 Which of the following operating arrangements allow an FCC-licensed US citizen and many Central and South American amateur operators to operate in each other's countries?

    A. CEPT agreement
    B. IARP agreement
    C. ITU agreement
    D. All of these choices are correct

Heading south for a vacation and want to take your ham equipment along to *Central and South America*? The following countries and the U.S. have an *IARP* (International Amateur Radio Permit) agreement: Argentina, Brazil, Peru, Uruguay, and Venezuela. Canada also is an IARP country, so you can take your gear north, too! [97.5] **ANSWER B** *Remember, CEPT is Europe and IARP is South America*.

South American IARP Countries

E1F16 What types of communications may be transmitted to amateur stations in foreign countries?

A. Business-related messages

B. Automatic retransmissions of any amateur communications

C. Communications incidental to the purpose of the amateur service and remarks of a personal nature

D. All of these choices are correct

With your new Extra Class privileges you will likely make even more foreign country contacts. Remember, no business communications allowed, so *keep your comms to purely personal remarks, or* communications of a *technical nature*, when talking with hams in foreign countries. [97.117] **ANSWER C** www.dxpub.com

Good To Know:

Going "down under?" The Australian Communications and Media Authority (ACMA) has issued a new class of license to allow visiting amateurs to operate in Australia for up to 90 days. All you have to do is use your home call sign followed by the suffix "VK" followed by "portable" and then announce the location of your station, without doing anything more.

E1F06 Which of the following geographic descriptions approximately describes "Line A"?

A. A line roughly parallel to and south of the US-Canadian border

B. A line roughly parallel to and west of the US Atlantic coastline

C. A line roughly parallel to and north of the US-Mexican border and Gulf coastline

D. A line roughly parallel to and east of the US Pacific coastline

The United States and Canada have adopted the *"Line A" as a buffer zone for* certain types of radio stations. This keeps normally "line of sight" radio energy from interfering with *Canadian communications*. US amateurs are restricted on the 70-cm band between 420-430 MHz from transmitting if they are located north of "Line A." This is because Canada has a different type of radio allocation in the bottom part of the 70-cm band. [97.3] **ANSWER A**

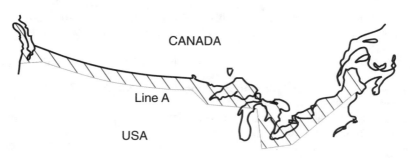

Amateur Radio Restrictions

E1F07 Amateur stations may not transmit in which of the following frequency segments if they are located north of Line A?

A. 440 - 450 MHz.

B. 53 - 54 MHz

C. 222 - 223 MHz

D. 420 - 430 MHz

Frequencies between 420-430 MHz are normally used for digital modes, fast-scan television, and auxiliary links. *North of "Line A"* next to the Canadian border, U.S. hams are *prohibited from operating below 430 MHz*. [97.303] **ANSWER D**

E1B05 What height restrictions apply to an amateur station antenna structure not close to a public use airport unless the FAA is notified and it is registered with the FCC?

A. It must not extend more than 300 feet above average height of terrain surrounding the site

B. It must be no higher than 200 feet above ground level at its site

C. There are no height restrictions because the structure obviously would not be a hazard to aircraft in flight

D. It must not extend more than 100 feet above sea level or the rim of the nearest valley or canyon

An amateur antenna must be *no higher than 200 feet*. This is measured from the ground level at the base of the tower up to the top of the antenna structure. Even if you live deep in a valley or canyon, you still cannot exceed the base-to-tip 200-feet height restriction. If you need more elevation, reconsider where you are going to mount your antenna tower. [97.15] **ANSWER B**

MAXIMUM ANTENNA HEIGHT WITHOUT FCC APPROVAL – 200 FT.

Antenna Height

E1B06 Which of the following additional rules apply if you are installing an amateur station antenna at a site within 20,000 feet of a public use airport?

A. You may have to notify the Federal Aviation Administration and register it with the FCC

B. No special rules apply if your antenna structure will be less than 300 feet in height

C. You must file an Environmental Impact Statement with the EPA before construction begins

D. You must obtain a construction permit from the airport zoning authority

If you are located within 20,000 feet (about 4 miles) of an airport, you need to take a look at FCC Part 17 regulations that talk about the height of an antenna near an airport. The closer you are to the airport, the lower your antenna system must be, according to FCC Part 17. Make sure you talk *to the FAA and register* your tower *with the FCC*. [97.15] **ANSWER A**

E1B07 Whose approval is required before erecting an amateur station antenna located at or near a public use airport if the antenna would exceed a certain height depending upon the antenna's distance from the nearest active runway?

    A. The FAA must be notified and it must be registered with the FCC
    B. Approval must be obtained from the airport manager
    C. Approval must be obtained from the local zoning authorities
    D. The FAA must approve any antenna structure that is higher than 20 feet

As a new Amateur Extra Class operator, you will likely be erecting a tower and getting that beam high up in the air. *Remember the airport 4-mile rule* – if you are closer to an airport than 4 miles, it could have a negative impact on how tall your antenna structure may be. [97.15] **ANSWER A**

E1F10 When may an amateur station send a message to a business?

    A. When the total money involved does not exceed $25
    B. When the control operator is employed by the FCC or another government agency
    C. When transmitting international third-party communications
    D. When neither the amateur nor his or her employer has a pecuniary interest in the communications

In 1993, the prohibited business communications rules were redefined by the FCC to allow an amateur to *send a message to a business as long as neither the amateur nor his or her employer has a pecuniary interest in the communications.* If you run a tree-trimming business, it would not be legal to use an autopatch to call your answering machine to find out where your next customer is waiting. On the other hand, if you are a school teacher and discover that a big pine tree has fallen down across the school's driveway, it would be perfectly acceptable to place an autopatch call to a tree-trimmer and have them come out to do their job. But could the school teacher call into the school district and tell them that she is going to be late for work? Probably NOT legal. [97.113] **ANSWER D**

E1F11 Which of the following types of amateur-operator-to-amateur-operator communications are prohibited?

    A. Communications transmitted for hire or material compensation, except as otherwise provided in the rules
    B. Communications that have a political content, except as allowed by the Fairness Doctrine
    C. Communications that have a religious content
    D. Communications in a language other than English

This question deals with permissible communications from one ham to another. Political, religious, and foreign language communications ARE permitted, but *communications transmitted for hire* or material compensation *are normally prohibited.* [97.113] **ANSWER A**

E1F09 When may the control operator of a repeater accept payment for providing communication services to another party?

    A. When the repeater is operating under portable power
    B. When the repeater is operating under local control
    C. During Red Cross or other emergency service drills
    D. Under no circumstances

Under no circumstances can someone pay you for handling a ham radio call. Even if they want to give you a tip, tell the stranded motorist to learn more about the great hobby of Amateur Radio. [97.113] **ANSWER D**

E1A10 If a station in a message forwarding system inadvertently forwards a message that is in violation of FCC rules, who is primarily accountable for the rules violation?
A. The control operator of the packet bulletin board station
B. The control operator of the originating station
C. The control operators of all the stations in the system
D. The control operators of all the stations in the system not authenticating the source from which they accept communications

A few years ago, dozens of amateur operators were sent "greetings" from the FCC for taking part in forwarding a packet radio message that contained material specifically prohibited by the rules and regulations. The hams forwarding the messages claimed everything was in the automatic mode and it was not up to them to censor what was coming down the electronic data line! Hence, new rules hold the *control operator of the station originating the message as primarily accountable* for any rule violation, and the control operator of the first forwarding station also must accept accountability for any violation of the rules. More specifically, everyone else "down the line" is no longer responsible for the message content, but must shut down their packet bulletin boards if informed that there is a message being automatically forwarded in violation of the rules. [97.219] **ANSWER B**

E1A11 What is the first action you should take if your digital message forwarding station inadvertently forwards a communication that violates FCC rules?
A. Discontinue forwarding the communication as soon as you become aware of it
B. Notify the originating station that the communication does not comply with FCC rules
C. Notify the nearest FCC Field Engineer's office
D. Discontinue forwarding all messages

If you are advised that your packet station is automatically forwarding communications in violation of the rules, get into the computer and *discontinue forwarding this specific communication as soon as you become aware of it*. You may continue to forward all other messages. [97.219] **ANSWER A**

E1C07 What is meant by local control?
A. Controlling a station through a local auxiliary link
B. Automatically manipulating local station controls
C. Direct manipulation of the transmitter by a control operator
D. Controlling a repeater using a portable handheld transceiver

Local control is *the actual place where you turn on your equipment*, press the microphone and transmit. This is called "direct manipulation of the transmitter" by a control operator. [97.3] **ANSWER C**

E1C01 What is a remotely controlled station?
A. A station operated away from its regular home location
B. A station controlled by someone other than the licensee
C. A station operating under automatic control
D. A station controlled indirectly through a control link

Popular amateur radio IRLP stations located high atop mountains or buildings do not have the control operator sitting right in the repeater room. The station is controlled through a control link station. Most control link frequencies are found on UHF 420-430 MHz, or up on 1.2 GHz. *"Control link" is the key for remote control* of an amateur station or repeater. [97.3] **ANSWER D**

FIXED
CONTROL
STATION

REPEATER
RECEIVES ON f$_1$
TRANSMITS ON f$_2$

T2 R2

Repeater

Source: *Mobile 2-Way Radio Communications*, G. West, Copyright ©1992 Master Publishing, Inc., Niles, IL

E1C08 What is the maximum permissible duration of a remotely controlled station's transmissions if its control link malfunctions?

A. 30 seconds
B. 3 minutes
C. 5 minutes
D. 10 minutes

If a distant, remotely-controlled station is undergoing remote control tone commands from an auxiliary station and the control link on microwave fails, that remotely-controlled station must *shut down within three minutes*. [97.213] **ANSWER B**

E1C06 Which of the following statements concerning remotely controlled amateur stations is true?

A. Only Extra Class operators may be the control operator of a remote station
B. A control operator need not be present at the control point
C. A control operator must be present at the control point
D. Repeater and auxiliary stations may not be remotely controlled

To remotely control another ham station, the control *operator must be present at the control point*. Only under AUTOMATIC control, like a repeater, may the control operator get some sleep! [97.109] **ANSWER C**

E1C02 What is meant by automatic control of a station?

A. The use of devices and procedures for control so that the control operator does not have to be present at a control point
B. A station operating with its output power controlled automatically
C. Remotely controlling a station's antenna pattern through a directional control link
D. The use of a control link between a control point and a locally controlled station

Ham operators have come up with *devices and procedures* so they don't have to stand guard at the repeater block house on a mountain top. [97.3, 97.109] **ANSWER A**

E1C04 When may an automatically controlled station retransmit third party communications?
A. Never
B. Only when transmitting RTTY or data emissions
C. When specifically agreed upon by the sending and receiving stations
D. When approved by the National Telecommunication and Information Administration

A good example of *third party messages from an automatically-controlled station* is *PACKET* radio. PACKET, along with *RTTY*, is a *data emission* which has specific spots reserved on the high frequency radio dial when operated in the automatic mode. For instance, on 15 meters, an automatically controlled digital station has 10 kHz at 21.090 – 21.100 MHz. On 20 meters, the automatically controlled station may only pass third party communications between 14.1005 -14.1120 MHz. These automatic digital stations are unattended, but there still must be a control operator who will ensure absolute compliance with the rules and regulations. This automatically controlled RTTY or data emission will respond to interrogation by a ham station that is under local or remote control. Also, the automatically-controlled station may not occupy a bandwidth of more than 500Hz. The very popular Winlink 2000 running relatively narrow PACTOR 1 and PACTOR 2 may be found anywhere below the SSB bands, but the wider PACTOR 3 has a control operator to initiate an unattended "autostart" station under FCC rules. [97.109] **ANSWER B**
www.winlink.org

E1C03 How do the control operator responsibilities of a station under automatic control differ from one under local control?
A. Under local control there is no control operator
B. Under automatic control the control operator is not required to be present at the control point
C. Under automatic control there is no control operator
D. Under local control a control operator is not required to be present at a control point

Repeaters under *automatic control don't have anyone sitting up* there *at that distant control point.* [97.3, 97.109] **ANSWER B**

E1C05 When may an automatically controlled station originate third party communications?
A. Never
B. Only when transmitting RTTY or data emissions
C. When specifically agreed upon by the sending and receiving stations
D. When approved by the National Telecommunication and Information Administration

An example of third party and third party traffic would be messages from one control operator to another ham station control operator on behalf of a close friend or relative who may not have their own ham license. If we read this question correctly, it asks "may an automatically controlled station ORIGINATE third party communications." The answer is *never, because a third party without a ham license may not be* designated by the first control operator to assume the *control operator* function required to ORIGINATE that third party communication. Even though the station may be automatically controlled and sending data emissions, a third party is not allowed to electronically key up your station and begin messaging. It takes a licensed control operator to initiate an unattended "auto-start" station that may be handling third party traffic. [97.109] **ANSWER A**

E1C10 What types of amateur stations may automatically retransmit the radio signals of other amateur stations?
A. Only beacon, repeater or space stations
B. Only auxiliary, repeater or space stations
C. Only earth stations, repeater stations or model crafts
D. Only auxiliary, beacon or space stations

Automatically retransmitting the radio signals of other ham stations takes place with a common *repeater*, and can also take place from *satellite and space stations*, and can also take place from an *auxiliary station*, such as one handling IRLP. [97.113] **ANSWER B** www.winsystem.org

E1C09 Which of these frequencies are available for automatically controlled ground-station repeater operation?
A. 18.110 - 18.168 MHz   C. 10.100 - 10.150 MHz
B. 24.940 - 24.990 MHz   D. 29.500 - 29.700 MHz

Repeater operation on high frequency is limited *only to the top of the 10 meter band*, between 29.5 MHz to 29.7 MHz. No other high frequency (3-30MHz) bands permit repeater operation. [97.205] **ANSWER D**

E1F15 Who may be the control operator of an auxiliary station?
A. Any licensed amateur operator
B. Only Technician, General, Advanced or Amateur Extra Class operators
C. Only General, Advanced or Amateur Extra Class operators
D. Only Amateur Extra Class operators

An amateur radio auxiliary station is a transceiver under your local control, which remotely controls another station, like a mountaintop repeater, or a distant high-ridge cross-band system, part of a cooperating amateur station network. *Any amateur radio operator, EXCEPT NOVICE CLASS*, may set up an auxiliary station and be the control operator of that station. But here is the BIG NEWS: as of 2007 Auxiliary operation, originally restricted to ham bands above 222 MHz, may now take place on the popular 2 meter band, above 144.50 MHz, except the satellite sub-band 145.8-146.0 MHz. The FCC noted that there was no apparent basis to conclude that allowing auxiliary stations to transmit on the 2 meter band would cause harmful interference to other stations' communications. This new ruling now makes dual band handheld transceivers, with a built-in TNC, take on some additional benefits of auxiliary operation, other than for the Novice operator who may NOT be a control operator of an auxiliary station. (While Novice and Advanced Class licenses are no long being issued, there are hams who still hold valid Novice and Advanced Class licenses.) [97.201] **ANSWER B**

E1F17 Under what circumstances might the FCC issue a "Special Temporary Authority" (STA) to an amateur station?
A. To provide for experimental amateur communications
B. To allow regular operation on Land Mobile channels
C. To provide additional spectrum for personal use
D. To provide temporary operation while awaiting normal licensing

Ham radio operators are always on the prowl for new types of emissions, and vacant frequencies that the *FCC* may allow us to use with special temporary authority. While obtaining the FCC's STA requires diligence and numerous filings, ham operators have been successful in obtaining *permission to experiment with new emissions not* even *found in the rules* as well as *operation on unused very low frequencies* (VLF) for specific propagation studies. These experimental communications may lead to future rule makings on our behalf! [1.931b2] **ANSWER A**

E1B09 What is the Radio Amateur Civil Emergency Service (RACES)?
A. A radio service using amateur service frequencies on a regular basis for communications that can reasonably be furnished through other radio services
B. A radio service of amateur stations for civil defense communications during periods of local, regional, or national civil emergencies
C. A radio service using amateur service frequencies for broadcasting to the public during periods of local, regional or national civil emergencies
D. A radio service using local government frequencies by Amateur Radio operators for civil emergency communications

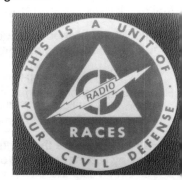

Remember Civil Defense? The C in *RACES is for Civil Defense Communications.* [97.3] **ANSWER B**
www.fema.gov/emergency/nims 🖑

The RACES Logo

E1B10 Which amateur stations may be operated in RACES?
A. Only those club stations licensed to Amateur Extra class operators
B. Any FCC-licensed amateur station except a Technician class operator's station
C. Any FCC-licensed amateur station certified by the responsible civil defense organization for the area served
D. Any FCC-licensed amateur station participating in the Military Affiliate Radio System (MARS)

All amateurs are eligible for RACES membership. [97.407] **ANSWER C**

E1B11 What frequencies are normally authorized to an amateur station participating in RACES?
A. All amateur service frequencies otherwise authorized to the control operator
B. Specific segments in the amateur service MF, HF, VHF and UHF bands
C. Specific local government channels
D. Military Affiliate Radio System (MARS) channels

Anyone with a valid amateur service license, including a Novice Class license, is eligible to be certified by a civil defense organization as a RACES operator. However, *you do not gain any out-of-band privileges as a RACES operator.* [97.407] **ANSWER A**

E1B13 What communications are permissible in RACES?

A. Any type of communications when there is no emergency
B. Any Amateur Radio Emergency Service communications
C. Authorized civil defense emergency communications affecting the immediate safety of life and property
D. National defense and security communications authorized by the President

For communications concerning national defense and security, *or immediate safety of life and property*, your area civil defense organization may decide on its own when RACES operation begins. They may also allow specific periods for testing and drills. [97.407] **ANSWER C** www.emcomm.org/em

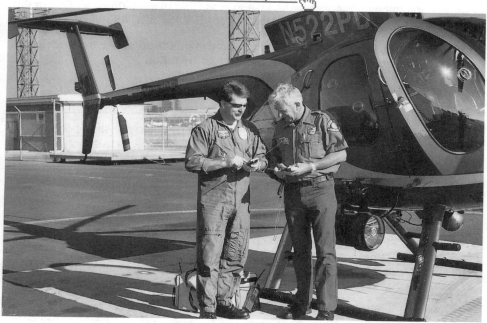

In an emergency, authorized hams participating in a RACES organization may communicate from a police helicopter.

E1B12 What are the frequencies authorized to an amateur station participating in RACES during a period when the President's War Emergency Powers are in force?

A. All frequencies in the amateur service authorized to the control operator
B. Specific amateur service frequency segments authorized in FCC Part 214
C. Specific local government channels
D. Military Affiliate Radio System (MARS) channels

If a war should break out, RACES operators may be authorized *specific segments* in the amateur service MF, HF, VHF, and UHF bands, *as defined in FCC Part 214* rules. Look at the incorrect answers, and see how good they look, and then memorize the correct answer! [97.407] **ANSWER B**

www.training.fema.gove/emiweb/is/crslist.asp

E1E04 What is a Volunteer Examiner Coordinator?

A. A person who has volunteered to administer amateur operator license examinations

B. A person who has volunteered to prepare amateur operator license examinations

C. An organization that has entered into an agreement with the FCC to coordinate amateur operator license examinations

D. The person that has entered into an agreement with the FCC to be the VE session manager

A Volunteer Examiner Coordinator is *an organization* that has *an agreement with the FCC* to coordinate amateur radio license exams. Two of the biggest VECs are the American Radio Relay League, and the W5YI-VEC. [97.521] **ANSWER C**

E1E03 Who is responsible for maintaining the question pools from which all amateur license examination questions must be taken?

A. All of the VECs

B. The VE team

C. The VE question pool team

D. The FCC's Wireless Telecommunications Bureau

All of the Volunteer Examiner Coordinators contribute to the question pool and insure it is up to date. If a rule change occurs that disqualifies a question, *all VECs* will eliminate that question from the question pool. [97.523] **ANSWER A**

E1E02 Where are the questions for all written US amateur license examinations listed?

A. In FCC Part 97

B. In an FCC-maintained question pool

C. In the VEC-maintained question pool

D. In the appropriate FCC Report and Order

The Extra Class exam, like all ham tests, may only take questions verbatim from the *VEC-maintained question pool*. [97.523] **ANSWER C** www.ncvec.org

---

E1E05 What is a VE?

A. An amateur operator who is approved by three or more fellow volunteer examiners to administer amateur license examinations

B. An amateur operator who is approved by a VEC to administer amateur operator license examinations

C. An amateur operator who administers amateur license examinations for a fee

D. An amateur operator who is approved by an FCC staff member to administer amateur operator license examinations

A volunteer examiner coordinator (VEC) will accredit *amateur operators as volunteer examiners* (VEs). [97.525, 97.3] **ANSWER B**

Working with kids as an Elmer or VE is both fun and a great way to help ham radio grow.

E1E08 Which of the following best describes the Volunteer Examiner accreditation process?

A. Each General, Advanced and Amateur Extra Class operator is automatically accredited as a VE when the license is granted

B. The amateur operator applying must pass a VE examination administered by the FCC Enforcement Bureau

C. The prospective VE obtains accreditation from a VE team

D. The procedure by which a VEC confirms that the VE applicant meets FCC requirements to serve as an examiner

VE accreditation is received from a Volunteer Examiner Coordinator *(VEC)* who *makes sure that each VE meets specific FCC requirements*, and has a clean record. [97.5091, 97.525] **ANSWER D** www.w5yi.org/vec

E1E07 Which of the following persons seeking to become VEs cannot be accredited?

A. Persons holding less than an Advanced Class operator license

B. Persons less than 21 years of age

C. Persons who have ever had an amateur operator or amateur station license suspended or revoked

D. Persons who are employees of the Federal government

Any amateur who has ever had his or her *license suspended or revoked may not serve* as an accredited volunteer examiner. [97.509] **ANSWER C**

E1E20 What is the minimum age to be a volunteer examiner?

A. 13 years old   C. 18 years old
B. 16 years old   D. 21 years old

Volunteer Examiners must be accredited by a VEC, and the *minimum age* for accreditation *as a VE is 18 years old*. When you pass your Extra, I encourage you to become an accredited Volunteer Examiner. Then, join a VE team and begin exam administration. Work over examination paperwork carefully, and NEVER pre-sign any passing certificates (CSCE) until you have proof that each and every applicant on the manifest has indeed passed the specific element for which you are signing. [97.509] **ANSWER C**

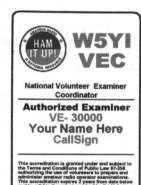

VE badge

E1E06 What is a VE team?

A. A group of at least three VEs who administer examinations for an amateur operator license

B. The VEC staff

C. One or two VEs who administer examinations for an amateur operator license

D. A group of FCC Volunteer Enforcers who investigate Amateur Rules violations

It takes a minimum of *3 accredited volunteer examiners* to conduct an examination session. [97.509] **ANSWER A**

E1E01 What is the minimum number of qualified VEs required to administer an Element 4 amateur operator license examination?

A. 5   C. 4
B. 2   D. 3

It takes a team of *3 Extra Class accredited examiners to administer an Element 4* amateur Extra Class test. It also takes these three Extra Class VEs to administer the General Class, Element 3, exam. [97.509] **ANSWER D**

E1E12 To which of the following examinees may a VE not administer an examination?

A. Employees of the VE
B. Friends of the VE
C. The VE's close relatives as listed in the FCC rules
D. All these answers are correct

As a volunteer examiner, *you may not test your own close relatives.* [97.509]
ANSWER C

E1E10 Who is responsible for the proper conduct and necessary supervision during an amateur operator license examination session?

A. The VEC coordinating the session
B. The FCC
C. Each administering VE
D. The VE session manager

Each one of the administering Volunteer Examiners must continuously supervise everyone in the room taking the tests. Administering VEs should not talk amongst themselves as the examinees are pouring over the test questions. [97.509]
ANSWER C

E1E09 Where must the VE team be while administering an examination?

A. All of the administering VEs must be present where they can observe the examinees throughout the entire examination
B. The VEs must leave the room after handing out the exam(s) to allow the examinees to concentrate on the exam material
C. The VEs may be elsewhere provided at least one VE is present and is observing the examinees throughout the entire examination
D. The VEs may be anywhere as long as they each certify in writing that examination was administered properly

As a VE, you must be *present and in a location to physically observe the candidate taking the test* throughout the entire examination. [97.509] **ANSWER A**

E1E14 What must the VE team do with the examinee's test papers once they have finished the examination?

A. The VE team must collect and send them to the NCVEC
B. The VE team must collect and send them to the coordinating VEC for grading
C. The VE team must collect and grade them immediately
D. The VE team must collect and send them to the FCC for grading

After the exam, the VE team must *collect and grade all papers immediately.* [97.509]
ANSWER C

E1E15 What must the VE team do if an examinee scores a passing grade on all examination elements needed for an upgrade or new license?

A. Photocopy all examination documents and forward them to the FCC for processing
B. Three VEs must certify that the examinee is qualified for the license grant and that they have complied with the VE requirements
C. Issue the examinee the new or upgrade license
D. All these answers are correct

When an examinee upgrades to a new, higher license, *the 3-member VE team must certify the exam paperwork and sign the CSCE* (Certificate of Successful Completion of Examination) showing that they have complied with the VE requirements. The applicant holds onto the CSCE until such time as the license is issued by the FCC. [97.509] **ANSWER B**

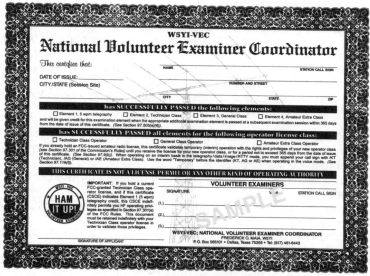

Don't Lose Your CSCE – It Is Proof of Your Privileges Until Your License Arrives

E1E16 What must the VE team do with the application form if the examinee does not pass the exam?

A. Return the application document to the examinee
B. Maintain the application form with the VEC's records
C. Send it to the FCC
D. Destroy the application form

You will *return the application to the examinee* and inform the candidate of the failing grade. Try to do this compassionately, urging the candidate to continue to study and try again soon. [97.509] **ANSWER A**

E1E11 What should a VE do if a candidate fails to comply with the examiner's instructions during an amateur operator license examination?
- A. Warn the candidate that continued failure to comply will result in termination of the examination
- B. Immediately terminate the candidate's examination
- C. Allow the candidate to complete the examination, but invalidate the results
- D. Immediately terminate everyone's examination and close the session

If an *examinee fails to comply* with your instructions, you should immediately *terminate that candidate's examination*. [97.509] **ANSWER B**

E1E18 For which types of out-of-pocket expenses may VEs and VECs be reimbursed?
- A. Preparing, processing, administering and coordinating an examination for an amateur radio license
- B. Teaching an amateur operator license examination preparation course
- C. No expenses are authorized for reimbursement
- D. Providing amateur operator license examination preparation training materials

Volunteer examiners and VECs are allowed to *recoup out-of-pocket expenses for preparing, processing, administering, and coordinating* an examination for an amateur radio license. There is a set fee that each applicant pays for the entire exam session. [97.527] **ANSWER A**

E1E19 How much reimbursement may the VE team and VEC accept for preparing, processing, administering and coordinating an examination?
- A. Actual out-of-pocket expenses
- B. The national minimum hourly wage for time spent providing examination services
- C. Up to the maximum fee per examinee announced by the FCC annually
- D. As much as the examinee is willing to donate

The fee collected is for actual *out-of-pocket expenses*. [97.509, 97.527] **ANSWER A**

E1E17 What are the consequences of failing to appear for re-administration of an examination when so directed by the FCC?
- A. The licensee's license will be cancelled
- B. The person may be fined or imprisoned
- C. The licensee is disqualified from any future examination for an amateur operator license grant
- D. All of the above

Occasionally, the FCC asks an applicant to appear for re-administration of an exam. This occurs if the exam session appears to have been flawed. *If the licensee fails to appear for the re-exam, the licensee's license will be canceled* and a new license will be issued that is consistent with examination elements not invalidated. [97.519] **ANSWER A**

E1E13 What may be the penalty for a VE who fraudulently administers or certifies an examination?

A. Revocation of the VE's amateur station license grant and the suspension of the VE's amateur operator license grant

B. A fine of up to $1000 per occurrence

C. A sentence of up to one year in prison

D. All of these choices are correct

Any *VE who is caught administering a fraudulent exam* may have his or her station *license revoked and the VE's amateur radio license grant suspended.* [97.509]

ANSWER A

The Effect of the Ionosphere on Radio Waves

To help you with the questions on radio wave propagation, here is a brief explanation on the effect the ionosphere has on radio waves.

The ionosphere is the electrified atmosphere from 40 miles to 400 miles above the Earth. You can sometimes see it as "northern lights." It is charged-up daily by the Sun, and does some miraculous things to radio waves that strike it. Some radio waves are absorbed during daylight hours by the ionosphere's D layer. Others are bounced back to Earth. Yet others penetrate the ionosphere and never come back again. The wavelength of the radio waves determines whether the waves will be absorbed, refracted, or will penetrate. Here's a quick way to memorize what the different layers do during day and nighttime hours:

The D layer is about 40 miles up. The D layer is a Daylight layer; it almost disappears at night. D for Daylight. The D layer absorbs radio waves between 1 MHz to 7 MHz. These are long wavelengths. All others pass through.

The E layer is also a daylight layer, and it is very Eccentric. E for Eccentric. Patches of E layer ionization may cause some surprising reflections of signals on both high frequency as well as very-high frequency. The E layer height is usually 70 miles.

The F1 layer is one of the layers farthest away. The F layer gives us those Far away signals. F for Far away. The F1 layer is present during daylight hours, and is up around 150 miles. The F2 layer is also present during daylight hours, and it gives us the Furthest range. The F2 layer is 250 miles high, and it's best for the Farthest range on medium and short waves. The F2 layer is strongest in the summer months. During winter months, both the F1 and F2 layers may become unpredictable, but always strong enough to support exciting skywaves! At nighttime, the F1 and F2 layers combine to become just the F layer at 180 miles. This F layer at nighttime will usually bend radio waves between 1 MHz and 15 MHz back to earth. At night, the D and E layers disappear.

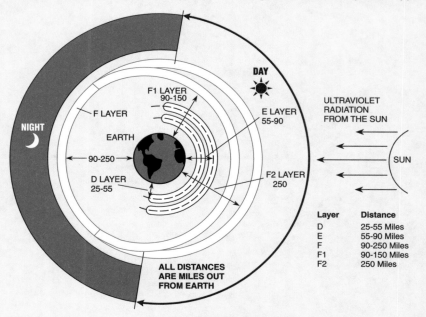

Ionosphere Layers

Source: *Antennas — Selection and Installation*, © 1986, Master Publishing, Inc., Niles, Illinois

E8D07 What is an electromagnetic wave?
A. Alternating currents in the core of an electromagnet
B. A wave consisting of two electric fields at right angles to each other
C. A wave consisting of an electric field and a magnetic field oscillating at right angles to each other
D. A wave consisting of two magnetic fields at right angles to each other

When you think of an *electromagnetic radio wave*, think of it as a *combination of an electric field and a magnetic field* at right angles to one another traveling in waves through the atmosphere at the same time. One field is vertically polarized and the other is horizontally polarized. If the antenna is vertically polarized, the electric field will be vertical, and the magnetic field will be horizontal. **ANSWER C**

www.ips.gov.au/hf_systems/4/1/2

a. Electric and Magnetic Fields Radiating from Antenna

b. Radiation Pattern of Radio Waves Around Antenna

Radio Waves

Source: Basic Electronics © 1994, 2000 Master Publishing, Inc., Niles, Illinois

E8D08 Which of the following best describes electromagnetic waves traveling in free space?

A. Electric and magnetic fields become aligned as they travel
B. The energy propagates through a medium with a high refractive index
C. The waves are reflected by the ionosphere and return to their source
D. Changing electric and magnetic fields propagate the energy

Electromagnetic radio waves, traveling in free space, contain both *an electric field and a magnetic field propagating the energy*. The fields are at a right angle to each other, and it is both the electric field and the magnetic field that makes up the radio wave energy traveling at the speed of light in a vacuum. **ANSWER D**

E8D10 What is the polarization of an electromagnetic wave if its magnetic field is parallel to the surface of the Earth?

A. Circular   C. Elliptical

B. Horizontal   D. Vertical

Watch out for this one! *Polarization is always the electric field.* Here they are asking about the magnetic field which is parallel to the surface of the earth. If the magnetic field is parallel, the *electric field is vertical, so polarization is vertical.* **ANSWER D**

E8D11 What is the polarization of an electromagnetic wave if its magnetic field is perpendicular to the surface of the Earth?

A. Horizontal   C. Elliptical

B. Circular   D. Vertical

If the magnetic field is perpendicular (vertical) to the surface of the earth, the *electric* lines of force would be *horizontal*, and this would give us *horizontal polarization.* **ANSWER A**

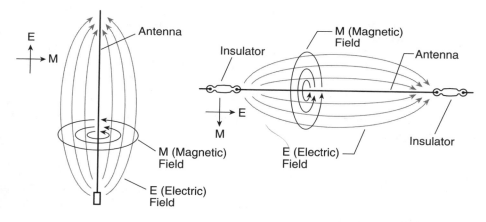

a. Vertically-Polarized Antenna   b. Horizontally-Polarized Antenna

Horizontal and Vertical Polarization

E8D09 What is meant by circularly polarized electromagnetic waves?

A. Waves with an electric field bent into a circular shape

B. Waves with a rotating electric field

C. Waves that circle the Earth

D. Waves produced by a loop antenna

Some satellite enthusiasts will use circular polarization to improve their transmission and reception through an orbiting satellite. With *circular polarization, the electric field rotates.* It could be right-hand circular, or left-hand circular, depending on the antenna feed system. **ANSWER B**

E8D12 At approximately what speed do electromagnetic waves travel in free space?

A. 300 million meters per second   C. 186,300 feet per second

B. 186,300 meters per second   D. 300 million miles per second

Electromagnetic radio waves and light waves travel at *300 million meters per second* in free space. Watch out for answer D! **ANSWER A**

www.qsl.net/w6elprop

E3B04 What type of propagation is probably occurring if an HF beam antenna must be pointed in a direction 180 degrees away from a station to receive the strongest signals?

A. Long-path   C. Transequatorial

B. Sporadic-E   D. Auroral

If two stations wish to communicate on high frequency when the sun is ionizing the F1 and F2 layers, both stations would normally aim their antennas at each other for an excellent *"short path"* contact. But if the sun is on the other side of the Earth to both stations, the stations may wish to try long-path propagation by aiming their antennas in the opposite direction – *180 degrees away from the station with which they wish to communicate*. They are actually sending their signals all the way around the World, the long way, to get a signal to the other station. Many times you can hear a tell-tale echo when a station is being received via a long path. **ANSWER A** www.arrl.org/tis/info/propagation.html

E3B05 Which amateur bands typically support long-path propagation?

A. 160 to 40 meters   C. 160 to 10 meters

B. 30 to 10 meters   D. 6 meters to 2 meters

Long-range, *long-path propagatio*n can be found on the worldwide bands from *10 meters down to 160 meters*. Twenty meters is always the best band to expect almost daily long-path propagation, which is best in the late evening or early morning hours. **ANSWER C** http://propagation.hfradio.org

E3B06 Which of the following amateur bands most frequently provides long-path propagation?

A. 80 meters   C. 10 meters

B. 20 meters   D. 6 meters

The amateur radio *20-meter band is the best one for long-path* DX with a relatively modest directional antenna system. When you pass your upcoming Extra Class exam, you will gain an exclusive 20-meter CW window from 14.000-14.025 MHz, and an exclusive Extra Class window from 14.150 MHz to 14.175 MHz, just for working rare 20-meter DX on a band shared only by other Extra Class operators in the United States. **ANSWER B** www.ips.gov.au/hf_systems/4/1/2

E3B07 Which of the following could account for hearing an echo on the received signal of a distant station?

A. High D layer absorption

B. Meteor scatter

C. Transmit frequency is higher than the MUF

D. Receipt of a signal by more than one path

When *long-path* conditions exist, European ham stations and even European shortwave stations will be received with a *noticeable echo on the signal*. The echo is the slight delay of the signal coming in long-path from what you are also hearing sooner as a short-path signal. **ANSWER D**
http://tf.nist.gov/stations/wwv.html

E3C08 What is the name of the high-angle wave in HF propagation that travels for some distance within the F2 region?

A. Oblique-angle ray
B. Pedersen ray
C. Ordinary ray
D. Heaviside ray

The *Pedersen ray* is a very-high-angle signal path, occurring in the *F-layer region* and when band conditions are quiet it provides a strong first hop between Northeastern states and all of Europe. Best signal strengths occur when it is afternoon in Europe and early morning here in the US, with excitement from 20 meters all the way up through six meters! If you could visualize the Pedersen ray, it almost looks like it uses the F-layer as a waveguide on HF! **ANSWER B**
http://prop.hfradio.org

E2C12 In North America during low sunspot activity, when signals from Europe become weak and fluttery across an entire HF band two to three hours after sunset, what might help to contact other European DX stations?

A. Switch to a higher frequency HF band
B. Switch to a lower frequency HF band
C. Wait 90 minutes or so for the signal degradation to pass
D. Wait 24 hours before attempting another communication on the band

We are on the upward side of solar cycle 24, and the 20-meter band begins to hold propagation two to three hours after sunset. When *signals begin to become too weak to work, switch to a lower frequency* HF band to compensate for the lower maximum useable frequency (MUF). **ANSWER B** www.dxatlas.com

E3B08 What type of propagation is probably occurring if radio signals travel along the terminator between daylight and darkness?

A. Transequatorial
B. Sporadic-E
C. Long-path
D. Gray-line

Once you earn your Extra Class license, you will stay up for long hours working rare DX. Just as the sun is rising here, it may be setting over Europe or Asia, and working stations in the *twilight at both ends* of the circuit may lead to some extraordinary *gray-line DX contacts* that can last up to 30 minutes. **ANSWER D**

E3B10 What is the cause of gray-line propagation?

A. At midday, the Sun, being directly overhead, superheats the ionosphere causing increased refraction of radio waves
B. At twilight, solar absorption drops greatly, while atmospheric ionization is not weakened enough to reduce the MUF
C. At darkness, solar absorption drops greatly, while atmospheric ionization remains steady
D. At mid afternoon, the Sun heats the ionosphere, increasing radio wave refraction and the MUF

During twilight, the D layer quickly disappears resulting in less absorption, while the E and F layers continue relatively strong. This same condition holds true during solar eclipses. **ANSWER B** www.dxlabsuite.com/propagation

E3B11 What communications are possible during gray-line propagation?

A. Contacts up to 2,000 miles only on the 10-meter band
B. Contacts up to 750 miles on the 6- and 2-meter bands
C. Contacts up to 8,000 to 10,000 miles on three or four HF bands
D. Contacts up to 12,000 to 15,000 miles on the 2 meter and 70 centimeter bands

It is not uncommon to reach beyond *8,000 miles up to 10,000 miles* on three or four high-frequency bands *using gray-line propagation*. **ANSWER C**
http://geoclock.hom.att.net

E3B09 At what time of day is gray-line propagation most prevalent?
A At sunrise and sunset
B. When the Sun is directly above the location of the transmitting station
C. When the Sun is directly overhead at the middle of the communications path between the two stations
D. When the Sun is directly above the location of the receiving station

Gray-line propagation occurs when the Sun is just setting to our west, and just coming up nearly halfway around the world to THEIR east. Our signal travels along the gray-line "terminator" and provides about twenty minutes of exciting, stronger-than-usual propagation. There are numerous computer programs that show gray-line DX opportunities. If you enjoy working DX *just before the Sun rises*, turn your antennas to the EAST and maybe work a station that is just enjoying *THEIR sunset*. The *twilight contacts* can really be a thrill! A *gray-line communications* path, by definition, follows the daylight/dark "terminator" wherever it happens to exist at any given moment. This means that the communications path involved with gray-line propagation is constrained within the boundaries of the gray-line. The condition that creates the gray-line, specifically "twilight," requires that the sun be below the horizon. Therefore, the sun cannot at the same time be "overhead at the middle of the communications path." The gray-line communications path also is a type of great circle; therefore, the shortest distance between the two end points. The fact that the sun might appear to be overhead at the point between the end points on a planar map does not mean that it is overhead on a great-circle route. **ANSWER A**

A Geo Clock shows the gray-line area.

E3A09 When a meteor strikes the Earth's atmosphere, a cylindrical region of free electrons is formed at what layer of the ionosphere?
 A. The E layer
 B. The F1 layer
 C. The F2 layer
 D. The D layer

It is within the *E-layer* of the ionosphere that 6- and 2-meter excitement like *Sporadic-E and meteor scatter* contacts take place. *Think mEtEor!* **ANSWER A**
www.spaceweather.com

E3A10 Which range of frequencies is well suited for meteor-scatter communications?
 A. 1.8 - 1.9 MHz
 B. 10 - 14 MHz
 C. 28 - 148 MHz
 D. 220 - 450 MHz

During a recent meteor shower, I was able to maintain 30-second meteor-scatter QSOs on the 10-meter band; 10-second QSOs on the 6-meter band, and 3-second QSOs on the 2-meter band. The higher you go in frequency, the shorter the contact time. *28-148 MHz are the best* areas to hear the effects of *meteor-scatter*. If you live within 100 miles of an airport, listen to 75 MHz on a scanner for airport radio navigation signals to bounce off of meteor trails. **ANSWER C**

E3A11 What transmit and receive time sequencing is normally used on 144 MHz when attempting a meteor-scatter contact?
 A. Two-minute sequences, where one station transmits for a full two minutes and then receives for the following two minutes
 B. One-minute sequences, where one station transmits for one minute and then receives for the following one minute
 C. 15-second sequences, where one station transmits for 15 seconds and then receives for the following 15 seconds
 D. 30-second sequences, where one station transmits for 30 seconds and then receives for the following 30 seconds

On meteor-scatter, stations transmitting from the west to the east using voice or CW go for the first *15 seconds* and the third 15 seconds of a minute. East calls west on the second and fourth 15 seconds of the minute. This is the pattern used for voice and CW scheduled contacts. This pattern is not used for random meteor-scatter calls. Digital FSK 441 contacts require longer duration sequences. **ANSWER C**

E3B01 What is transequatorial propagation?
 A. Propagation between two points at approximately the same distance north and south of the magnetic Equator
 B. Propagation between any two points located on the magnetic Equator
 C. Propagation between two continents by way of ducts along the magnetic Equator
 D. Propagation between two stations at the same latitude

A TE (transequatorial) signal is *propagated* between stations *north and south of the magnetic Equator*. Some of the best contacts have been between Florida and countries in South America. Any stations in contact with each other are about the same distance away from the Equator – ideal conditions for a TE contact. Both CW as well as SSB are the normal modes for TE on VHF and UHF bands. **ANSWER A**

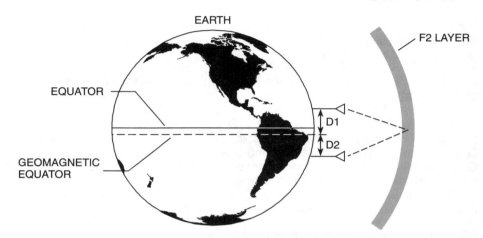

For transequatorial propagation to occur, stations at D1 and D2 must be equidistant from geomagnetic equator. Popular theory is that reflections occur in and off the F2 layer during peak sunspot activity.

Transequatorial Propagation

E3B02 What is the approximate maximum range for signals using transequatorial propagation?

A. 1000 miles   C. 5000 miles
B. 2500 miles   D. 7500 miles

The maximum total distance for a *TE (transequatorial)* contact is about *5,000 miles*. **ANSWER C**

E3B03 What is the best time of day for transequatorial propagation?

A. Morning   C. Afternoon or early evening
B. Noon   D. Late at night

Similar to Sporadic-E, the best time of day for *TE propagation* is *mid-afternoon or early evening*. By this time of day, the Sun's ultraviolet radiation has had time to "warm up" the possible propogation path. **ANSWER C**

E3C01 What effect does auroral activity have on radio communications?

A. Signals experience long-delay echo
B. FM communications are clearer
C. CW signals have a clearer tone
D. CW signals have a fluttery tone

If you live in the Northwest, Northeast, or along the Great Lakes, chances are you have seen some auroral activity. The aurora is a visual glowing of the lower ionospheric layers, and will cause VHF and UHF signals to reflect off of this shimmering curtain. Since the aurora is always changing, *CW signals will sound like a fluttery tone*, or none at all! **ANSWER D** www.csuhfs.org

E3C02 What is the cause of auroral activity?

A. Reflections in the solar wind
B. A low sunspot level
C. The emission of charged particles from the Sun
D. Meteor showers concentrated in the northern latitudes

During periods of major *sunspots, auroral activity* will be high. When a giant solar flare occurs on the face of the Sun, we see it here on earth about eight minutes later and feel the effects of its ultraviolet radiation. About two days later, slower moving *charged particles* begin to pump up the ionosphere, many times creating spectacular auroral light shows. It's the charged particles that take a couple of days to finally reach us that *give us an aurora.* **ANSWER C**
www.aurorasentry.net

Solar flares and sunspots affect radiowave propagation

Photo courtesy of N.A.S.A.

E3C03 Where in the ionosphere does auroral activity occur?

A. At F-region height
B. In the equatorial band
C. At D-region height
D. At E-region height

Have you been to Canada or Alaska to watch an *aurora*? These light shows occur in our ionospheric *"E" layer*. On worldwide signals, the aurora will many times degrade good skip conditions. But on VHF and UHF, the aurora may provide some exciting fluttery "E" layer bounces. **ANSWER D**
http://umtof.umd.edu/pm/latest2day.gif

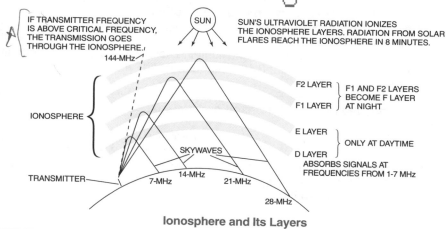

IF TRANSMITTER FREQUENCY IS ABOVE CRITICAL FREQUENCY, THE TRANSMISSION GOES THROUGH THE IONOSPHERE.

SUN

SUN'S ULTRAVIOLET RADIATION IONIZES THE IONOSPHERE LAYERS. RADIATION FROM SOLAR FLARES REACH THE IONOSPHERE IN 8 MINUTES.

144-MHz

F2 LAYER
F1 LAYER
} F1 AND F2 LAYERS BECOME F LAYER AT NIGHT

IONOSPHERE

E LAYER
D LAYER
} ONLY AT DAYTIME

SKYWAVES

ABSORBS SIGNALS AT FREQUENCIES FROM 1-7 MHz

TRANSMITTER
7-MHz
14-MHz
21-MHz
28-MHz

Ionosphere and Its Layers

E3C04 (A) Which emission mode is best for auroral propagation?

A. CW
B. SSB
C. FM
D. RTTY

Bouncing a signal off of an aurora is difficult. *CW always provides the best* opportunity for someone hearing raspy sounds coming into their receiver. On many *auroral contacts* on CW, we don't even hear a tone – all that can be heard are just short and long rushes of super-imposed noise. Play my audio CD Extra Class course and listen for yourself. **ANSWER A**

E3C11 From the contiguous 48 states, in which approximate direction should an antenna be pointed to take maximum advantage of auroral propagation?

A. South
B. North
C. East
D. West

You would aim your directional antenna *north* at the aurora in order to pick up VHF and UHF fluttery auroral CW sounds. Also, with big auroras, you can sometimes even transmit SSB. Forget about FM or RTTY as they usually will not work off of an aurora. **ANSWER B**

Geomagnetic disturbances caused by the Sun result in the Northern Lights.

E3C05 What causes selective fading?

A. Small changes in beam heading at the receiving station
B. Phase differences in the received signal caused by different paths
C. Large changes in the height of the ionosphere
D. Time differences between the receiving and transmitting stations

Phase differences in an incoming signal caused by receiving that signal via different paths will result in distorted sound due to selective fading of the sidebands. **ANSWER B**

E4E06 What is a major cause of atmospheric static?

A. Solar radio frequency emissions
B. Thunderstorms
C. Geomagnetic storms
D. Meteor showers

Thunderstorms carry lightning activity, and lightning noise can be received from as far away as 800 miles on the 80- and 40-meter bands. **ANSWER B**

www.benito.net

E3C14 Why does the radio-path horizon distance exceed the geometric horizon?

A. E-region skip
B. D-region skip
C. Auroral skip
D. Radio waves may be bent

Because of the difference in the air's refractive index at higher altitudes, *radio waves will bend slightly,* giving them a longer horizon than the optical horizon. See the explanation at E3C06. **ANSWER D**

E3C06 How much farther does the VHF/UHF radio-path horizon distance exceed the geometric horizon?

A. By approximately 15% of the distance
B. By approximately twice the distance
C. By approximately one-half the distance
D. By approximately four times the distance

Radio waves bend slightly over the horizon because of the difference in the air's refractive index at higher altitudes. You can calculate your approximate VHF range to the horizon with the formula: D (miles) = 1.415 × √2H (in feet). Determine the height (in feet) of the station you are wishing to communicate with, calculate its distance to the horizon, and add the two answers together for your rock-solid communications range. *Depending on local weather conditions, a 15% to 30% range enhancement over the optical horizon will usually take place at VHF and UHF radio frequency bands.* **ANSWER A**

VHF Range Nomograph

E3C09 What effect is usually responsible for propagating a VHF signal over 500 miles?

A. D-region absorption
B. Faraday rotation
C. Tropospheric ducting
D. Moonbounce

Some incredible extra-long-range VHF and UHF propagation may take place in the presence of a high-pressure system. Sinking warm air, called a subsidence, overlays cool air just above the surface of the Earth and over water. *A well-defined inversion layer occurs* when there is a sharp boundary between the sinking warm air and the cool air beneath. Over big cities, we call it smog. To the VHF and UHF DX enthusiast, we call it a for-sure key to super range contacts via VHF *tropospheric ducting*. I've communicated many times from my station in California to Hawaii on the 2-meter band during summer months when tropospheric ducting is at its best! **ANSWER C** http://dx.qsl.net/propagation/tropospheric

Tropospheric Ducting

E3C12 As the frequency of a signal is increased, how does its ground wave propagation change?
A. It increases
B. It decreases
C. It stays the same
D. Radio waves don't propagate along the Earth's surface

Ground waves travel further on lower frequencies, so as the *frequency of a signal is increased, ground wave propagation decreases*. This same propagation phenomena occurs with audio frequencies. Lower audio frequencies travel further than higher audio frequencies. That's why fog horns always blast out a very low audio tone.
ANSWER B

E3C13 What type of polarization does most ground-wave propagation have?
A. Vertical   C. Circular
B. Horizontal   D. Elliptical

We use *vertical polarization for best ground-wave propagation*. Knife-edge bending is a good example of vertically-polarized ground waves that drag the bottom half of the wave over a mountain top, resulting in the ground-wave signal getting into valleys where there normally would be no reception. **ANSWER A**

RADIO ENERGY
DIFFRACTED

RECEIVER

TRANSMITTER

MOUNTAIN

Knife-Edge Diffraction

E2C01 Which of the following is true about contest operating?
A. Operators are permitted to make contacts even if they do not submit a log
B. Interference to other amateurs is unavoidable and therefore acceptable
C. It is mandatory to transmit the call sign of the station being worked as part of every transmission to that station
D. Every contest requires a signal report in the exchange

Many of you are preparing for Extra Class to gain valuable, exclusive Extra Class frequencies for contesting. Contesting hones our capability to pick weak signals out of the noise, and enhances speedy operating techniques, essential in some emergency communication situations. *There is no requirement to submit a contest log* when participating in a contest. However, sending in a log lets contest officials know the popularity of their specific contest. **ANSWER A**
www.hornucopia.com/contestcal/index.html

E2C05 Which of the following frequencies would generally be acceptable for U.S. stations to work other U.S. stations in a phone contest?
A. 5405 kHz   C. 50.050 MHz
B. 14.310 MHz   D. 146.52 MHz

For this question, let's eliminate those frequencies where it would NOT be acceptable for contesting. Don't contest on 5405 kHz, because this is a channel center in the 60 meter band, where contesting does not normally take place. 50.050 would be taboo for phone contesting because this is in the CW only portion of the band. 146.520 MHz on 2 meters FM is generally not allowed for contesting as it is the national calling frequency. This leaves a good *contest* pick hit at *14.310 MHz, the 20 meter band*, a great place to contest in working other US stations on phone. [97.301] **ANSWER B** www.arrl.org/contests

E2C11 How should you generally sign your call when attempting to contact a DX station working a "pileup" or in a contest?
    A. Send your full call sign once or twice
    B. Send only the last two letters of your call sign until you make contact
    C. Send your full call sign and grid square
    D. Send the call sign of the DX station three times, the words "this is", then your call sign three times
Always make sure to send your full call sign when operating DX, not just the last letter or 2 in your call sign, which is technically not legal. Full call sign. Rules also require that you momentarily listen to your offset transmit frequency to ensure the frequency is not in use. **ANSWER A** www.arrl.org/awards/dxcc

E2C10 Why might a phone DX station state that he is listening on another frequency?
    A. Because the DX station may be transmitting on a frequency that is prohibited to some responding stations
    B. To separate the calling stations from the DX station
    C. To reduce interference, thereby improving operating efficiency
    D. All of these choices are correct
As a new Extra Class operator, learn from listening during your first contest in the Extra Class portion of the band. If it is an international contest, you will hear rare DX stations calling for a contact, "listening up 10." This means they are not listening on their own transmit frequency, but are listening 10 kHz higher for a response. An example might be a foreign DX station operating just below your Extra Class band limits on 20 meters, at 14.145, listening "up 10." This means you would transmit back to them on 14.155 MHz. To do this, you tune VFO-A to the receive frequency of 14.145, and put VFO-B on your transmit frequency of 14.155. Now SPLIT VFO OPERATION and make sure you are transmitting on VFO-B, yet receiving on VFO-A. You must be in SPLIT for this to occur. If you transmit back to the foreign station outside of your Extra Class lower band edge you are illegally out of band and the foreign station can't hear you because they are listening "up 10 kHz" within the Extra USA band. *Split operation reduces interference, separates calling stations from the DX station, and lets the DX station stay in the clear, out of our USA phone band.* **ANSWER D**

E2C07 What is the Cabrillo format?
    A. A standard for organizing information in contest log files
    B. A method of exchanging information during a contest QSO
    C. The most common set of contest rules
    D. The rules of order for meetings between contest sponsors
The various computer logging programs (such as CT by K1EA, TR Log, N1MM, etc.) have built-in utilities that *automatically generate a Cabrillo-formatted log* after

the contest is over. It's one of those features where you click on a box and the program automatically ker-chunks out a Cabrillo file for submission to the ARRL, CQ, or other contest sponsor. **ANSWER A**

E2C02 Which of the following best describes "self spotting" in regards to contest operating?
A. The generally prohibited practice of posting one's own call sign and frequency on a call sign spotting network
B. The acceptable practice of manually posting the call signs of stations on a call sign spotting network
C. A manual technique for rapidly zero beating or tuning to a station's frequency before calling that station
D. An automatic method for rapidly zero beating or tuning to a station's frequency before calling that station

Most avid contesters, looking for a high contest score, will stay glued to a computer call sign spotting network. This allows them to see rare stations and where they are operating on the radio dial. It is considered *poor practice to spot yourself on a computer posting* of contest activity, called "self spotting." **ANSWER A**

E2C06 During a VHF/UHF contest, in which band segment would you expect to find the highest level of activity?
A. At the top of each band, usually in a segment reserved for contests
B. In the middle of each band, usually on the national calling frequency
C. In the weak signal segment of the band, with most of the activity near the calling frequency
D. In the middle of the band, usually 25 kHz above the national calling frequency

During a VHF/UHF contest, *most of the activity is found on each side of the calling frequency.* **ANSWER C** www.swotrc.org

Band	Calling Frequency
6 meters	50.125 MHz
2 meters	144.200 MHz
1.25	222.1 MHz
70 cm	432.100 MHz
35 cm	902.100 MHz
23 cm	1296.100 MHz

E2C04 On which of the following frequencies is an amateur radio contest contact generally discouraged?
A. 3.525 MHz   C. 28.330 MHz
B. 14.020 MHz   D. 146.52 MHz

On the 2 meter band, *146.520 MHz is the national simplex calling frequency.* Most VHF contests preclude any operation on this important calling channel, so don't use "52" for contesting. **ANSWER D**

E2C03 From which of the following bands is amateur radio contesting generally excluded?
A. 30 meters   C. 2 meters
B. 6 meters   D. 33 cm

The 30 meter, 10 MHz band allows CW and data ONLY with a maximum power of 200 watts output. *There is no contesting allowed on the 30 meter band.* **ANSWER A**

E1D02 What is the amateur-satellite service?
    A. A radio navigation service using satellites for the purpose of self-training, intercommunication and technical studies carried out by amateurs
    B. A spacecraft launching service for amateur-built satellites
    C. A radio communications service using amateur stations on satellites
    D. A radio communications service using stations on Earth satellites for weather information gathering

The amateur satellite service allows hams to *communicate through amateur station repeaters and translators* located *on orbiting satellites*. [97.3] **ANSWER C**
www.amsat.org

E2A02 What is the direction of a descending pass for an amateur satellite?
    A. From north to south   C. From east to west
    B. From west to east   D. From south to north

The satellite will pass over the Equator *from our northern hemisphere into the southern hemisphere*. **ANSWER A**

E2A01 What is the direction of an ascending pass for an amateur satellite?
    A. From west to east   C. From south to north
    B. From east to west   D. From north to south

Ground tracking on an ascending pass will have the ham satellite going over the Equator *from the southern hemisphere to the northern hemisphere*. **ANSWER C**

E2A03 What is the orbital period of a satellite?
A. The point of maximum height of a satellite's orbit
B. The point of minimum height of a satellite's orbit
C. The time it takes for a satellite to complete one revolution around the Earth
D. The time it takes for a satellite to travel from perigee to apogee

One complete orbit is the period of a satellite. **ANSWER C**

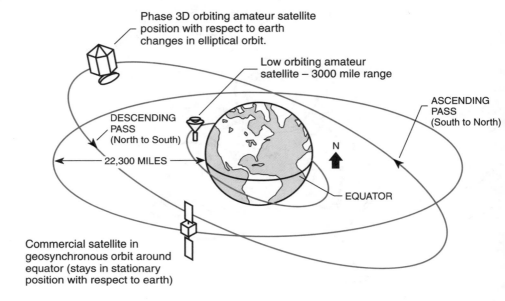

Phase 3D orbiting amateur satellite position with respect to earth changes in elliptical orbit.

Low orbiting amateur satellite – 3000 mile range

ASCENDING PASS (South to North)

DESCENDING PASS (North to South)

22,300 MILES

N

EQUATOR

Commercial satellite in geosynchronous orbit around equator (stays in stationary position with respect to earth)

Orbiting Satellites

E1D04 What is an Earth station in the amateur satellite service?
A. An amateur station within 50 km of the Earth's surface for communications with amateur stations by means of objects in space
B. An amateur station that is not able to communicate using amateur satellites
C. An amateur station that transmits telemetry consisting of measurement of upper atmosphere data from space
D. Any amateur station on the surface of the Earth

Below 50 kilometers, you're considered an *earth station* when you are communicating via the amateur satellite service. [97.3] **ANSWER A**

E1D11 Which amateur stations are eligible to operate as Earth stations?
A. Any amateur station whose licensee has filed a pre-space notification with the FCC's International Bureau
B. Only those of General, Advanced or Amateur Extra Class operators
C. Only those of Amateur Extra Class operators
D. Any amateur station, subject to the privileges of the class of operator license held by the control operator

An amateur Earth station is located down here on planet Earth. Operating as an *Earth station* for space communications is *available to all amateur stations*. Be sure to use only those frequency privileges allowed by your license class. [97.209] **ANSWER D**

E1D03 What is a telecommand station in the amateur satellite service?
A. An amateur station located on the Earth's surface for communications with other Earth stations by means of Earth satellites
B. An amateur station that transmits communications to initiate, modify or terminate certain functions of a space station
C. An amateur station located more than 50 km above the Earth's surface
D. An amateur station that transmits telemetry consisting of measurements of upper atmosphere data from space

Telecommand means *initiating, modifying, or terminating a function of another station*, such as a space station. [97.3] **ANSWER B**

E1D01 What is the definition of the term telemetry?
A. One-way transmission of measurements at a distance from the measuring instrument
B. A two-way interactive transmission
C. A two-way single channel transmission of data
D. One-way transmission that initiates, modifies, or terminates the functions of a device at a distance

We hear the word "telemetry" a lot in satellite service. Satellite telemetry may give ground controllers vital information on satellite battery power, power loads, and satellite solar power charging. *Telemetry* is a one-way transmission of *measurements at a distance* from the measuring instrument. [97.3] **ANSWER A**

E1D10 Which amateur stations are eligible to be telecommand stations?
A. Any amateur station designated by NASA
B. Any amateur station so designated by the space station licensee
C. Any amateur station so designated by the ITU
D. All of these choices are correct

Any amateur station so designated by the space station licensee *may be a telecommand station.* [97.211] **ANSWER B**

E2A04 What is meant by the term "mode" as applied to an amateur radio satellite?
A. The type of signals that can be relayed through the satellite
B. The satellite's uplink and downlink frequency bands
C. The satellite's orientation with respect to the Earth
D. Whether the satellite is in a polar or equatorial orbit

Working through amateur satellites is exciting, challenging, and fun! Our *transmit and receive frequencies for satellite operation* are on separate bands. Each band has its own designator:

Frequency Bands	Frequency Range	Modes
High Frequency	21 - 30 MHz	Mode H
VHF	144 - 146 MHz	Mode V
UHF	435 - 438 MHz	Mode U
L band	1.26 - 1.27 GHz	Mode L
S band	2.4 - 2.45 GHz	Mode S
C band	5.8 GHz	Mode C
X band	10.4 GHz	Mode X
K band	24 GHz	Mode K

The satellite receives on one frequency band, and transmits on another frequency band. Since two bands are involved, we will have two mode designators to best describe our transmit and receive bands, and the satellite receive and transmit bands. We call our Earth transmit band an "uplink", and our receive band the "downlink." **ANSWER B**

E2A05 What do the letters in a satellite's mode designator specify?
A. Power limits for uplink and downlink transmissions
B. The location of the ground control station
C. The polarization of uplink and downlink signals
D. The uplink and downlink frequencies

The *two mode designators indicate* our transmit *uplink frequency and* our receive *downlink frequency* band. **ANSWER D**

E2A09 What do the terms L band and S band specify with regard to satellite communications?
A. The 23 centimeter and 13 centimeter bands
B. The 2 meter and 70 centimeter bands
C. FM and Digital Store-and-Forward systems
D. Which sideband to use

You can work this out by recalling the MHz to meters and meters to MHz formula, but there are lots of conversions because we are working with centimeters and GHz. The *L band* at 1.26 GHz works out to be *23 centimeters*, and the *S band*, at 2.4 GHz, works out to be *13 centimeters*. You can rule out Answer B as that would be VHF and UHF, with C and D having nothing to do with band specifics. 23 centimeters is L band, and 13 centimeters is S band. **ANSWER A**

E2A06 On what band would a satellite receive signals if it were operating in mode U/V?
A. 432 MHz   C. 50 MHz
B. 144 MHz   D. 28 MHz

Watch out on this question – I don't want you to miss it even though you THOUGHT they might be trying to trick you. The question asks on what band would a satellite receive signals – this is the same as asking on what band would an Earth station transmit to the satellite. Since the *mode* begins with the letter *U*, we transmit, and the satellite simultaneously receives, on UHF 435 - 438 MHz, 70 cm, sometimes called the *"432"* band. **ANSWER A**

E2A07 Which of the following types of signals can be relayed through a linear transponder?
A. FM and CW   C. PSK and Packet
B. SSB and SSTV   D. All these answers are correct

Thanks to AMSAT, many of our OSCAR satellites offer a "bent pipe" re-transmission of many modes of our uplink signal. If we uplink FM and CW, it comes back down FM and CW through the satellite linear transponder. Same thing with single sideband, slow scan television, and the digital modes – *all of these signals* are relayed by the satellite through the onboard linear transponder. **ANSWER D**

E2A10 Why may the received signal from an amateur satellite exhibit a rapidly repeating fading effect?

A. Because the satellite is rotating
B. Because of ionospheric absorption
C. Because of the satellite's low orbital altitude
D. Because of the Doppler effect

Many amateur satellites continuously rotate to keep all sides of the "bird" equally bathed in sunlight. This distributes the heat build-up, and allows all of the solar panels to receive energy from the Sun. *Because of the rotation*, we hear a characteristic *rapid pulse in and out on the downlink*. **ANSWER A**

E2A11 What type of antenna can be used to minimize the effects of spin modulation and Faraday rotation?

A. A linearly polarized antenna
B. A circularly polarized antenna
C. An isotropic antenna
D. A log-periodic dipole array

The *circular polarized antenna* will give you best results when working amateur satellites. Although you lose approximately 3 dB gain over a horizontal antenna, circular polarization minimizes fading. **ANSWER B**

Tracking and communicating through amateur satellites can be done with a cross-polarized satellite antenna

E2A12 What is one way to predict the location of a satellite at a given time?

A. By means of the Doppler data for the specified satellite
B. By subtracting the mean anomaly from the orbital inclination
C. By adding the mean anomaly to the orbital inclination
D. By calculations using the Keplerian elements for the specified satellite

You can log onto many satellite web pages and learn the *Keplerian elements for* a specific satellite or a specific *day and time* for the location of the satellite. You can find this information on the AMSAT website at www.AMSAT.org. **ANSWER D**

Computer programs and websites can show you where and when an amateur satellite or the Space Station will be in range of your ham station

E2A14 What happens to a satellite's transmitted signal due to the Doppler Effect?
A. The signal strength is reduced as the satellite passes overhead
B. The signal frequency shifts lower as the satellite passes overhead
C. The signal frequency shifts higher as the satellite passes overhead
D. The polarization of the signal continually rotates

Have you worked our orbiting satellites? As they come up over the horizon, *Doppler Effect* may cause their transmit (our receive) signal to appear higher. Just before the pass is over, the received signal appears lower. We can always tell when the satellite is near its overhead position because the *signal frequency shifts* from higher (approaching us) to progressively lower (overhead and going away). **ANSWER B**

F is higher as satellite approaches.

F = Frequency of signal when satellite is right at hand.

F is lower as satellite moves away.

Doppler Effect

E2A08 What is the primary reason for satellite users to limit their transmit ERP?
A. For RF exposure safety
B. Because the satellite transmitter output power is limited
C. To avoid limiting the signal of the other users
D. To avoid interfering with terrestrial QSOs

Our satellites are powered by on-board batteries, charged by solar panels. On some older satellites, still operational, a very strong uplink signal received by the satellite will put more power into the transmit downlink. *Help conserve satellite battery power* by always monitoring your own downlink signal and try to reduce your uplink effective radiated power to a minimum level. True, some linear satellites actually AGC-downsize the strength of overly-strong signals but, overall, answer B is best for the test! **ANSWER B**

E2D04 What is the purpose of digital store-and-forward functions on an Amateur satellite?
A. To upload operational software for the transponder
B. To delay download of telemetry until the satellite is over the control station
C. To store digital messages in the satellite for later download by other stations
D. To relay messages between satellites

Amateur orbiting satellites make great *store-and-forward messengers* to hold messages that may be downloaded later by other stations. **ANSWER C**

E2D05 Which of the following techniques is normally used by low-Earth orbiting digital satellites to relay messages around the world?
A. Digipeating
B. Store-and-forward
C. Multi-satellite relaying
D. Node hopping

Store-and-forward is a popular way of sending a wireless e-mail that may be received halfway around the world when the satellite passes over the distant station. **ANSWER B**

E2A13 What type of satellite appears to stay in one position in the sky?
A. HEO
B. Geosynchronous
C. Geomagnetic
D. LEO

Great news from AMSAT – they are in discussion with Intelsat to place an amateur radio payload on a future Intelsat GEOSTATIONARY satellite in a "rideshare" arrangement. We could end up with a *GEOSYNCHRONOUS satellite* that could provide 500 voice channels and the ability to provide video and other digital services, 24 hours a day, with dishes for S band and C band aimed in just one fixed direction! We currently have NO ham satellites in geosynchronous orbit, but with this "rideshare" agreement with Intelsat, a "geo" may be in our future! Watch out for incorrect answer "geomagnetic". **ANSWER B**

E1D12 Who must be notified before launching an amateur space station?
A. The National Aeronautics and Space Administration, Houston, TX
B. The FCC's International Bureau, Washington, DC
C. The Amateur Satellite Corp., Washington, DC
D. All of these answers are correct

The *FCC's International Bureau* in Washington, DC, handles the notification before the launch of an amateur satellite station into orbit. [97.207] **ANSWER B**

E1D06 Which of the following special provisions must a space station incorporate in order to comply with space station requirements?
A. The space station must be capable of effecting a cessation of transmissions by telecommand when so ordered by the FCC
B. The space station must cease all transmissions after 5 years
C. The space station must be capable of changing its orbit whenever such a change is ordered by NASA
D. The station call sign must appear on all sides of the spacecraft

All space stations must be capable of receiving a telecommand to *shut them down* if ordered to do so by the FCC. [97.207] **ANSWER A**

E1D07 Which amateur service HF bands have frequencies authorized to space stations?
A. Only 40m, 20m, 17m, 15m, 12m and 10m
B. Only 40m, 20m, 17m, 15m and 10m bands
C. 40m, 30m, 20m, 15m, 12m and 10m bands
D. All HF bands

By international agreement, all high-frequency ITU voice bands plus most of our regular high-frequency ham bands are available for space operation. This includes *40 meters, 20 meters, 17 meters ITU, 15 meters, 12 meters ITU, and 10 meters.* [97.207] **ANSWER A**

E1D05 What class of licensee is authorized to be the control operator of a space station?
A. Any except those of Technician Class operators
B. Only those of General, Advanced or Amateur Extra Class operators
C. A holder of any class of license
D. Only those of Amateur Extra Class operators

There is no longer a specific higher grade license requirement for space operation. *Any grade of license* may now qualify. (Originally, only an Extra Class operator could transmit from space.) [97.207] **ANSWER C**

E1D08 Which VHF amateur service bands have frequencies available for space stations?
A. 6 meters and 2 meters
B. 6 meters, 2 meters, and 1.25 meters
C. 2 meters and 1.25 meters
D. 2 meters

On VHF 30-300 MHz, only the 2-meter band allows space station operation. Space station operation is prohibited on 1.25 meters (the 222 MHz band) and 6 meters. You can find the right answer by looking at the wrong answers. [97.207] **ANSWER D**

E1D09 Which amateur service UHF bands have frequencies available for a space station?
A. 70 cm
B. 70 cm, 23 cm, and 13 cm
C. 70 cm and 33 cm
D. 33 cm and 13 cm

On UHF, 300-3000 MHz, the 33 cm (900 MHz) band is NOT allowed for space station, but all other bands are allowed. This includes *70 cm (435 MHz), 23 cm (1260 MHz), and 13 cm* (2300 MHz). [97.207] **ANSWER B**

E3A01 What is the approximate maximum separation along the surface of the Earth between two stations communicating by moonbounce?
A. 500 miles if the moon is at perigee
B. 2000 miles, if the moon is at apogee
C. 5000 miles, if the moon is at perigee
D. 12,000 miles, as long as both can "see" the moon

It takes a minimum of a pair of long-boom Yagis, plus the maximum legal power output, to establish a moonbounce QSO on CW or SSB phone. If you are working a station with a huge dish antenna, you might get by with a single long-boom Yagi and a good VHF or UHF kilowatt amplifier. Moonbounce is most common on the bottom edge of the 2-meter band, and to communicate over any distance, *both stations must be able to see the moon* in the sky. Monthly ham magazines publish the best EME (Earth-Moon-Earth) days. **ANSWER D**

E3A04 What type of receiving system is desirable for EME communications?
A. Equipment with very wide bandwidth
B. Equipment with very low dynamic range
C. Equipment with very low gain
D. Equipment with very low noise figures

For EME communications, it's best to use a receiver with front-end transistors that have extremely *high gain and extremely low noise* (a "hot front end"). For my station, I use GaAsFET transistors for maximum gain and minimum noise. **ANSWER D**

EME communications require specialized equipment and patience.

E3A07 What frequency range would you normally tune to find EME stations in the 2 meter band?
A. 144.000 - 144.001 MHz   C. 144.100 - 144.300 MHz
B. 144.000 - 144.100 MHz   D. 145.000 - 145.100 MHz

Moon-bounce is found in the CW weak-signal portion of the band. I prefer 144.074 MHz, but *anywhere between 144.000 to 144.100 is the spot for Moon-bounce*. (WSJT EME can be found on 144.1 – 144.2 MHz.) **ANSWER B**

E3A05 What transmit and receive time sequencing is normally used on 144 MHz when attempting an EME contact?
A. Two-minute sequences, where one station transmits for a full two minutes and then receives for the following two minutes
B. One-minute sequences, where one station transmits for one minute and then receives for the following one minute
C. Two-and-one-half minute sequences, where one station transmits for a full 2.5 minutes and then receives for the following 2.5 minutes
D. Five-minute sequences, where one station transmits for five minutes and then receives for the following five minutes

Moon-bounce communication takes plenty of power, a hot receiver with digital signal processing, big antennas, and plenty of patience. Most successful contacts are made by a prearranged schedule. *One station transmits two minutes, and then listens to the other station that will transmit for two minutes*. (When EME conditions are "hot," a shorter transmit/receive sequence usually is used.) **ANSWER A**

E3A08 What frequency range would you normally tune to find EME stations in the 70 cm band?
A. 430.000 - 430.150 MHz
C. 431.100 - 431.200 MHz
B. 430.100 - 431.100 MHz
D. 432.000 - 432.100 MHz

The 70-cm band is again the 432-MHz band – everything *below 432.100 is within the weak-signal (only) portion of the band* where CW and SSB can be found.
ANSWER D

E3A06 What transmit and receive time sequencing is normally used on 432 MHz when attempting an EME contact?
A. Two-minute sequences, where one station transmits for a full two minutes and then receives for the following two minutes
B. One-minute sequences, where one station transmits for one minute and then receives for the following one minute
C. Two-and-one-half minute sequences, where one station transmits for a full 2.5 minutes and then receives for the following 2.5 minutes
D. Five-minute sequences, where one station transmits for five minutes and then receives for the following five minutes

At 432-MHz, on the 70-cm band, conditions are even more rough than what you would find on 2 meters, so you need to send *two-and-one-half-minute sequences*, rather than just two minutes. **ANSWER C**

E3A02 What characterizes libration fading of an Earth-Moon-Earth signal?
A. A slow change in the pitch of the CW signal
B. A fluttery irregular fading
C. A gradual loss of signal as the Sun rises
D. The returning echo is several Hertz lower in frequency than the transmitted signal

Remember, EME means Earth-Moon-Earth and that the Moon is not a perfect reflector of radio signals. All those craters on the *Moon will cause your return signal to sound fluttery, with rapid, irregular fading.* **ANSWER B**

E3A03 When scheduling EME contacts, which of these conditions will generally result in the least path loss?
A. When the Moon is at perigee
C. When the Moon is at apogee
B. When the Moon is full
D.
When the MUF is above 30 MHz

PERigee is the time when the Moon is closest to the Earth. This is *the PERfect condition for EME to* occur, and a PERfect day to schedule an EME contact. A Moon at perigee, just appearing above the horizon, will give you the best opportunity for Moon-bounce. **ANSWER A**

Ground-mounted antennas, like this 10GHz EME dish in Alaska, should be surrounded by a wood safety fence . And make sure to stay a safe distance away from any antenna on transmit!

E2B01 How many times per second is a new frame transmitted in a fast-scan (NTSC) television system?

A. 30

B. 60

C. 90

D. 120

Operating fast-scan television is fun on the 420-MHz and higher bands. *A new frame is created 30 times per second* by two complete fields for each frame. This gives you a picture just like home television. In fact, older analog cable-ready TVs can still directly receive local ATV signals! **ANSWER A**

Amateur Television

E2B02 How many horizontal lines make up a fast-scan (NTSC) television frame?

A. 30   C. 525
B. 60   D. 1080

A total of *525 lines from two fields make up a complete frame*. **ANSWER C**

E2B03 How is an interlace scanning pattern generated in a fast-scan (NTSC) television system?

A. By scanning two fields simultaneously
B. By scanning each field from bottom to top
C. By scanning lines from left to right in one field and right to left in the next
D. By scanning odd numbered lines in one field and even numbered ones in the next

Each field is 262.5 lines, and *the frame is created by scanning even numbered lines in one field and odd numbered lines in the second field*. **ANSWER D**

E2B04 What is blanking in a video signal?

A. Synchronization of the horizontal and vertical sync pulses
B. Turning off the scanning beam while it is traveling from right to left or from bottom to top
C. Turning off the scanning beam at the conclusion of a transmission
D. Transmitting a black and white test pattern

The scanning beam is turned off when it completes its travel from left to right, and is returning from right to left to start another line. The scanning beam is also blanked when the beam reaches the bottom and is returning to the top to begin the next field. **ANSWER B** www.atn-tv.org

E2B08 Which of the following is a common method of transmitting accompanying audio with amateur fast-scan television?

A. Frequency-modulated sub-carrier
B. A separate VHF or UHF audio link
C. Frequency modulation of the video carrier
D. All of these choices are correct

Besides the standard 4.5 MHz sound subcarrier used by most ATV and analog broadcast stations, *there are a variety of ways to pass audio while transmitting an amateur radio fast-scan "live action" video signal*. Remember, no analog fast-scan TV down on the worldwide bands, or bands below 420 MHz due to bandwidth regulations. To add audio to a fast-scan signal, we could frequency modulate the video carrier itself, known as "on carrier" sound, which was used in the early days when hams added video modulators to FM voice transceivers. Audio can also be simultaneously sent using FM audio on a dedicated VHF or UHF audio link in another band. This link also can be used as an ATV calling, coordination and talkback channel from the receiving stations. On the 2 meter band, most ATV stations use 144.340 MHz or 146.430 MHz for this link. **ANSWER D**
www.hamtv.com

E2B21 If 100 IRE units correspond to the most-white level in the NTSC standard video format, what is the level of the most-black signal?

A. 140 IRE units   C. 0 IRE units
B. 7.5 IRE units   D. -40 IRE units

The composite baseband video signal out of a camera is 1 volt peak-to-peak into 75 ohms. This 1 volt peak-to-peak is broken down into NTSC IRE units of approximately 7.14 mV each and therefore totaling 140 IRE. *Zero IRE units is the blanking level* with the sync tip at -40 IRE. *7.5 IRE units would represent black*, and white is 100 IRE units. **ANSWER B** www.hampubs.com

a. A TV Composite Video Signal
Source: *Using Video in Your Home,* G. McComb. © 1989, Master Publishing, Inc., Niles, IL.

b. Bandwidth for a TV Channel
Source: *Antennas,* A. Evans, K. Britain,. © 1988, Master Publishing, Inc., Niles, IL.

The video signal is composed of three major components: picture, timing, and color. Television sets "know" how to decode this stream of information into pictures that reproduce the changing scenes captured by the video camera.

E2B07 What is the name of the video signal component that carries color information?

A. Luminance

B. Chroma

C. Hue

D. Spectral Intensity

Chroma is the video component contained in a phase modulated 3.58 MHz subcarrier *that varies with the instantaneous color* in the scene being scanned by the video camera. **ANSWER B** www.cq-tv.com

E2B06 What is vestigial sideband modulation?

A. Amplitude modulation in which one complete sideband and a portion of the other sideband is transmitted

B. A type of modulation in which one sideband is inverted

C. Narrow-band FM transmission achieved by filtering one sideband from the audio before frequency modulating the carrier

D. Spread spectrum modulation achieved by applying FM modulation following single sideband amplitude modulation

Vestigial sideband modulation (VSB) is amplitude modulation of a carrier in which *one complete sideband is transmitted* (upper VSB is standard) *and a vestigial sideband filter is used to attenuate the other sideband* video energy greater than 1.25 MHz and the 3.58 MHz color and 4.5 MHz sound sub-carrier frequencies. This helps reduce occupied bandwidth to 6 MHz and provides better spectrum efficiency than full double sideband AM modulation. **ANSWER A**

atv-newsletter@hotmail.com

E2B05 Which of the following is an advantage of using vestigial sideband for standard fast scan TV transmissions?

A. The vestigial sideband carries the audio information

B. The vestigial sideband contains chroma information

C. Vestigial sideband reduces bandwidth while allowing for simple video detector circuitry

D. Vestigial sideband provides high frequency emphasis to sharpen the picture

Vestigal sideband (VSB) cuts off the lower color and sound subcarriers at -3.58 and -4.50 MHz from the video carrier respectively as they are unnecessary. Therefore the frequencies below 1.25 MHz from the video carrier in a VSB transmitter will have very low energy radiated and this *frees up room for more users of the band*. Total TV channel bandwidth is +4.75 / -1.25 MHz from the video carrier, equaling 6 MHz. Simple analog video detectors are used in the TV receiver with most of the work being done by the VSB filter in the IF ahead of the detector. Even though commercial TV signals are switching from analog to digital, many ham fast scan TV signals remain fast scan analog. New TVs will still employ an analog tuner and vestigal sideband receiver *with a simple video detector* in addition to the digital system, for some time, to allow compatibility with older VCRs and DVD players. **ANSWER C** www.qsl.net/k6ccc

E2B19 On which of the following frequencies is one likely to find FMTV transmissions?

A. 14.230 MHz

C. 52.525 MHz

B. 29.6 MHz

D. 1255 MHz

FM fast-scan television is found on the 902 MHz and higher bands because it occupies a whopping 17- to 21-MHz of bandwidth, depending on the sound subcarrier frequency used. US standard is 4 MHz deviation and 5.5 MHz sound in the *902 MHz and 1240 MHz bands*, resulting in an occupied bandwidth of 19 MHz. The center frequency must then be at least 9.5 MHz from the band edge so the sideband energy does not fall outside the band limits. 1255 MHz is a reasonable frequency to use given these parameters. The beauty of FM ATV, thanks to signal-to-noise limiter multiplication, is a snow-free picture that can be received up to 12 dB weaker in signal strength than an AM ATV picture. **ANSWER D** www.atco.com

E2B17 Which of the following is NOT a characteristic of FMTV (Frequency-Modulated Amateur Television) as compared to vestigial sideband AM television?
A. Immunity from fading due to limiting
B. Poor weak signal performance
C. Greater signal bandwidth
D. Greater complexity of receiving equipment

Here is one of the test questions that needs a "negative" answer – you solve this by looking for the correct answers, leaving only the one they are looking for, a "not" negative answer! FM amateur radio television does require a complex receiver at the other end of the circuit, and it does require greater bandwidth, and FM TV does not do well under weak signal conditions. But the "not" answer they are looking for is, *is FM TV is immune from fading? Absolutely NOT –* FM TV has NO immunity from fading due to limiting. **ANSWER A** www.ac6rb.com

---

E2B16 Which of the following is the video standard used by North American fast-scan ATV stations?
A. PAL
B. DRM
C. Scottie
D. NTSC

North American fast-scan analog ATV stations transmit NTSC, National Television System Committee, identical to analog over-the-air broadcast TV signals. Broadcast will soon be all digital. PAL is the analog broadcast TV system used primarily in Europe and other countries. DRM and Scottie are SSTV modes. They ask for *the North American fast-scan video standard, which is NTSC.* **ANSWER D**

E2B12 How are analog slow-scan television images typically transmitted on the HF bands?
A. Video is converted to equivalent Baudot representation
B. Video is converted to equivalent ASCII representation
C. Varying tone frequencies representing the video are transmitted using FM
D. Varying tone frequencies representing the video are transmitted using single sideband

Transmitting a slow scan picture requires not much more than your HF transceiver, a sound card, SSTV ultra–inexpensive software, and your favorite camcorder to freeze frame your smiling mug. The *varying tone frequencies* you hear on a transmitted signal, on SSB, *represent the video* going out over the airwaves. To receive a color SSTV signal, all you need to add to your HF transceiver is a patch cable to your computer's sound card mic input, and the rest is mostly SSTV ultra-inexpensive software! **ANSWER D** www.k9uvy.camstreams.com

---

E2B18 What is the approximate bandwidth of a slow-scan TV signal?
A. 600 Hz
B. 3 kHz
C. 2 MHz
D. 6 MHz

We can find slow scan television on both high frequency as well as on VHF/UHF. On high frequency, look for *slow scan* at 14.230 MHz, and notice that it *takes only 3 kHz of bandwidth*, but up to 45 seconds for a complete single picture. **ANSWER B**

E2B20 What special operating frequency restrictions are imposed on slow scan TV transmissions?

A. None; they are allowed on all amateur frequencies
B. They are restricted to 7.245 MHz, 14.245 MHz, 21.345, MHz, and 28.945 MHz
C. They are restricted to phone band segments and their bandwidth can be no greater than that of a voice signal of the same modulation type
D. They are not permitted above 54 MHz

Slow-scan TV transmissions, as well as facsimile, are allowed in phone band segments as long as their *bandwidth is no greater than that of a voice signal* of the same modulation type. You can easily hear 20-meter slow-scan signals by tuning in 14.230 and 14.233, a hot-bed of SSTV activity that is easily seen on a computer program or on your little handheld SSTV transmit/receive equipment. **ANSWER C**

Amateur slow-scan TV pictures can be displayed
on a tube, or an LCD display like this one

E2B13 How many lines are commonly used in each frame on an amateur slow-scan color television picture?

A. 30 to 60
B. 60 or 100
C. 128 or 256
D. 180 or 360

It takes *128 lines to make up a complete frame. 256 lines increases the resolution* of the color. **ANSWER C** www.bonito.net

E2B15 What signals SSTV receiving equipment to begin a new picture line?

A. Specific tone frequencies
B. Elapsed time
C. Specific tone amplitudes
D. A two-tone signal

Depending on which SSTV mode you are using, *new picture LINES are started by specific tone frequencies.* **ANSWER A**

E2B14 What aspect of an amateur slow-scan television signal encodes the brightness of the picture?

A. Tone frequency
B. Tone amplitude
C. Sync amplitude
D. Sync frequency

Brightness of an SSTV picture *depends on the higher tone frequencies* received.
ANSWER A

E2B09 What hardware, other than a transceiver with SSB capability and a suitable computer, is needed to decode SSTV based on Digital Radio Mondiale (DRM)?

A. A special IF converter
B. A special front end limiter
C. A special notch filter to remove synchronization pulses
D. No other hardware is needed

The term "Digital Radio Mondiale" (DRM) is NOT a special kind of circuit with a big chip in the middle – rather, DRM is a panel of commercial and non-commercial radio users who have developed the sole standard for sending broadcasts over worldwide low-frequency and high-frequency bands. SSTV (slow scan television) is easy to hear at 14.230 MHz, and *it's easy to capture a full-color*, high resolution picture *with* just *your HF transceiver and a suitably-equipped computer with a sound card* running SSTV software. It's easy to get great pictures on high frequency. **ANSWER D**

E2B10 Which of the following is an acceptable bandwidth for Digital Radio Mondiale (DRM) based voice or SSTV digital transmissions made on the HF amateur bands?

A. 3 kHz
B. 10 kHz
C. 15 kHz
D. 20 kHz

The typical high-frequency, *slow-scan signal* occupies no more room than a conventional single sideband voice signal, *3 kHz or less*. **ANSWER A**

E2B11 What is the function of the Vertical Interval Signaling (VIS) code transmitted as part of an SSTV transmission?

A. To lock the color burst oscillator in color SSTV images
B. To identify the SSTV mode being used
C. To provide vertical synchronization
D. To identify the call sign of the station transmitting

There are over a dozen individual methods of sending a color slow scan television signal over HF and VHF airwaves. The most common are Martin and Scottie. These popular modes require the initial reception of *the 300 ms VIS code, which is necessary for your computer to know which SSTV mode it is being sent.* **ANSWER B**

E6D06 What function does a charge-coupled device (CCD) serve in a modern video camera?

A. It stores photogenerated charges as signals corresponding to pixels
B. It generates the horizontal pulses needed for electron beam scanning
C. It focuses the light used to produce a pattern of electrical charges corresponding to the image
D. It combines audio and video information to produce a composite RF signal

The charge-coupled device is continually clocking the data out, or the data "dissipates" like a dynamic RAM. The CCD converts photo-generated charges into signals corresponding to pixels. **ANSWER A**

http://electronics.howstuffworks.com/camcorder2.htm

E6D05 Which of the following is true of a charge-coupled device (CCD)?
    A. Its phase shift changes rapidly with frequency
    B. It is a CMOS analog-to-digital converter
    C. It samples an analog signal and passes it in stages from the input to the output
    D. It is used in a battery charger circuit

The charge-coupled device *(CCD) samples an analog signal* and pass it in stages from input to output. **ANSWER C** www.computer-int.com

Amateur TV signals can be received on a variety
of equipment – even a small hand-held monitor

E6D16 Which is NOT true of a charge-coupled device (CCD)?
    A. It uses a combination of analog and digital circuitry
    B. It can be used to make an audio delay line
    C. It is commonly used as an analog-to-digital converter
    D. It samples and stores analog signals

This question asks which is NOT true of a *CCD*. A charge-coupled device *cannot be used as an analog-to-digital converter*. **ANSWER C**

E6D01 How is the electron beam deflected in a vidicon?
    A. By varying the beam voltage
    B. By varying the bias voltage on the beam forming grids inside the tube
    C. By varying the beam current
    D. By varying electromagnetic fields

The electron beam is deflected by *varying electromagnetic fields* in coils surrounding the tube. **ANSWER D**

E6D02 What is cathode ray tube (CRT) persistence?
    A. The time it takes for an image to appear after the electron beam is turned on
    B. The relative brightness of the display under varying conditions of ambient light
    C. The ability of the display to remain in focus under varying conditions
    D. The length of time the image remains on the screen after the beam is turned off

The term *"persistence"* in a cathode-ray tube is the *length of time that an image will remain on the screen* after the beam gets turned off. **ANSWER D**

E6D15 What type of CRT deflection is better when high-frequency waves are to be displayed on the screen?

A. Electromagnetic
B. Tubular
C. Radar
D. Electrostatic

Cathode-ray tube *(CRT) electrostatic deflection* is better for high-frequency signals. Horizontal and vertical deflection plates, similar to capacitor plates, deflect the electron beam onto the screen according to signal voltages applied to the plates. **ANSWER D**

E6D04 Exceeding what design rating can cause a cathode ray tube (CRT) to generate X-rays?

A. The heater voltage
B. The anode voltage
C. The operating temperature
D. The operating frequency

X-rays can be emitted from a cathode-ray tube *if the anode voltage is increased beyond the* value at which the tube is *safely rated.* **ANSWER B**

E6D03 If a cathode ray tube (CRT) is designed to operate with an anode voltage of 25,000 volts, what will happen if the anode voltage is increased to 35,000 volts?

A. The image size will decrease
B. The image size will increase
C. The image will become larger and brighter
D. There will be no apparent change

If the anode voltage on a cathode-ray tube is increased from a normal 25,000 volts to 35,000 volts, you will see that the *over voltage will actually decrease the size of the image on the screen*, and the CRT could also produce harmful radiation because of this excessive voltage. **ANSWER A**

E6D07 What is a liquid-crystal display (LCD)?

A. A modern replacement for a quartz crystal oscillator which displays its fundamental frequency
B. A display that uses a crystalline liquid to change the way light is refracted
C. A frequency-determining unit for a transmitter or receiver
D. A display that uses a glowing liquid to remain brightly lit in dim light

A liquid-crystal display, found on most amateur radio handheld units, *uses a crystalline liquid to change the way light is refracted* from a rear mirror through the liquid. **ANSWER B** www.hamtv.org

Liquid Crystal Displays are popular because of their large size and low power consumption

---

75

E6D17 What is the principle advantage of liquid-crystal display (LCD) devices over other types of display devices?

A. They consume less power
B. They can display changes instantly
C. They are visible in all light conditions
D. They can be easily interchanged with other display devices

It takes *very little current* to sustain a liquid crystal display segment. **ANSWER A**

E2E01 What is a common method of transmitting data emissions below 30 MHz?

A. DTMF tones modulating an FM signal
B. FSK/AFSK
C. Pulse modulation
D. Spread spectrum

Frequency Shift Keying (FSK) is the changing of the carrier frequency in step with your computer's data pulses during transmit. With Audio Frequency Shift Keying (AFSK), your transmit frequency remains steady with audio tones sent to represent data pulses. Both *FSK and AFSK are the common modes below 30 MHz*, with AFSK now more popular than FSK. The reason? Computer sound cards, and smart data controllers! Teletype (RTTY) is an example of Frequency Shift Keying. If a teleprinter is attached to a rig, it has to be connected to the FSK connector and FSK mode must be selected. AFSK includes the digital modes PSK31/63, MFSK8 and 16, SSTV, Olivia, and other digital modes that are created in sound card programs such as MultiPSK. The output of the sound card is connected to the "packet" connector on the rear panel, and the front panel will have "Packet" or "PKT" selected. AFSK modes operate in SSB mode, typically USB, and require careful adjustment of the audio level for ZERO ALC level. Transmitter output power in watts will typically be 1/2 of the full rating. **ANSWER B**

E2E06 What is the most common data rate used for HF packet communications?

A. 48 baud   C. 300 baud
B. 110 baud   D. 1200 baud

High frequency packet must labor along at a relatively slow *300 baud* so as not to exceed signal bandwidth limits below 30 MHz. 300 baud seems pretty slow compared to higher speeds on VHF and UHF, and high-frequency packet is not necessarily a "right now" transmission method. However, it is highly accurate and even binary files may be sent around the world via HF packet! **ANSWER C**

E2D03 Which of the following is true when comparing HF and 2-meter packet operations?

A. HF packet typically uses FSK with a data rate of 300 baud; 2-meter packet uses AFSK with a data rate of 1200 baud
B. HF packet and 2-meter packet operations use different codes for information exchange
C. HF packet is limited to Amateur Extra class amateur licensees; 2-meter packet is open to all but Novice Class amateur licensees
D. HF and 2-meter packet operations are both limited to CW/Data-only band segments

On *high frequency*, our packet signal typically use frequency shift keying (FSK) with a data rate of *300 baud maximum*. On *2 meters*, we can operate up to *1200 baud* and we use audio frequency shift keying (AFSK). **ANSWER A**

E2D09 Under clear communications conditions, which of these digital communications modes has the fastest data throughput?

A. AMTOR   C. PSK31
B. 170-Hz shift, 45 baud RTTY   D. 300-baud packet

Although *300-baud packet* sounds relatively slow, *on the worldwide bands* it's faster than most other modes. **ANSWER D**

E2D02 What is the definition of "baud"?

A. The number of data symbols transmitted per second
B. The number of characters transmitted per second
C. The number of characters transmitted per minute
D. The number of words transmitted per minute

The term *"baud"* is the *number of data symbols transmitted per second*. With Baudot signaling speeds, the character count will not match the data symbol rate. We call those symbols transmitted per second as a number of events or discreet conditions per second. In the Baudot code, one character may be represented by five bits. **ANSWER A**

E2E11 What is the Baudot code?

A. A code used to transmit data only in modern computer-based data systems using seven data bits
B. A binary code consisting of eight data bits
C. An alternate name for Morse code
D. The International Telegraph Alphabet Number 2 (ITA2) which uses five data bits

The original name for *transmitting and receiving letters and numbers* over the air was a code called International Teletype Alphabet Number 2. We now call it *Baudot*, giving us the on-air capability to produce both letters and numbers, plus punctuation symbols, with the *5-bit code*. Everything is sent upper case. **ANSWER D**

E2D01 What does "command mode" mean in packet operations?
A. Your computer is ready to run packet communications software
B. The TNC is ready to receive instructions via the keyboard
C. Your TNC has received a command packet from a remote TNC
D. The computer is ready to be set up to communicate with the TNC

When the prompt *"CMD"* shows up on the monitor when you are in the packet mode, it indicates that *the terminal node controller (TNC) is ready to receive keyboard instructions.* **ANSWER B**

Packet Terminal Node Controller (TNC)
Courtesy of MFJ Enterprises, Inc.

E2E08 Which of the following HF digital modes can be used to transfer binary files?
A. Hellschreiber
B. PACTOR
C. RTTY
D. AMTOR

PACTOR is more than 20 years old, and the transmission sounds like 2 birds chirping. Using PACTOR, data is sent in blocks and the receiving station sends ACK for acknowledging everything sent, or NAK indicating the request to send the block again. *PACTOR may be used to transfer binary files*, allowing you to download programs from a BBS and then work the program on your laptop or home computer. **ANSWER B**

E8C02 What are some of the differences between the Baudot digital code and ASCII?
A. Baudot uses four data bits per character, ASCII uses seven; Baudot uses one character as a shift code, ASCII has no shift code
B. Baudot uses five data bits per character, ASCII uses seven; Baudot uses two characters as shift codes, ASCII has no shift code
C. Baudot uses six data bits per character, ASCII uses seven; Baudot has no shift code, ASCII uses two characters as shift codes
D. Baudot uses seven data bits per character, ASCII uses eight; Baudot has no shift code, ASCII uses two characters as shift codes

Baudot is a 5-bit code; ASCII is a 7-bit code. In actuality, ASCII is an 8-bit code with only 7 bits uniformly defined. There are 2 shift codes in Baudot, an up-shift and a down-shift. **ANSWER B**

E2E02 What do the letters FEC mean as they relate to digital operation?

A. Forward Error Correction
C. Fatal Error Correction
B. First Error Correction
D. Final Error Correction

The word "AMTOR" stands for amateur teleprinting over radio. This is a digital mode with error correction leading to perfect copy when band conditions are favorable on worldwide frequencies. *"FEC" stands for forward-error correction*, AMTOR Mode B, where each character is sent twice. **ANSWER A**

E2E03 How is Forward Error Correction implemented?

A. By the receiving station repeating each block of three data characters
B. By transmitting a special algorithm to the receiving station along with the data characters
C. By transmitting extra data that may be used to detect and correct transmission errors
D. By varying the frequency shift of the transmitted signal according to a predefined algorithm

During *AMTOR FEC, each data character is sent twice* with no acknowledgment by the receiving station. **ANSWER C**

E2E05 How does ARQ accomplish error correction?

A. Special binary codes provide automatic correction
B. Special polynomial codes provide automatic correction
C. If errors are detected, redundant data is substituted
D. If errors are detected, a retransmission is requested

ARQ (Automatic Repeat reQuest) is a digital protocol that acknowledges individual data blocks, and *requests a repeat of any missed block*. ARQ is part of the PACTOR and CLOVER digital signaling systems. **ANSWER D**

E2E04 What is indicated when one of the ellipses in an FSK crossed-ellipse display suddenly disappears?

A. Selective fading has occurred
B. One of the signal filters has saturated
C. The receiver has drifted 5 kHz from the desired receive frequency
D. The mark and space signal have been inverted

Most high-frequency stations feature a companion station monitor oscilloscope that will display two crossed ellipses, indicating a properly tuned-in digital signal. *If one of the ellipses disappears*, the phenomenon known as selective fading has occurred, and will cause your received copy to stall until the signal comes out of the fade and is then printed out on the screen or on paper. Don't touch the receiver during *selective fading* – you are on frequency; it's just that propagation is causing the signal to fade in and out. **ANSWER A**

E8C03 What is one advantage of using the ASCII code for data communications?

A. It includes built-in error-correction features
B. It contains fewer information bits per character than any other code
C. It is possible to transmit both upper and lower case text
D. It uses one character as a shift code to send numeric and special characters

ASCII code allows upper and lower case text to be transmitted; Baudot does not.
ANSWER C

E8C14 What is the advantage of including a parity bit with an ASCII character stream?

A. Faster transmission rate
B. The signal can overpower interfering signals
C. Foreign language characters can be sent
D. Some types of errors can be detected

The *parity bit* is used for error detection when sending data. A parity bit 1 or 0 might indicate the odd or even number of 1's or 0's in the data block. It is not foolproof – if a pair of 1's or a pair of 0's are missed, the error detection circuit might consider no errors. Yet this simple *error detection* method is commonly used and works surprisingly well to confirm the other station received the character intact, or needs a repeat. **ANSWER D**

Bit Position

							0	1	0	1	1	0	0	1
							0	0	1	1	1	1	0	0
1	2	3	4	5	6	7	1	1	1	1	0	0	0	0
0	0	0	0				@	P	'	p	0	sp	NUL	DLE
1	0	0	0				A	Q	a	q	1	!	SOH	DC1
0	1	0	0				B	R	b	r	2	"	STX	DC2
1	1	0	0				C	S	c	s	3	#	ETX	DC3
0	0	1	0				D	T	d	t	4	$	EOT	DC4
1	0	1	0				E	U	e	u	5	%	ENQ	NAK
0	1	1	0				F	Z	f	v	6	&	ACK	SYN
1	1	1	0				G	W	g	w	7	'	BEL	ETB
0	0	0	1				H	X	h	x	8	(	BS	CAN
1	0	0	1				I	Y	i	y	9	)	HT	EM
0	1	0	1				J	Z	j	z	:	*	LF	SUB
1	1	0	1				K	[	k	{	;	+	VT	ESC
0	0	1	1				L	\	l	l	<	,	FF	FS
1	0	1	1				M	]	m	}	=	-	CR	GS
0	1	1	1				N	^	n	~	>	.	SO	RS
1	1	1	1				O	_	o	DEL	?	/	SI	US

American Standard Code for Information Interchange

E8C07 What is the necessary bandwidth of a 170-hertz shift, 300-baud ASCII transmission?

A. 0.1 Hz
B. 0.3 kHz
C. 0.5 kHz
D. 1.0 kHz

Digital bandwidth is:
BW = baud rate + (1.2 × f shift)
BW = 300 + (1.2 × 170) = 504 Hz = *0.504 kHz.* **ANSWER C**

⌐C08 What is the necessary bandwidth of a 4800-Hz frequency shift, 9600-baud ASCII FM transmission?

A. 15.36 kHz

B. 9.6 kHz

C. 4.8 kHz

D. 5.76 kHz

Digital bandwidth again – use the formula at question E8C07. In this problem, the baud rate is 9600 and the frequency shift is 4800. *Bandwidth = 9600 + (1.2 × 4800) = 15360.* The answer is 15,360 Hz, and when the decimal point is moved three places to the left, the bandwidth works out to be *15.36 kHz*, matching answer A. **ANSWER A**

E8C05 What technique is used to minimize the bandwidth requirements of a PSK-31 signal?

A. Zero-sum character encoding

B. Reed-Solomon character encoding

C. Use of sinusoidal data pulses

D. Use of trapezoidal data pulses

Phase shift keying at 31 bit rate – actually 31.25 – *uses sinusoidal data pulses*, allows for synchronous reception through the demodulation of the signal with no delay, to the signal delayed by 1 bit as polarity is shifted. The number "0" represents a phase reversal and a "1" represents the steady carrier. The PSK-31 VARICODE allocates just a few 1's and 0's for the more common letters, and a long string of 1's and 0's for less used characters. For example, E is Varicode 11 while Q is Varicode 110111111. Some new, big ticket HF transceivers now include a PSK-31 decoder for on-screen, no-computer-required reading of messages. The use of 31 Hz sinusoidal data pulses provides sidebands with carrier phase excursions of less than 31.25 Hz, *resulting in near-perfect copy using very little bandwidth*. One critical component is a rock-solid receiver that can follow the signal with no less than 2 or 3 Hz error. **ANSWER C**

E2E09 Which of the following HF digital modes uses variable-length coding for bandwidth efficiency?

A. RTTY

B. PACTOR

C. MT63

D. PSK31

PSK31 stands for Phase Shift Keying with a bit rate slightly over 31. It is a little bit like Morse code, with the more common letters represented by a short count of bits for that character:

E 11	A 1011
T 101	O 111

The less used characters, such as Q and X, might contain up to 10 bits. This *Varicode is transmitted* with audio phase shifts, occupying a mere 31 Hz of bandwidth, leading to bandwidth efficiency. *When using PSK31*, you cannot copy PSK63 signals, although they might be visible on the waterfall as "wider" PSK31 signals. Similarly, when using PSK63, you might see more narrow PSK31 signals on the waterfall, but you will not be able to copy tem without switching to PSK31. PSK63 is just like PSK31, except that it is twice as fast and twice as wide. Macros and Brag files will transmit at 100 wpm on PSK63, instead of 50 wpm on PSK31. Using PSK63, the turnover and exchange times for contesting will be twice as fast as on PSK31, and even faster than RTTY. Weak signal performance of PSK63 is similar to PSK31, except that twice the power needs to be run compared to PSK31 for the same signal-to-noise ratio **ANSWER D**

E2E07 What is the typical bandwidth of a properly modulated MFSK16 signal?

A. 31 Hz
C. 550 Hz
B. 316 Hz
D. 2 kHz

MFSK refers to a super-charged RTTY signal, Millennium Frequency Shift Keying. Instead of simple RTTY with two tones, *MFSK 16 uses* 16 tones, one at a time at 15.625 baud, spaced at 15.625 Hertz apart. This works out to a relatively narrow *316 Hertz bandwidth*, just like RTTY, and offers higher non-error rates with improved reception under noisy conditions. It is an ideal mode for 40-, 80-, and 160-meters. **ANSWER B** www.ykc.com/wa5ufh/wsjtgroup

E2E12 Which of these digital communications modes has the narrowest bandwidth?

A. MFSK16
C. PSK31
B. 170-Hz shift, 45 baud RTTY
D. 300-baud packet

Phase shift keying is the type of modulation that generates *PSK*, and the *"31"* means the bit rate at 31.25. There is no mistaking the whistle sound of PSK 31, and the modern transceiver with adaptive digital signal processing can pull a signal out of the noise when you think you might not get any reception at all. If you have a modern ham set and a computer, working PSK 31 at around 50 wpm requires only a relatively inexpensive matching device and the readily-available software and a sound card. You will be fascinated when you eavesdrop on two operators running PSK 31, and I expect that it will ultimately become one of the most popular computer-to-computer digital modes, going well beyond RTTY. **ANSWER C**

E4A09 Which of the following is most important when adjusting PSK31 transmitting levels?

A. Power output
C. ALC level
B. PA current
D. SWR

The PSK31 mode is exciting to tune in at 14.070 MHz or 7.070 MHz. Just listen to the whistle, get your computer on to the PSK31 waterfalls, and watch the message read out. Every so often, you'll notice a computer waterfall signature that looks extra wide, and with multiple sidebands – a common occurrence in the presence of excessive drive. Likely, the *ALC (automatic limiter control)* readout on the transmitter is going into the red – time to immediately decrease drive level either at the transmitter, or at the software in the computer. Keep drive levels down and output power down and you will have a great PSK signal on the air! **ANSWER C**

E8C15 What is one advantage of using JT-65 coding?

A. Uses only a 65 Hz bandwidth
B. Virtually perfect decoding of signals well below the noise
C. Easily copied by ear if necessary
D. Permits fast-scan TV transmissions over narrow bandwidth

Weak signal VHF/UHF and microwave operators know well the popular WSJT software to enable miraculous reception of digital signals well below a normal noise floor. *JT-65 coding allows your computer to capture everything from meteor scatter CQ's to conversations off the surface of the moon!* Just because YOU can't hear anything coming out of the speaker, many times your computer's sound card program can deliver enough meaningful audio to decode programs that will utterly amaze you. **ANSWER B**

Good to know:

Weak Signal Band Plan Recommendations

Over the past few years, tremendous advances have been made in weak-signal communications on the VHF and UHF bands using computer-generated data modes. These modes enable communications at or below the noise floor. Amateurs with modest stations are now making contacts over thousands of kilometers via EME and Meteor Scatter using these new modes. However, these very-weak data signals often cannot be detected by ear, which makes them incompatible with normal analog SSB or CW signals. There have been instances of interference caused by SSB operators who obviously can't hear the data signals. The recent EME Conference held in Germany recommended the creation of worldwide VHF and UHF sub-bands for JT-65, the weak signal data protocol. The suggested segments are 50.185 to 50.195 MHz on 6 meters; 144.115 to 44.135 MHz on 2 meters; 432.060 to 432.070 MHz on 70 centimeters; and 1296.060 to 1296.070 MHz.

E2D10 How can an APRS station be used to help support a public service communications activity?

A. An APRS station with an emergency medical technician can automatically transmit medical data to the nearest hospital
B. APRS stations with General Personnel Scanners can automatically relay the participant numbers and time as they pass the check points
C. An APRS station with a GPS unit can automatically transmit information to show a mobile station's position during the event
D. All of these choices are correct

Many marathons are supported by ham operators on foot, bicycles, and motorcycles with an APRS station tied into a GPS to automatically transmit position information along the course route. All this can be done without the operator needing to do a thing – *simply set the time interval you want your APRS packets transmitted and, presto!, everyone with the right equipment can easily see the APRS position information.* **ANSWER C**

E2D07 Which of the following digital protocols is used by APRS?

A. AX.25   C. PACTOR
B. 802.11   D. AMTOR

The digital packet protocol in use for *APRS is described as AX.25*, the ham version of commercial packet networks operating X.25. The AX.25 protocol is recognized and authorized by the Federal Communications Commission with specific speed limitations depending on what band you are operating on. **ANSWER A**
www.winlink.org/positions

E2D08 Which of the following types of packet frames is used to transmit APRS beacon data?

A. Connect frames   C. Acknowledgement frames
B. Disconnect frames   D. Unnumbered Information frames

The packet frames used to transmit APRS beacon data are called UIF – Un-numbered Information Frames. Networking systems could allow an APRS position and short message to be transmitted and relayed throughout the country. One manufacturer produces a dual-band handheld with the APRS terminal node controller already built-in. Handheld GPS equipment that outputs NMEA data is available for under $99, and mapping GPS can also show ham call signs and locations. **ANSWER D** www.geosat.us

Kenwood dual bander plugged into the Avmap G5 GPS position plotter.

E2D11 Which of the following data sources are needed to accurately transmit your geographical location over the APRS network?

    A. The NMEA-0183 formatted data from a Global Positioning System (GPS) satellite receiver

    B. The latitude and longitude of your location, preferably in degrees, minutes and seconds, entered into the APRS computer software

    C. The NMEA-0183 formatted data from a LORAN navigation system

    D. Any of these choices is correct

Hooking up your APRS transmitter to a Global Positioning System receiver will give you much better performance over the older Loran navigation system, but Loran could also work. In real-world APRS, Answer B should be refined to show that the latitude and longitude is sent in degrees, minutes, and FRACTIONS OF A MINUTE. But *any of these data sources will work*. **ANSWER D** www.aprs.fi

E2D06 Which of the following is a commonly-used 2-meter APRS frequency?

    A. 144.20 MHz   C. 145.02 MHz

    B. 144.39 MHz   D. 146.52 MHz

APRS stands for Automatic Position Reporting System. APRS links a portable or fixed-mount Global Positioning System (GPS) receiver to a ham transmitter or transceiver. APRS allows the ham radio to transmit pre-set timed packet bursts of the GPS position, either on worldwide high frequencies, or on the VHF and UHF bands. *On 2 meters, the most common APRS frequency is 144.390 MHz*. **ANSWER B** www.findu.com

E8C09 What term describes a wide-bandwidth communications system in which the transmitted carrier frequency varies according to some predetermined sequence?

A. Amplitude compandored single sideband
B. AMTOR
C. Time-domain frequency modulation
D. Spread-spectrum communication

Spread spectrum communications are becoming more popular. You may not realize it, but your new cordless phone may use *spread-spectrum* communications. The *frequency hops in a pre-arranged sequence*, eliminating interference and eavesdropping. **ANSWER D**

E1F01 On what frequencies are spread spectrum transmissions permitted?

A. Only on amateur frequencies above 50 MHz
B. Only on amateur frequencies above 222 MHz
C. Only on amateur frequencies above 420 MHz
D. Only on amateur frequencies above 144 MHz

Spread spectrum is still new to ham radio operators, and *is confined to the 222 MHz band and above*. For the time being, spread spectrum is not allowed on 2- or 6-meters. [97.305] **ANSWER B**

E8C10 Which of these techniques causes a digital signal to appear as wide-band noise to a conventional receiver?

A. Spread-spectrum
B. Independent sideband
C. Regenerative detection
D. Exponential addition

Do you own a GPS receiver? If you could listen to 1575 MHz, the GPS public channel, all you would hear is noise. *It takes a specific spread spectrum receiver to translate this wide-band noise into meaningful reception.* Ham radio operators are allowed spread spectrum from 222 MHz and above. Power output of 100 watts is allowed, but any more than 1 watt of spread spectrum requires automatic transmitter power control circuits that identify a strong signal and reduce its own transmit power. Spread spectrum (SS) is just one more exciting "new mode" that hams are encouraged to explore above 222 MHz. **ANSWER A**

E8C11 What spread-spectrum communications technique alters the center frequency of a conventional carrier many times per second in accordance with a pseudo-random list of channels?

A. Frequency hopping
B. Direct sequence
C. Time-domain frequency modulation
D. Frequency compandored spread-spectrum

Spread spectrum communications alters the center frequency of an RF carrier in a pseudo-random manner causing the *frequency to "hop" around* from channel to channel. This is termed "frequency hopping," a form of spread spectrum communications that alters the center frequency. **ANSWER A**

E8C12 What spread-spectrum communications technique uses a high speed binary bit stream to shift the phase of an RF carrier?

A. Frequency hopping
B. Direct sequence
C. Binary phase-shift keying
D. Phase compandored spread-spectrum

The term *"direct sequence" is used to describe a system where a fast binary stream shifts the phase of an RF carrier. This is another form of spread spectrum* communications. Using only a single carrier frequency and then modulating the signal by shifting the phase in accordance with a high-speed binary bit stream results in a signal whose pattern on a spectrum analyzer spreads out into a pattern of hills and valleys. This is called direct sequence spread spectrum. **ANSWER B**

E8C13 What makes spread-spectrum communications resistant to interference?

    A. Interfering signals are removed by a frequency-agile crystal filter
    B. Spread-spectrum transmitters use much higher power than conventional carrier-frequency transmitters
    C. Spread-spectrum transmitters can hunt for the best carrier frequency to use within a given RF spectrum
    D. Only signals using the correct spreading sequence are received

Just like that new cordless 900-MHz spread-spectrum telephone, spread-spectrum communications are resistant to interference because only those signals with the correct spreading sequence are received. With the carrier signal spread out over a broad bandwidth, either because of using a direct-sequence spreading code, or from frequency hopping, the signal is much more resistant to interference from random noise. However, *the receiver must know the spreading code or the hopping sequence in order to recover the signal.* **ANSWER D**

E2C09 How does the spread-spectrum technique of frequency hopping (FH) work?

    A. If interference is detected by the receiver it will signal the transmitter to change frequencies
    B. If interference is detected by the receiver it will signal the transmitter to wait until the frequency is clear
    C. A pseudo-random binary bit stream is used to shift the phase of an RF carrier very rapidly in a particular sequence
    D. The frequency of the transmitted signal is changed very rapidly according to a particular sequence also used by the receiving station

Frequency hopping depends on a particular signaling sequence, and *the frequency of the RF carrier is changed* so *quickly* that it is almost indistinguishable except to other spread-spectrum receivers locked on to the same signaling sequence. **ANSWER D**

900MHz cordless phones use spread-spectrum technology.

E2C08 Why are received spread-spectrum signals resistant to interference?
A. Signals not using the spectrum-spreading algorithm are suppressed in the receiver
B. The high power used by a spread-spectrum transmitter keeps its signal from being easily overpowered
C. The receiver is always equipped with a digital blanker circuit
D. If interference is detected by the receiver it will signal the transmitter to change frequencies

Amateur operators transmitting and receiving spread-spectrum signals are just pioneering one more way that hams can serve our valuable frequency resources. Although spread-spectrum may utilize an entire band, the hopping technique won't disturb other signals on the band, and *all other signals not using the same spread-spectrum algorithm are suppressed in the receiver.* So just when you thought there was no more room for any more signals on a particular band, spread-spectrum gets through! **ANSWER A**

E1F12 FCC-licensed amateur stations may use spread spectrum (SS) emissions to communicate under which of the following conditions?
A. When the other station is in an area regulated by the FCC
B. When the other station is in a country permitting SS communications
C. When the transmission is not used to obscure the meaning of any communication
D. All of these choices are correct

Spread-spectrum communications are allowed to any other station under FCC regulation, and to stations in foreign countries that have specifically permitted spread-spectrum communications to their country from ours. Spread-spectrum may not be used to obscure the meaning of any communication. If these 3 requirements are met, and as long as you *stay below 100 watts, you are entitled to use spread spectrum on 222 MHz and up.* [97.311] **ANSWER D**

E1F13 What is the maximum transmitter power for an amateur station transmitting spread spectrum communications?
A. 1 W   C. 100 W
B. 1.5 W   D. 1.5 kW

Since hams are still in the early stages of experimenting with *spread spectrum,* the FCC limits *maximum power output to 100 watts.* [97.311] **ANSWER C**

E8C01 Which one of the following digital codes consists of elements having unequal length?

A. ASCII

C. Baudot

B. AX.25

D. Morse code

Morse Code is made up of unequal length elements. Dits are short, and dahs are long. **ANSWER D** www.dxatlas.com/morserunner

Morse Code

E8C06 What is the necessary bandwidth of a 13-WPM international Morse code transmission?

A. Approximately 13 Hz

C. Approximately 52 Hz

B. Approximately 26 Hz

D. Approximately 104 Hz

To determine the bandwidth of a Morse code signal, use this formula – bandwidth equals:

$$BW_{cw} = baud\ rate \times wpm \times fading\ factor$$

For CW, the baud rate is 0.8 and the fading factor is 5, therefore, *multiply 0.8 times 13 wpm times 5. The answer works out to be 52 Hz.* **ANSWER C**

E8B01 What is the term for the ratio between the frequency deviation of an RF carrier wave and the modulating frequency of its corresponding FM-phone signal?
A. FM compressibility
B. Quieting index
C. Percentage of modulation
D. Modulation index

Be careful with this one. Since they don't say the highest modulating frequency, but say only "modulating frequency," they are looking for the *modulation index*. Notice that there is not any answer that says "deviation ratio" to get you in trouble. **ANSWER D**

E8B02 How does the modulation index of a phase-modulated emission vary with RF carrier frequency (the modulated frequency)?
A. It increases as the RF carrier frequency increases
B. It decreases as the RF carrier frequency increases
C. It varies with the square root of the RF carrier frequency
D. It does not depend on the RF carrier frequency

This is one of those answers that has a "not" in it that makes it correct. When you calculate the *modulation index*, you *do not look at the actual RF carrier frequency* as part of your calculations. **ANSWER D**

On-line calculator site:
www.calculatoredge.com/index.htm

FM versus AM

Greater Number of Sidebands

In FM modulation, one sine wave is used to modify another sine wave and multiple sums and differences result, depending on the deviation ratio. This is illustrated in Figure a. Sidebands appear on either side of f_c at f_m, $2 f_m$, $3 f_m$, etc., depending upon the deviation ratio. Figure b *shows that there are five significant sidebands for a deviation ratio of 3, and* Figure c *shows three significant sidebands for a deviation ratio of 1.67. The multiple sidebands are formed in both the upper and lower sideband positions, separated by the modulating frequency.*

a. General Spectrum

b. Deviation Ratio of 3

c. Deviation Ratio of 1.67

Frequency spectrum of FM signals.

Source: *Basic Communications Electronics*, Hudson & Luecke, © 1999 Master Publishing, Inc., Niles, IL

E8B03 What is the modulation index of an FM-phone signal having a maximum frequency deviation of 3000 Hz either side of the carrier frequency, when the modulating frequency is 1000 Hz?

A. 3

B. 0.3

C. 3000

D. 1000

3000 divided by 1000 gives you a *modulation index of 3.* ANSWER A

▶ $\text{Modulation Index } (\chi) = \dfrac{\text{Peak Deviation (D)}}{\text{Modulation Frequency } (m)}$ or $\chi = \dfrac{D}{m}$

E8B04 What is the modulation index of an FM-phone signal having a maximum carrier deviation of plus or minus 6 kHz when modulated with a 2-kHz modulating frequency?

A. 6000

B. 3

C. 2000

D. 1/3

6 kHz divided by 2 kHz gives us a *modulation index of 3.* ANSWER B

E8B10 What is meant by deviation ratio?

A. The ratio of the audio modulating frequency to the center carrier frequency

B. The ratio of the maximum carrier frequency deviation to the highest audio modulating frequency

C. The ratio of the carrier center frequency to the audio modulating frequency

D. The ratio of the highest audio modulating frequency to the average audio modulating frequency

It's important to set the deviation ratio properly on your FM transceiver to prevent splatter and a signal bandwidth that is too wide. *Deviation ratio* is the ratio of the *maximum carrier swing to your highest audio modulating frequency* when you speak into the microphone. ANSWER B

E8B05 What is the deviation ratio of an FM-phone signal having a maximum frequency swing of plus-or-minus 5 kHz and accepting a maximum modulation rate of 3 kHz?

A. 60

B. 0.167

C. 0.6

D. 1.67

Deviation ratio is the ratio of the maximum carrier swing to your highest audio modulating frequency when you speak into the microphone. To calculate the deviation ratio, divide the maximum carrier frequency swing by the maximum modulation frequency. *5 kHz frequency swing divided by 3 kHz modulation frequency* gives you a *deviation ratio of 1.67.* ANSWER D

▶ $\text{Deviation Ratio} = \dfrac{\text{Maximum Carrier Frequency Deviation in kHz}}{\text{Maximum Modulation Frequency in kHz}}$

E8B06 What is the deviation ratio of an FM-phone signal having a maximum frequency swing of plus or minus 7.5 kHz and accepting a maximum modulation frequency of 3.5 kHz?

A. 2.14

B. 0.214

C. 0.47

D. 47

To calculate deviation ratio of an FM signal, simply divide the maximum carrier frequency swing by the maximum modulation frequency. The small number goes into the larger number. *3.5 kHz into 7.5 kHz ends up with a deviation ratio of 2.14.* Simple, huh? **ANSWER A**

E8B08 What parameter does the modulating signal vary in a pulse-position modulation system?
A. The number of pulses per second
B. The amplitude of the pulses
C. The duration of the pulses
D. The time at which each pulse occurs

This question is about a pulse-position modulation system. The position is the time at which each pulse occurs. *The modulating signal varies the time when pulses occur.* **ANSWER D**

E8B09 How are the pulses of a pulse-modulated signal usually transmitted?
A. A pulse of relatively short duration is sent; a relatively long period of time separates each pulse
B. A pulse of relatively long duration is sent; a relatively short period of time separates each pulse
C. A group of short pulses are sent in a relatively short period of time; a relatively long period of time separates each group
D. A group of short pulses are sent in a relatively long period of time; a relatively short period of time separates each group

During pulse modulation, *the duration of each pulse is relatively short* and there is a *long period of time between each* of these *separate pulses*. The long separation time is between each pulse; there are no groups of pulses separated by long periods of time. **ANSWER A**

E8B07 When using a pulse-width modulation system, why is the transmitter's peak power greater than its average power?
A. The signal duty cycle is less than 100%
B. The signal reaches peak amplitude only when voice modulated
C. The signal reaches peak amplitude only when voltage spikes are generated within the modulator
D. The signal reaches peak amplitude only when the pulses are also amplitude modulated

In pulse-width modulation, the output signal is composed of pulses of carrier wave of varying widths. Each pulse is at the transmitter's peak power, but between pulses the transmitter is at zero power. The *average power is* determined by the percent of time the transmitter is on – *the duty cycle*. **ANSWER A**

E8B11 Which of these methods can be used to combine several separate analog information streams into a single analog radio frequency signal?

A. Frequency shift keying   C. Frequency division multiplexing
B. A diversity combiner   D. Pulse compression

In *frequency division multiplexing (FDM)*, each analog signal is used to modulate a different sub-carrier signal, and then these sub-carriers are used to modulate the actual carrier. A good example of this is the way stereo is transmitted on FM broadcast signals – the stereo channel is modulated onto a 38 kHz sub-carrier, and both the monaural and stereo signals are then used to modulate the carrier. In the

---

receiver, the sub-carrier is removed from the incoming signal by a filter and recovered. **ANSWER C**

E8B12 Which of the following describes frequency division multiplexing?
    A. The transmitted signal jumps from band to band at a predetermined rate
    B. Two or more information streams are merged into a "baseband," which then modulates the transmitter
    C. The transmitted signal is divided into packets of information
    D. Two or more information streams are merged into a digital combiner, which then pulse position modulates the transmitter

The *"information streams" are the baseband.* Each information stream is modulated onto a sub-carrier (up-converting it), which is then used to modulate the carrier. In the receiver, the sub-carriers are removed by pass band filters, then each information stream is recovered by down-converting the sub-carrier to baseband. **ANSWER B**

E8B13 What is time division multiplexing?
    A. Two or more data streams are assigned to discrete sub-carriers on an FM transmitter
    B. Two or more signals are arranged to share discrete time slots of a digital data transmission
    C. Two or more data streams share the same channel by transmitting time of transmission as the sub-carrier
    D. Two or more signals are quadrature modulated to increase bandwidth efficiency

Time division multiplexing (TDM) allows multiple users to share the same transmit and receive channel, divided into *discreet time slots*, for the sending of data. Again, this modern form of signaling is most used by commercial and telecommunications point-to-point broadcasting, but hams with the right equipment could take advantage of this frequency conserving technology. The two signals don't actually share discrete time slots – rather, they are separated by each using a different time slot. **ANSWER B**

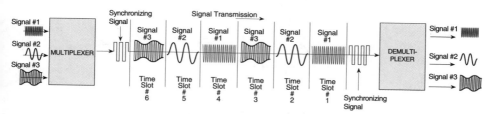

Time multiplexing and demultiplexing.
Source: *Basic Communications Electronics*, Hudson & Luecke, © 1999 Master Publishing, Inc., Niles, IL

E8D01 What is the easiest voltage amplitude parameter to measure when viewing a pure sine wave signal on an oscilloscope?
    A. Peak-to-peak voltage   C. Average voltage
    B. RMS voltage   D. DC voltage

Looking at a pure sine wave signal on a scope, it is *easy to identify the peak-to-peak voltage* measured from the maximum positive excursion of the signal to the maximum negative excursion of the signal. **ANSWER A**

Peak, Peak-to-Peak and RMS Voltages

Sine Wave   Pulse Waveform   Irregular Waveform

V_P = Peak voltage

V_{PP} = Peak-to-peak voltage

V_{RMS} = Root-mean-square voltage

Equations for Sinewaves

$$V_P = \frac{V_{PP}}{2} \qquad V_{PP} = 2V_P$$

$$V_{RMS} = 0.707\, V_P$$

$$V_P = 1.414\, V_{RMS}$$

E8D02 What is the relationship between the peak-to-peak voltage and the peak voltage amplitude in a symmetrical waveform?

  A. 0.707:1   C. 1.414:1
  B. 2:1   D. 4:1

The relationship between peak-to-peak voltage and peak voltage is 2:1. It is important to realize that the waveform must be symmetrical – and a sine wave certainly is. $V_{PP} = 2V_P$. **ANSWER B**

E8A01 What type of wave is made up of a sine wave plus all of its odd harmonics?

  A. A square wave   C. A cosine wave
  B. A sine wave   D. A tangent wave

If you're *odd*, you're probably *square*. **ANSWER A**

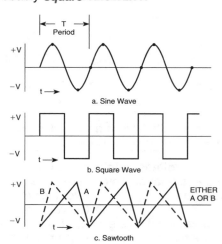

a. Sine Wave

b. Square Wave

c. Sawtooth

Sine, Square and Sawtooth Waveforms

E8A02 What type of wave has a rise time significantly faster than its fall time (or vice versa)?

A. A cosine wave   C. A sawtooth wave

B. A square wave   D. A sine wave

The *sawtooth wave* can be backwards, too – an immediate *rise time* significantly *faster than the fall time*. **ANSWER C**

E8A03 What type of wave is made up of sine waves of a given fundamental frequency plus all its harmonics?

A. A sawtooth wave   C. A sine wave

B. A square wave   D. A cosine wave

If it has *all the harmonics* the answer is a *sawtooth wave*. **ANSWER A**

E8A04 What is the equivalent to the root-mean-square value of an AC voltage?

A. The AC voltage found by taking the square of the average value of the peak AC voltage

B. The DC voltage causing the same amount of heating in a given resistor as the corresponding peak AC voltage

C. The DC voltage causing the same amount of heating in a resistor as the corresponding RMS AC voltage

D. The AC voltage found by taking the square root of the average AC value

You sometimes see this as RMS, also called effective value of an AC voltage. Since AC voltage is constantly changing continuously in amplitude, we must look at its *root mean square value* before we can come up with the *same heating effect in a given resistor as a constant DC voltage*. **ANSWER C**

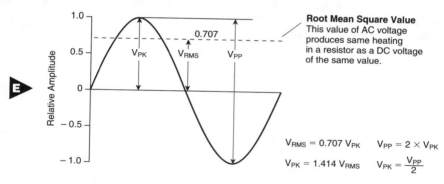

Root Mean Square Value
This value of AC voltage produces same heating in a resistor as a DC voltage of the same value.

$$V_{RMS} = 0.707 \, V_{PK} \quad\quad V_{PP} = 2 \times V_{PK}$$
$$V_{PK} = 1.414 \, V_{RMS} \quad\quad V_{PK} = \frac{V_{PP}}{2}$$

RMS (VRMS), Peak (VPK), and Peak-to-Peak (VPP) Voltage

E8A05 What would be the most accurate way of measuring the RMS voltage of a complex waveform?

A. By using a grid dip meter

B. By measuring the voltage with a D'Arsonval meter

C. By using an absorption wavemeter

D. By measuring the heating effect in a known resistor

In a very complex wave form, one way to determine its effective value is to *measure the heating effect in a known resistor*, compared to a known DC voltage. **ANSWER D**

E8A07 What determines the PEP-to-average power ratio of a single-sideband phone signal?
A. The frequency of the modulating signal
B. The characteristics of the modulating signal
C. The degree of carrier suppression
D. The amplifier gain

It's not all that easy to determine the ratio of peak envelope power to average power in your worldwide SSB set because your speech characteristics (the *characteristics of the modulating signal*) may vary from those of another operator when using the same equipment. **ANSWER B**

On SSB transmit, peak envelope power (PEP) is determined by your speech characteristics.

E8A06 What is the approximate ratio of PEP-to-average power in a typical voice-modulated single-sideband phone signal?
A. 2.5 to 1   C. 1 to 1
B. 25 to 1   D. 100 to 1

When you talk about power output from your SSB worldwide set, we normally refer to power as peak envelope power. Depending on your modulation, the *ratio of PEP to average power is about 2.5 to 1*. You can remember 2.5 because that's very close to 2.5 kHz of bandwidth occupancy for a properly-modulated SSB signal. **ANSWER A**

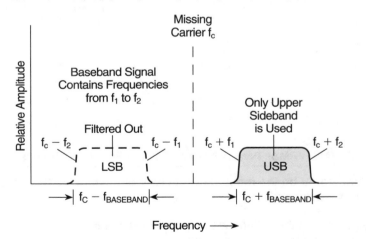

Spectral plot of a SSB signal.

Source: *Basic Communications Electronics*, Hudson & Luecke, © 1999 Master Publishing, Inc., Niles, IL

E8D13 What type of meter should be used to monitor the output signal of a voice-modulated single-sideband transmitter to ensure you do not exceed the maximum allowable power?
A. An SWR meter reading in the forward direction
B. A modulation meter
C. An average reading wattmeter
D. A peak-reading wattmeter

The peak-reading watt meter momentarily holds the highest amount of output signal — in order for you to double check that you are not exceeding the maximum allowable power. Many newer, worldwide ham sets have a *peak-reading power output meter* with an LCD display built in. **ANSWER D**

E8D06 What is the advantage of using a peak-reading wattmeter to monitor the output of a SSB phone transmitter?
A. It is easier to determine the correct tuning of the output circuit
B. It gives a more accurate display of the PEP output when modulation is present
C. It makes it easier to detect high SWR on the feed-line
D. It can determine if any "flat-topping" is present during modulation peaks

When you transmit on your brand-new, high-frequency transceiver you got yourself as a reward for passing your Extra class exam, it is likely you will see that transceiver's average power output indicator not going much above 70 watts as you are speaking. There is nothing wrong with you equipment – you may be transmitting 100 watts peak envelope power with the meter showing only about 70 watts due to the latency in the meter movement, or the slower reaction time that some LCD meters employ to average out their readouts. A *peak-reading watt meter* compensates for this seemingly lower-than-usual power output indication and faithfully gathers enough power output information on your varying voice waveform to show you your *true peak envelope power (PEP) output*. Most transceivers have an aggressive ALC (automatic limiting control) modulation setting, so don't expect any panel meter built in to the gear to instantly fly off the scale above 100 watts.
ANSWER B

E8D04 What is the PEP output of a transmitter that has a maximum peak of 30 volts to a 50-ohm load as observed on an oscilloscope?
A. 4.5 watts   C. 16 watts
B. 9 watts   D. 18 watts

The first step in solving this problem is to take the peak voltage and reduce it to average by multiplying $30 \times 0.707 = 21.21$ volts.

Average volts $\times$ average current = average power
Average power, $P = E^2/R$
$P = (21.21)^2 \div 50 = 8.99 \text{ watts}$

ANSWER B

E8D14 What is the average power dissipated by a 50-ohm resistive load during one complete RF cycle having a peak voltage of 35 volts?
A. 12.2 watts   C. 24.5 watts
B. 9.9 watts   D. 16 watts

The first step in solving this problem is to take the peak voltage and reduce it to the RMS voltage by multiplying 35 volts × 0.707 = 24.745 volts.

 Average volts × average current = average power
Average power, P = E²/R
P = (24.745)² ÷ 50 = 12.2463 watts, or 12.2 watts

ANSWER A

E8D15 If an RMS reading voltmeter reads 34 volts on a sinusoidal waveform, what is the peak voltage?
A. 123 volts   C. 55 volts
B. 96 volts   D. 48 volts
In this question, *34 volts RMS is multiplied by 1.414 = 48.076 peak volts.* Remember, to go from average to peak, multiple by 1.414. Going from peak to average, you would multiply by 0.707, as we did in the earlier problem. **ANSWER D**

E8D16 Which of the following is a typical value for the peak voltage at a common household electrical outlet?
A. 240 volts   C. 120 volts
B. 170 volts   D. 340 volts
When you measure your house line voltage with a volt meter, you are measuring RMS. If you were to look at it on an oscilloscope, and look at the electrical peaks, it would be *1.414 times higher than 120 volts*, or a total of *170 volts peak.* **ANSWER B**

E8D17 Which of the following is a typical value for the peak-to-peak voltage at a common household electrical outlet?
A. 240 volts   C. 340 volts
B. 120 volts   D. 170 volts
If you really want to impress your friends about your house line voltage, tell them that you have *340 volts* coming out of the socket. If they bet you don't, tell them you are stating the voltage as *peak-to-peak*, which is twice as much as peak voltage. **ANSWER C**

E8D18 Which of the following is a typical value for the RMS voltage at a common household electrical power outlet?
A. 120-V AC   C. 85-V AC
B. 340-V AC   D. 170-V AC
Household AC line voltage is rated at *120-V AC RMS.* **ANSWER A**

E8D19 What is the RMS value of a 340-volt peak-to-peak pure sine wave?
A. 120-V AC   C. 240-V AC
B. 170-V AC   D. 300-V AC
340 volts peak-to-peak divided in half is 170 volts peak. Multiply the peak voltage by 0.707, and you end up with *120 volts AC, RMS.* **ANSWER A**

E8D05 If an RMS-reading AC voltmeter reads 65 volts on a sinusoidal waveform, what is the peak-to-peak voltage?
A. 46 volts   C. 130 volts
B. 92 volts   D. 184 volts
Vp = 1.414 × V$_{RMS}$, and Vpp = 2Vp. We will first change 65 volts RMS to peak voltage by multiplying *65 × 1.414 = 91.91.* Since they want peak-to-peak voltage, *multiply this by 2*, and you end up with *184 volts.* **ANSWER D**

E8A08 What is the period of a wave?

A. The time required to complete one cycle
B. The number of degrees in one cycle
C. The number of zero crossings in one cycle
D. The amplitude of the wave

The period of a wave is the *time required to complete one cycle* of that wave. It is the reciprocal of the frequency T = 1÷f. If the frequency is 1 MHz, then T = 1÷1MHz = 1ms. If a wave goes through one million cycles in one second, then each cycle takes 1 one-millionth of a second. **ANSWER A**

E8A09 What type of waveform is produced by human speech?

A. Sinusoidal
B. Logarithmic
C. Irregular
D. Trapezoidal

Sound waves between 300 and 3000 Hz are the most useful by radio modulator circuits to transmit the human voice. Unlike pure tones going into the microphone circuit, our *human speech word tones form irregular waves* with constantly changing amplitude and frequency. **ANSWER C**

E8A13 What is an advantage of using digital signals instead of analog signals to convey the same information?

A. Less complex circuitry is required for digital signal generation and detection
B. Digital signals always occupy a narrower bandwidth
C. Digital signals can be regenerated multiple times without error
D. All of these answers are correct

An advantage of digital signals is the capability of *relaying the signals multiple times* without error. Digital signals in a noisy environment may also be forward-error-corrected, giving your equipment and computer a second chance at decoding an incoming noisy data signal. Many times you can't even HEAR the data signal, yet your equipment can faithfully decode that incoming digital signal. Noise isn't absent in digital signals, but the fact that the signal is either in one state or another (sometimes either on or off, or other times at one discrete frequency or another) means that it is easier to detect the exact state it is in. In comparison, analog signals vary over a very wide range of amplitudes and frequencies, and thus are more prone to becoming lost among the noise and interference. Because when you recover a digital signal you recover only the discrete states, you can faithfully reproduce the original signal without distortion. **ANSWER C**

E8A12 What type of information can be conveyed using digital waveforms?

A. Human speech
B. Video signals
C. Data
D. All of these answers are correct

Even analog voice may be converted into data, just like what happens inside your cell phone. Over-the-air television signals are now digital and, of course, data is digital, so *all of the answers are correct.* **ANSWER D**

E8A14 Which of these methods is commonly used to convert analog signals to digital signals?

A. Sequential sampling
B. Harmonic regeneration
C. Level shifting
D. Phase reversal

Changing an *analog signal to a digital signal* takes place in the analog-to-digital converter through *sequential sampling* of the waveform. Thousands of tiny audio slices are held in a sequential sample-and-hold circuit where they are converted into binary numbers. Some ADCs count with a staircase generator while others convert analog voltage into digital values with multiple comparators, yet others in DSS use a phase accumulator to identify points on a specific waveform cycle. Sequential sampling of the incoming waveform is the heart of converting analog signals to digital. **ANSWER A**

E8A15 What would the waveform of a digital data stream signal look like on a conventional oscilloscope?
A. A series of sine waves with evenly spaced gaps
B. A series of pulses with varying patterns
C. A running display of alpha-numeric characters
D. None of the above; this type of signal cannot be seen on a conventional oscilloscope

When you look at a *digital signal on* a conventional *oscilloscope*, you will see a series of *sharp pulses with varying patterns*, illustrating a string of data bits, 1's and 0's. **ANSWER B**

E8A10 Which of the following is a distinguishing characteristic of a pulse waveform?
A. Regular sinusoidal oscillations
B. Narrow bursts of energy separated by periods of no signal
C. A series of tones that vary between two frequencies
D. A signal that contains three or more discrete tones

Sending Morse code is a good example of a *pulse waveform – short bursts of energy separated by spaces*. Intermittent Continuous Wave (ICW) still continues to be a popular amateur radio activity, even though the FCC has completely eliminated any Morse code testing. **ANSWER B**

E8A11 What is one use for a pulse modulated signal?
A. Linear amplification   C. Multiphase power transmission
B. PSK31 data transmission   D. Digital data transmission

Pulse modulation is used for some exciting data transmissions:

CW	WINLINK 2000
RTTY	HELLSCHREIBER
PACTOR	G-TOR
MFSK (MultiFrequency Shift Keying)	CLOVER

Many of the new high frequency transceivers may already have DSP capabilities to decode some of these *digital data transmissions*. Add a laptop or home computer to your radio and enjoy all of the excitement on you new Extra class sub-bands transmitting data. Remember, keep your power levels reduced, and keep your data gain controls at a minimum. **ANSWER D**

E7E01 Which of the following can be used to generate FM-phone emissions?
A. A balanced modulator on the audio amplifier
B. A reactance modulator on the oscillator
C. A reactance modulator on the final amplifier
D. A balanced modulator on the oscillator

The *reactance modulator* causes the oscillator to vary frequency in accordance with the modulation. It's *the oscillator that is modulated*. **ANSWER B**

E7E02 What is the function of a reactance modulator?

A. To produce PM signals by using an electrically variable resistance
B. To produce AM signals by using an electrically variable inductance or capacitance
C. To produce AM signals by using an electrically variable resistance
D. To produce PM signals by using an electrically variable inductance or capacitance

The *reactance modulator* is found in a frequency modulation transceiver, *varying inductance or capacitance to produce the phase modulation (PM) signal* where the phase of the carrier current is varied with the frequency of the modulating voltage. **ANSWER D**

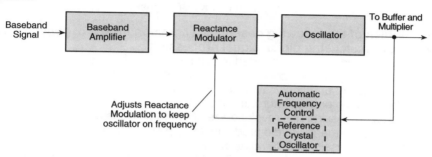

Block diagram for generating FM modulation
Source: *Basic Communications Electronics*, Hudson & Luecke, © 1999 Master Publishing, Inc., Niles, IL

E7E03 What is the fundamental principle of a phase modulator?

A. It varies the tuning of a microphone preamplifier to produce PM signals
B. It varies the tuning of an amplifier tank circuit to produce AM signals
C. It varies the tuning of an amplifier tank circuit to produce PM signals
D. It varies the tuning of a microphone preamplifier to produce AM signals

Phase modulation is developed by *varying the tuning of the amplifier tank circuit to produce phase modulation*, but never in the microphone preamp circuit. **ANSWER C**

E7E05 What circuit is added to an FM transmitter to proportionally attenuate the lower audio frequencies?

A. A de-emphasis network   C. An audio prescaler
B. A heterodyne suppressor   D. A pre-emphasis network

Pre-emphasis networks in modern FM transmitters help *improve the signal-to-noise ratio*. **ANSWER D**

E7E04 What is one way a single-sideband phone signal can be generated?

A. By using a balanced modulator followed by a filter
B. By using a reactance modulator followed by a mixer
C. By using a loop modulator followed by a mixer
D. By driving a product detector with a DSB signal

In a *single-sideband transceiver*, a lower or upper sideband *filter removes the unwanted sideband*. **ANSWER A**

Generating an SSB signal

E7E14 Which of the following describes a common means of generating a SSB signal when using digital signal processing?
A. Mixing products are converted to voltages and subtracted by adder circuits
B. A frequency synthesizer removes the unwanted sidebands
C. Emulation of quartz crystal filter characteristics
D. The phasing or quadrature method

Digital signal processing has revolutionized ham radio transmitters and receivers, and a host of after market audio products, to help clean up signal reception. For SSB signal transmissions, *DSP relies on phase shifting* carrier and audio components by 90 degrees, and sending this phased split to the SSB balanced modulator. The output is a DSP upper or lower sideband, with the carrier and unwanted sideband suppressed more than 40 dB. No heterodyning is required, and all of this *quadrature* occurs in the DSP chip. **ANSWER D**

E7C09 What type of digital signal processing filter might be used in generating an SSB signal?
A. An adaptive filter
B. A notch filter
C. A Hilbert-transform filter
D. An elliptical filter

In a *DSP* unit for transmit, we might use the *Hilbert-transform filter* – think of "transform" *for SSB transmit*. **ANSWER C**

Block diagram of a basic digital signal processing (DSP) system

E6E01 Which of these filter bandwidths would be a good choice for use in a SSB radiotelephone transmitter?

A. 6 kHz at -6 dB   C. 500 Hz at -6 dB

B. 2.4 kHz at -6 dB   D. 15 kHz at -6 dB

That new high frequency transceiver you just purchased as a reward for passing you upcoming Extra Class exam will likely have a pair of *SSB filters* for you to select when operating voice. Start off using the 2.4 kHz at -6dB filter first, as this is what most operators use for casual conversations. During a contest, you may wish to pinch the transmit audio and then drop down to 1.8 kHz, but *2.4 kHz is the common setting.* **ANSWER B**

E1B01 Which of the following constitutes a spurious emission?

A. An amateur station transmission made at random without the proper call sign identification

B. A signal transmitted in a way that prevents its detection by any station other than the intended recipient

C. Any transmitted bogus signal that interferes with another licensed radio station

D. An emission outside its necessary bandwidth that can be reduced or eliminated without affecting the information transmitted

May your spurious emissions be minimum! The FCC says so. A *spurious emission* could include random splatter to adjacent frequencies, second harmonics, and any other microvolt or millivolt emission that serves no purpose *outside of your necessary bandwidth.* [97.3] **ANSWER D**

E1B08 On what frequencies may the operation of an amateur station be restricted if its emissions cause interference to the reception of a domestic broadcast station on a receiver of good engineering design?

A. On the frequency used by the domestic broadcast station

B. On all frequencies below 30 MHz

C. On all frequencies above 30 MHz

D. On the interfering amateur service transmitting frequencies

Sometimes the FCC may allow you to continue to operate at any time, but may *restrict* what frequency or *frequencies you may operate on*, due to interference complaints. [97.121] **ANSWER D**

E7B11 What type of circuit is shown in Figure E7-1?

A. Switching voltage regulator   C. Common emitter amplifier

B. Linear voltage regulator   D. Emitter follower amplifier

In a *common emitter amplifier*, the input signal is applied between base and emitter. In this circuit, the emitter is at AC ground because of C3. The output is taken from the collector. **ANSWER C**

Figure E7-1

E7B09 In Figure E7-1, what is the purpose of R1 and R2?
A. Load resistors   C. Self bias
B. Fixed bias   D. Feedback
This reminds you a little bit of Thevenin's Theorem doesn't it? *R1 and R2* form a voltage divider to set the voltage and the current at the base of the transistor for *fixed bias*. **ANSWER B**

E7B10 In Figure E7-1, what is the purpose of R3?
A. Fixed bias   C. Output load resistor
B. Emitter bypass   D. Self bias
Current through *R3 produces* a voltage drop that affects the base-emitter bias voltage. Since the transistor's collector and base current (the emitter current) determine the voltage at the emitter, it is called *self bias*. **ANSWER D**

E7B12 In Figure E7-2, what is the purpose of R?
A. Emitter load   C. Collector load
B. Fixed bias   D. Voltage regulation
One end of the resistor R is connected to the emitter, the other end to ground. It is classified as an *emitter load resistor* in this circuit because the output is taken from the emitter. **ANSWER A**

Figure E7-2

E7B13 In Figure E7-2, what is the purpose of C2?
A. Output coupling   C. Input coupling
B. Emitter bypass   D. Hum filtering
Notice the little circle after C2? This denotes the output of the circuit, and *C2 is the output coupling capacitor*. **ANSWER A**

E7C01 How are the capacitors and inductors of a low-pass filter Pi-network arranged between the network's input and output?
A. Two inductors are in series between the input and output and a capacitor is connected between the two inductors and ground
B. Two capacitors are in series between the input and output and an inductor is connected between the two capacitors and ground
C. An inductor is in parallel with the input, another inductor is in parallel with the output, and a capacitor is in series between the two
D. A capacitor is in parallel with the input, another capacitor is in parallel with the output, and an inductor is in series between the two
The pi-network features a capacitor in parallel with the input, a second capacitor in parallel with the output, and an *inductor in series* between the two. It looks like the Greek letter p. **ANSWER D**

E7C02 A T-network with series capacitors and a parallel (shunt) inductor has which of the following properties?
A. It transforms impedance and is a low-pass filter
B. It transforms reactance and is a low-pass filter
C. It transforms impedance and is a high-pass filter
D. It transforms reactance and is a narrow bandwidth notch filter

The *T-network transforms impedances* and is also used as a *high-pass filter*.
ANSWER C

T-Network High-Pass

L Low-Pass

Pi Low-Pass

Pi-L Low-Pass

T-Network Low-Pass

Matching Networks

E7C03 What advantage does a Pi-L-network have over a Pi-network for impedance matching between the final amplifier of a vacuum-tube type transmitter and an antenna?
A. Greater harmonic suppression
B. Higher efficiency
C. Lower losses
D. Greater transformation range

Worldwide ham sets into a multi-band antenna system can generate harmonics. The *Pi-L-network* always gives us *greater harmonic suppression* inside the transceiver. **ANSWER A**

E7C11 Which of the following is the common name for a filter network which is equivalent to two L networks back-to-back?

A. Pi-L   C.   Omega
B. Cascode   D.   Pi

The *Pi network* looks like the Greek letter π, and consists of two variable capacitors, shunt to ground, for transmitter output impedance matching. The Pi network also has only a single inductor. **ANSWER D**

E7C12 What is a Pi-L network, as used when matching a vacuum-tube final amplifier to a 50-ohm unbalanced output?
  A. A Phase Inverter Load network
  B. A network consisting of two series inductors and two shunt capacitors
  C. A network with only three discrete parts
  D. A matching network in which all components are isolated from ground

The popular *Pi-L network* is characterized by *TWO series-adjustable inductors*, and *TWO variable shunt-to-ground capacitors*, providing the greatest harmonic attenuation and optimum matching capability to an unbalanced (coax) antenna output. **ANSWER B**

E7C13 What is one advantage of a Pi matching network over an L matching network?
  A. Q of Pi networks can be varied depending on the component values chosen
  B. L networks can not perform impedance transformation
  C. Pi networks have fewer components
  D. Pi networks are designed for balanced input and output

The big advantage of a *Pi matching network* over the L network is the shunt-to-ground variable capacitors that *can vary the Q*, depending on the value of the variable capacitors and adjustable tap coil chosen. **ANSWER A**

E7B08 Which of the following describes how the loading and tuning capacitors are to be adjusted when tuning a vacuum tube RF power amplifier that employs a Pi-network output circuit?
  A. The loading capacitor is set to maximum capacitance and the tuning capacitor is adjusted for minimum allowable plate current
  B. The tuning capacitor is set to maximum capacitance and the loading capacitor is adjusted for minimum plate permissible current
  C. The loading capacitor is adjusted to minimum plate current while alternately adjusting the tuning capacitor for maximum allowable plate current
  D. The tuning capacitor is adjusted for minimum plate current while the loading capacitor is adjusted for maximum permissible plate current

If you're going to be running a big power amplifier on the HF bands, chances are it will still use a vacuum tube for kilowatts of power output. Solid-state power amplifiers require no *tuning*, but most solid-state power amps only put out about 800 watts max. With *a tube power amplifier*, alternately tune and *increase the plate current with a loading capacitor*, and then *dip the plate current with a tuning capacitor*. Do this for short periods of time, and do it on a frequency that no one else is transmitting on. I first tune up into a dummy load to get me close in settings, and then switch over to the antenna, select a frequency which no one is using, announce, "I'm going to quickly tune up," and then quickly tune up. **ANSWER D**

E7C04 How does a network transform a complex impedance to a resistive impedance?
  A. It introduces negative resistance to cancel the resistive part of an impedance
  B. It introduces transconductance to cancel the reactive part of an impedance
  C. It cancels the reactive part of an impedance and transforms the resistive part to the desired value
  D. Network resistances are substituted for load resistances

Modulate Your Transmitters

In older worldwide sets, you could vary the matching network to *cancel the reactive (X) part of an impedance and change the value of the resistive part (R)* of an impedance. Newer transistorized sets have a fixed output, and there is no manual operator control of the fixed matching devices. However, manufacturers have come to the rescue in antenna matching by providing new worldwide ham sets with built-in automatic antenna tuners. **ANSWER C**

E4D03 How can intermodulation interference between two repeaters occur?

- A. When the repeaters are in close proximity and the signals cause feedback in one or both transmitter final amplifiers
- B. When the repeaters are in close proximity and the signals mix in one or both transmitter final amplifiers
- C. When the signals from the transmitters are reflected out of phase from airplanes passing overhead
- D. When the signals from the transmitters are reflected in phase from airplanes passing overhead

"Intermod," in its true sense, occurs within the *repeater final amplifier.* When signals mix in one or both repeater amplifiers, sum and difference signals on many different frequencies can be heard. **ANSWER B**

E4D08 What causes intermodulation in an electronic circuit?

- A. Too little gain
- B. Lack of neutralization
- C. Nonlinear circuits or devices
- D. Positive feedback

Intermodulation interference is minimized by a careful selection of linear circuits and components. If that newly-designed transceiver for 2 meters or 440 MHz, or that repaired repeater is experiencing high levels of intermodulation, the problem could be caused by *non-linear circuits*, devices, and components inside the receiver. **ANSWER C**

E4D06 If the signals of two transmitters mix together in one or both of their final amplifiers, and unwanted signals at the sum and difference frequencies of the original signals are generated, what is this called?

- A. Amplifier desensitization
- B. Neutralization
- C. Adjacent channel interference
- D. Intermodulation interference

Repeaters are fun to operate through, but a real headache to keep on the air with a clean signal. The problem is *intermodulation caused by* other close proximity transmitters. What you may hear are *two signals coming in at once*, and this is the effect commonly called "intermod." **ANSWER D**

E7C10 Which of the following filters would be the best choice for use in a 2-meter repeater duplexer?

- A. A crystal filter
- B. A cavity filter
- C. A DSP filter
- D. An L-C filter

For a *2-meter repeater* duplexer system, we need big filters. We call them *cavity filters* because they are hollowed out to form extremely narrow-band tuned resonant circuits. **ANSWER B**

4-Cavity Duplexer for 2-Meter Band
Courtesy of WACOM Products, Inc.

E4D04 What is an effective way to reduce or eliminate intermodulation interference between two repeater transmitters operating in close proximity to one another?
    A. By installing a band-pass filter in the feed line between the transmitter and receiver
    B. By installing a properly terminated circulator at the output of the transmitter
    C. By using a Class C final amplifier
    D. By using a Class D final amplifier

Your ham friends who regularly trek to mountaintops to maintain ham radio VHF/UHF repeaters deserve your organization's major support. Mountaintop repeaters are located in the worst RF environment possible – in the midst of hundreds of nearby signals that may desensitize the receiver, or create "gar-bage" on the input. Everything was fine when your team left the hill, but a new land-mobile radio system on the same tower is now causing *intermodulation* interference. One *solution is to install a terminated circulator* or ferrite isolator between your own transmitter and duplexer, which helps zero in on your own receive frequency and cancel out any other off-channel frequencies that seem to creep in only when your equipment is on transmit. A spectrum analyzer is an essential piece of equipment for mountaintop repeater maintenance. **ANSWER B**

E4E08 What type of signal is picked up by electrical wiring near a radio transmitter?
    A. A common-mode signal at the frequency of the radio transmitter
    B. An electrical-sparking signal
    C. A differential-mode signal at the AC power line frequency
    D. Harmonics of the AC power line frequency

Electrical wiring will many times pick up *common-mode radio signals* at the frequency of the radio transmitter. The question is slightly in error – the wiring near the radio antenna is where most of the signal gets picked up, not necessarily at the radio transmitter. **ANSWER A**

E7B18 What is a klystron?
    A. A high speed multivibrator
    B. An electron-coupled oscillator utilizing a pentode vacuum tube
    C. An oscillator utilizing ceramic elements to achieve stability
    D. A VHF, UHF, or microwave vacuum tube that uses velocity modulation

The *Klystron* was originally found mainly in RADARs, but a few have been adapted by ham operators for specific microwave frequency use. *Velocity modulation* refers to how this *high-powered tube* is modulated – electrons are beamed down a precisely-tuned tube which has tiny openings that may speed up or slow down the electrons when modulation voltages are applied to the openings. This causes the electron velocity flow to vary. **ANSWER D**

E1F04 What does it mean if an external RF amplifier is listed on the FCC database as certificated for use in the amateur service?

    A. The RF amplifier may be marketed for use in any radio service
    B. That particular RF amplifier may be marketed for use in the amateur service
    C. All similar RF amplifiers produced by other manufacturers may be marketed
    D. All RF amplifiers produced by that manufacturer may be marketed

Do you own a linear amplifier? If so, look at the *certification label* and see that it is marked as *approved for use in the amateur service*. All commercially-made RF amplifiers must be listed on the FCC database. [97.315] **ANSWER B**

E1F05 Under what circumstances may a dealer sell an external RF power amplifier capable of operation below 144 MHz if it has not been granted FCC certification?

    A. It was purchased in used condition from an amateur operator and is sold to another amateur operator for use at that operator's station
    B. The equipment dealer assembled it from a kit
    C. It was imported from a manufacturer in a country that does not require certification of RF power amplifiers
    D. It was imported from a manufacturer in another country, and it was certificated by that country's government

Amplifiers for frequencies below 144 MHz could be *purchased in used condition* by an equipment dealer *and then sold by that dealer to another amateur operator*. This rule prevents the sale of amplifiers really intended for CB use that are constructed without the FCC's blessing. [97.315] **ANSWER A**

E1F14 Which of the following best describes one of the standards that must be met by an external RF power amplifier if it is to qualify for a grant of FCC certification?
- A. It must produce full legal output when driven by not more than 5 watts of mean RF input power
- B. It must be capable of external RF switching between its input and output networks
- C. It must exhibit a gain of 0 dB or less over its full output range
- D. It must satisfy the FCC's spurious emission standards when operated at its full output power

Recently, the FCC revised its policy on RF amplifiers. In order for an RF power amplifier to be granted FCC certification, *the amp must meet tight spurious emission standards* when it is operating at full power. Tube amplifiers with large band switching filter networks meet the specs more easily than smaller all-solid-state amps. This may be why the solid state amplifiers are still relatively expensive compared to tube amps. [97.317] **ANSWER D**

This little 2-meter linear amplifier meets stringent FCC spurious emission standards.
2-Meter Power Amplifier

E8D03 What input-amplitude parameter is valuable in evaluating the signal-handling capability of a Class A amplifier?
- A. Peak voltage
- B. RMS voltage
- C. Average power
- D. Resting voltage

In a *Class A amplifier, peak voltage* provides a double-check on the capability and linearity of that amplifier. Many times, distortion occurs when the amplifier is handling a peak voltage. **ANSWER A**

E7B03 Where on the load line of a Class A common emitter amplifier would bias normally be set?
- A. Approximately half-way between saturation and cutoff
- B. Where the load line intersects the voltage axis
- C. At a point where the bias resistor equals the load resistor
- D. At a point where the load line intersects the zero bias current curve

The *Class A amplifier* offers the greatest linearity, but offers only marginal efficiency usually less then 25%. We normally find the Class A amplifier as a "small signal" amplifier, sometimes used in modulation circuits where perfect linearity is required. The input signal continuously varies the input current over the complete 360 degrees of the sine-wave signal, with *bias normally set approximately half-way between saturation and cutoff.* **ANSWER A**

E7B01 For what portion of a signal cycle does a Class AB amplifier operate?
A. More than 180 degrees but less than 360 degrees
B. Exactly 180 degrees
C. The entire cycle
D. Less than 180 degrees

The *Class AB amplifier* has some of the properties of both the Class A and the Class B amplifier. It has *output for more than 180 degrees of the cycle, but less than 360 degrees of the cycle.* **ANSWER A**

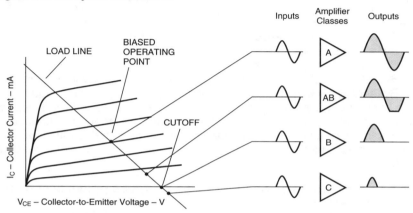

Various Classes of Transistorized Amplifiers

E7B05 Which of the following amplifier types reduces or eliminates even-order harmonics?
A. Push-push
C. Class C
B. Push-pull
D. Class AB

The Class-B amplifier may operate a pair of matched tubes in "push-pull" configuration, and operates only over one half of an input cycle. In transistorized Class B amplifiers, the circuit may be called "complimentary-symmetry" where NPN and PNP transistors each conduct over half the cycle. The advantage of the *push-pull circuit* is the *cancellation of even-order harmonics* – second, fourth, etc. It is important that you always change both output tubes together, never replacing one tube and leaving the older tube – always replace in pairs. **ANSWER B**

Push-Pull Amplifier

E7B17 Which of the following is a characteristic of a grounded-grid amplifier?

A. High power gain
B. High filament voltage
C. Low input impedance
D. Low bandwidth

The *grounded-grid amplifier* remains one of the most popular methods of achieving legal limit HF power output. Yes, vacuum tubes like the 8877 are still available, and the power supply may only require B+ plate voltage and a tap off the transformer for AC low filament voltage. Another benefit is a 50 ohm *low input impedance*, closely matching the output tuned circuit of your HF transceiver. That tube is literally loafing at a kW, and you'll have a nice clean signal on the air. **ANSWER C**

E7B07 How can a vacuum-tube power amplifier be neutralized?

A. By increasing the grid drive
B. By reducing the grid drive
C. By feeding back an out-of-phase component of the output to the input
D. By feeding back an in-phase component of the output to the input

We can keep our power amplified signal clean if the power *amplifier is neutralized*. For neutralization, follow the instructions in your amplifier manual. Chances are, you will be *feeding back an out-of-phase component of the output to the input* with neutralizing capacitors that are chosen to obtain the proper amount of feedback. **ANSWER C**

E7B16 Why are third-order intermodulation distortion products of particular concern in linear power amplifiers?

A. Because they are relatively close in frequency to the desired signal
B. Because they are relatively far in frequency from the desired signal
C. Because they invert the sidebands causing distortion
D. Because they maintain the sidebands, thus causing multiple duplicate signals

Third-order intermodulation distortion can be a big problem with power amplifiers with small amount of in-band *spurious emissions close to your operating frequency*. Third order IMD will likely elicit ham operators claiming your signal is wide or splattering, especially on 40 meters. **ANSWER A**

E7B04 What can be done to prevent unwanted oscillations in a power amplifier?

A. Tune the stage for maximum SWR
B. Tune both the input and output for maximum power
C. Install parasitic suppressors and/or neutralize the stage
D. Use a phase inverter in the output filter

As a new Extra soon, you will likely be operating with a tower and beam tied into a power amplifier to boost your transceiver's 100 watt output signal. But cautiously work yourself into high power amplifier operation. Big amps may cause interference to your home electronics, and big amps need to be tuned precisely to minimize parasitic oscillations. When viewed on a spectrum analyzer, parasitic oscillations look like a forest of trees surrounding your transmitted signal. *In tube amplifiers, RF chokes in the tube plate circuit, and small-value bypass and suppressor capacitors in the grid circuit, may help reduce unwanted oscillations*. With tube amplifiers, step by-step neutralization procedures are detailed in the instruction book. If the amplifier is brand new, you likely won't need to go through the neutralization process until you ultimately change out the final amplifier tube. **ANSWER C**

E7B02 Which class of amplifier, of the types shown, provides the highest efficiency?

A. Class A

B. Class B

C. Class C

D. Class AB

The *highest efficiency* comes out of a *Class C* amplifier. Since it operates the minimum time out of the cycle, it dissipates less power, but at the same time, produces narrow pulses which can cause loss of linearity. **ANSWER C**

E7B06 Which of the following is a likely result when a Class C rather than a Class AB amplifier is used to amplify a single-sideband phone signal?

A. Intermodulation products will be greatly reduced

B. Overall intelligibility will increase

C. Part of the transmitted signal will be inverted

D. The signal may become distorted and occupy excessive bandwidth

The Class AB amplifier will take an input signal and cause a field effect transistor or bipolar transistor to operate near cutoff, but not into cutoff. This will lead to a nearly linear reproduction of the input signal and using Class AB is common with careful attention to setting the bias just above the point where the signal base current goes into cutoff at zero. Once the transistor is biased beyond cutoff, efficiency continues to climb but at the cost of *distortion and excessive bandwidth*. This is why satellite operators using SSB caution against the use of non-linear FM-only solid state power amplifiers. The *Class C amp* is fine for data and FM. **ANSWER D**

Class-C power amplifier-modulator being modulated with baseband signal.

Source: *Basic Communications Electronics*, Hudson & Luecke, © 1999 Master Publishing, Inc., Niles, IL

E7B20 Which of the following devices is generally best suited for UHF or microwave power amplifier applications?

A. FET

B. Nuvistor

C. Silicon Controlled Rectifier

D. Triac

The *field effect transistor (FET)* controls current between the source and drain by voltage on the gate. Field effect transistors made with gallium arsenide (GaAs), an improvement over silicone, are preferred at *VHF and UHF* because of high gain and an extremely low noise factor. These are known as GaAs FETs, found in power amplifier receive preamp circuits. **ANSWER A**

E7B14 What is one way to prevent thermal runaway in a transistor amplifier?
A. Neutralization
B. Select transistors with high beta
C. Use degenerative emitter feedback
D. All of the above

UHF and microwave operators who homebrew their own amplifiers are cautious to protect against transistor thermal runaway – adding a fixed emitter resistor may slightly cut down on the transistor voltage gain, controlling transistor current without sacrificing linearity. In tube equipment, it is called cathode degeneration. In your *transistorized amplifier, thermal protection is provided using degenerative emitter feedback.* ANSWER C

Active Device — Provides Gain

NPN Transistor

Current Gain $= h_{fe} = \dfrac{\Delta\, ic}{\Delta\, ib}$

Passive Device — No Gain

Resistors R_1, R_2, R_3, R_4 and C_1

Δ means "change in"

Small-signal amplifier with an NPN transistor as the active device and resistors and a capacitor as passive devices that set the "no-signal" (DC) operating point.

Source: *Basic Communications Electronics*, Hudson & Luecke, © 1999 Master Publishing, Inc., Niles, IL

E6D11 What devices are commonly used as VHF and UHF parasitic suppressors at the input and output terminals of transistorized HF amplifiers?
A. Electrolytic capacitors
B. Butterworth filters
C. Ferrite beads
D. Steel-core toroids

If you look into the modern *VHF/UHF* single-band or dual-band *amplifier*, you'll see many leads dressed on a small *ferrite bead* to minimize parasitics coming down voltage or control lines. ANSWER C

E7B19 What is a parametric amplifier?
A. A type of bipolar operational amplifier with excellent linearity derived from use of very high voltage on the collector
B. A low-noise VHF or UHF amplifier relying on varying reactance for amplification
C. A high power amplifier for HF application utilizing the Miller effect to increase gain
D. An audio push-pull amplifier using silicon carbide transistors for extremely low noise

At VHF, UHF, and microwave frequencies, amplifier strip-line construction is common to minimize lead length capacitance. A common component within the parametric amplifier is the varactor diode, which behaves much like a variable capacitor, depending on the reverse bias voltage applied. Components are chosen carefully for *low-noise design*, and I personally use a *parametric amplifier* when I am up on a mountaintop operating 10 GHz microwave. ANSWER B

E7B15 What is the effect of intermodulation products in a linear power amplifier?

A. Transmission of spurious signals
B. Creation of parasitic oscillations
C. Low efficiency
D. All of the above

The effects of *intermodulation*, abbreviated IM, are *spurious signal products* usually traced to power amplifier stages or linear amplifiers with incorrect bias settings. Old time hams called any station with strong IM products "monkey chatter" that may travel up to 200 kHz up and down the band from the main transmitted signal. As a new Extra, with that new power amplifier turned on, start out your operation on extremely low power input to the amp, and suspect IM if another station drops down to your frequency and tells you that your signal is wide, splattering, and you sound like "monkey chatter." With careful tuning and monitoring of amp input drive power from your transceiver, intermodulation can usually be solved without having to completely field strip your station for repair. **ANSWER A**

E7D01 What is one characteristic of a linear electronic voltage regulator?

A. It has a ramp voltage as its output
B. It eliminates the need for a pass transistor
C. The control element duty cycle is proportional to the line or load conditions
D. The conduction of a control element is varied to maintain a constant output voltage

A *linear electronic voltage regulator varies the conduction of a circuit in* direct proportion to variations in the line voltage to or the load current from the device. You will find inside your base station power supply, which utilizes a big heavy transformer, a sophisticated voltage regulation circuit. **ANSWER D**

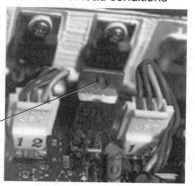

REGULATOR

Voltage Regulator IC
Mounted in Circuit Board

E7D03 What device is typically used as a stable reference voltage in a linear voltage regulator?

A. A Zener diode
B. A tunnel diode
C. An SCR
D. A varactor diode

For *voltage regulation* and a stable reference voltage, a *Zener diode* is found in most ham sets. **ANSWER A**

ANODE   CATHODE

Here is the schematic symbol of a Zener diode. Since a diode only passes energy in one direction, look for that one-way arrow, plus a "Z" indicating it is a Zener diode. Doesn't that vertical line look like a tiny "Z".

Zener Diode

E7D02 What is one characteristic of a switching electronic voltage regulator?
A. The resistance of a control element is varied in direct proportion to the line voltage or load current
B. It is generally less efficient than a linear regulator
C. The control device's duty cycle is controlled to produce a constant average output voltage
D. It gives a ramp voltage at its output

The *switching voltage regulator* actually *switches the control device* completely *on or off*. **ANSWER C**

E7D04 Which of the following types of linear regulator makes the most efficient use of the primary power source?
A. A constant current source
B. A series regulator
C. A shunt regulator
D. A shunt current source

A series regulator normally runs cool. It's *more efficient* than a shunt regulator. Everything passes through the *series regulator*. **ANSWER B**

E7D05 Which of the following types of linear voltage regulator places a constant load on the unregulated voltage source?
A. A constant current source
B. A series regulator
C. A shunt current source
D. A shunt regulator

In circuits where the load on the *unregulated input source* must be kept constant, we use the slightly less-efficient *shunt regulator*. These can sometimes get quite warm, and are usually mounted to the chassis of the equipment. The chassis acts as a heat sink. **ANSWER D**

E7D06 What is the purpose of Q1 in the circuit shown in Figure E7-3?
A. It provides negative feedback to improve regulation
B. It provides a constant load for the voltage source
C. It increases the current-handling capability of the regulator
D. It provides D1 with current

This *transistor can handle greater current* than a Zener diode. They sometimes call these transistors "series-pass transistors." **ANSWER C**

Figure E7-3

E7D07 What is the purpose of C2 in the circuit shown in Figure E7-3?
A. It bypasses hum around D1
B. It is a brute force filter for the output
C. To self-resonate at the hum frequency
D. To provide fixed DC bias for Q1

C2 provides additional filtering for the ripple frequency. It *bypasses* voltage changes around the Zener diode, *D1*, to keep the reference voltage stable. **ANSWER A**

E7D08 What type of circuit is shown in Figure E7-3?
A. Switching voltage regulator   C. Linear voltage regulator
B. Grounded emitter amplifier   D. Emitter follower
Components *D1 and Q1* give the answer away – *a linear voltage regulator*. This should give you a good, solid, regulated voltage output, even though the load current may be changing. **ANSWER C**

E7D09 What is the purpose of C1 in the circuit shown in Figure E7-3?
A. It resonates at the ripple frequency
B. It provides fixed bias for Q1
C. It decouples the output
D. It filters the supply voltage
C1 is an electrolytic filter capacitor which removes ripple frequency (60-cycle or 120-cycle) from the input voltage. **ANSWER D**

E7D10 What is the purpose of C3 in the circuit shown in Figure E7-3?
A. It prevents self-oscillation
B. It provides brute force filtering of the output
C. It provides fixed bias for Q1
D. It clips the peaks of the ripple
You might see a lot of *C3*-type circuits in your power supply. This *is an RF bypass capacitor*, keeping any stray RF energy from getting into the circuit, which could cause *self-oscillation*. **ANSWER A**

E7D11 What is the purpose of R1 in the circuit shown in Figure E7-3?
A. It provides a constant load to the voltage source
B. It couples hum to D1
C. It supplies current to D1
D. It bypasses hum around D1
R1 is connected to the power supply input voltage and *supplies the bias current to operate D1 and Q1* at a stable operating point for the voltage regulator output voltage and current desired. **ANSWER C**

E7D12 What is the purpose of R2 in the circuit shown in Figure E7-3?
A. It provides fixed bias for Q1
B. It provides fixed bias for D1
C. It decouples hum from D1
D. It provides a constant minimum load for Q1
R2 connected to the 12-volt output helps maintain voltage regulation by keeping a *constant minimum load for the transistor Q1*, and acts as a bleeder resistor to discharge capacitors after the power supply has been turned off. **ANSWER D**

E7D13 What is the purpose of D1 in the circuit shown in Figure E7-3?
A. To provide line voltage stabilization
B. To provide a voltage reference
C. Peak clipping
D. Hum filtering
D1 is a voltage regulator Zener diode, which is used to provide a voltage reference for Q1. If the load current increases (R2 gets smaller), the output voltage would tend to decrease. When this voltage change is compared to the reference voltage across D1 by Q1, Q1 adjusts its voltage drop from collector to emitter to raise the output voltage to the designed value with the new load current. **ANSWER B**

E7D14 What is one purpose of a "bleeder" resistor in a conventional (unregulated) power supply?
A. To cut down on waste heat generated by the power supply
B. To balance the low-voltage filament windings
C. To improve output voltage regulation
D. To boost the amount of output current

The *bleeder resistor* provides a stable load level in the power supply, and bleeds off current from the charged capacitors when the power supply is shut off. *Good output voltage regulation* is maintained by the bleeder resistor shunt grounded from the charged capacitors to chassis ground. **ANSWER C**

E7D15 What is the purpose of a "step-start" circuit in a high-voltage power supply?
A. To provide a dual-voltage output for reduced power applications
B. To compensate for variations of the incoming line voltage
C. To allow for remote control of the power supply
D. To allow the filter capacitors to charge gradually

The modern, high-voltage power supply likely contains a series resistor and capacitor in parallel in the high-voltage plate circuit of the tube in order to buffer the initial in-rush of startup current. This *allows the filter capacitors to slowly build their charges*, minimizing that dreaded arc sound when you turn on a high-voltage supply that has been turned off for several years! Some ham operators bring up high voltage on older equipment with a variable AC transformer. **ANSWER D**

E7D16 When several electrolytic filter capacitors are connected in series to increase the operating voltage of a power supply filter circuit, why should resistors be connected across each capacitor?
A. To equalize, as much as possible, the voltage drop across each capacitor
B. To provide a safety bleeder to discharge the capacitors when the supply is off
C. To provide a minimum load current to reduce voltage excursions at light loads
D. All of these answers are correct

Those *resistors* in parallel across power supply electrolytic filter capacitors help *equalize voltage drops* across each of the capacitors, *act as bleeder resistors* when the power supply is turned off, and *add a constant load if* there is minimal current required out of the power supply circuits. **ANSWER D**

E7D17 What is the primary reason that a high-frequency inverter type high-voltage power supply can be both less expensive and lighter in weight than a conventional power supply?
A. The inverter design does not require any output filtering
B. It uses a diode bridge rectifier for increased output
C. The high frequency inverter design uses much smaller transformers and filter components for an equivalent power output
D. It uses a large power-factor compensation capacitor to create "free" power from the unused portion of the AC cycle

Conventional, heavy-transformer power supplies that convert home AC power down to 12 volts DC weigh in at about 2 lbs. for every 12 volt DC ampere output. I have plenty of 20 amp power supplies that weigh about 40 lbs. each. These power supplies are characterized by a huge step-down transformer, diodes and big filter capacitors. The best efficiency you could hope for was about 50%. And, OHHH, would they get warm under load. The new power supply technology is called "switcher," and they are lightweight, small in size, give off little heat, and offer almost 90% efficiency. The output of a switching power supply (whether converting house power down to DC or switching house power up to various high voltage levels) is clean and pure thanks to high-speed field-effect transistors taking the place of that big heavy transformer. New switching power supplies also have minimal EMI (RF interference), and some may even take any detectable emitted spur and let you adjust it out of your favorite listening spot. The *switching power supply* is about the same cost as the old, big-transformer supplies, and the *very small transformer and filter components* easily fit in a relatively small package, either inside or outside the radio equipment. **ANSWER C**

E6E02 Which of these filter bandwidths would be a good choice for use with standard double-sideband AM transmissions?

A. 1 kHz at -6 dB
B. 500 Hz at -6 dB
C. 6 kHz at -6 dB
D. 15 kHz at -6 dB

Believe it or not, there are still some portions on the worldwide ham bands where *AM, double-sideband*, full-carrier phone emission still exists. This is twice as wide as SSB, and would *require a 6 kHz band-pass filter with -6 dB skirts* to pass the signal.
ANSWER C

E6E03 What is a crystal lattice filter?

A. A power supply filter made with interlaced quartz crystals
B. An audio filter made with four quartz crystals that resonate at 1-kHz intervals
C. A filter with wide bandwidth and shallow skirts made using quartz crystals
D. A filter with narrow bandwidth and steep skirts made using quartz crystals

The new worldwide set you purchase will probably have some good SSB and CW filters built in. The *filters have a nice narrow bandwidth and steep skirts*. The filters are *made up of quartz crystals*. You can buy accessory filters for a tighter response, but these many times will make your received signals sound pinched. Unless you do a lot of CW work, to get started, stay with the filters that come with the set.
ANSWER D

E6E06 What is one aspect of the piezoelectric effect?

A. Physical deformation of a crystal by the application of a voltage
B. Mechanical deformation of a crystal by the application of a magnetic field
C. The generation of electrical energy by the application of light
D. Reversed conduction states when a P-N junction is exposed to light

If you *apply a voltage to a quartz crystal*, it will vibrate at a specific frequency. This is the reason crystal oscillators are so accurate. They oscillate at the frequency, or harmonics of the frequency, of the crystal, and continue to do so with great accuracy unless the temperature changes outside design limits. **ANSWER A**

a. Schematic

AGC—Automatic
Gain Control
applied at the
points indicated.

b. Effect of Crystal Filter on Passband

Cascaded IF amplifiers. The active devices are JFETs. The value of most components depends upon the frequency of operation.

Source: *Basic Communications Electronics*, Hudson & Luecke, © 1999 Master Publishing, Inc., Niles, IL

E6E04 What technique is used to construct low-cost, high-performance crystal ladder filters?
  A. Obtain a small quantity of custom-made crystals
  B. Choose a crystal with the desired bandwidth and operating frequency to match a desired center frequency
  C. Measure crystal bandwidth to ensure at least 20% coupling
  D. Measure crystal frequencies and carefully select units with a frequency variation of less than 10% of the desired filter bandwidth

High-performance *crystal ladder filters* are made using crystals that have a frequency *variation of less than 10% of the desired filter bandwidth*. **ANSWER D**

E6E05 Which of the following factors has the greatest effect in helping determine the bandwidth and response shape of a crystal ladder filter?
  A. The relative frequencies of the individual crystals
  B. The DC voltage applied to the quartz crystal
  C. The gain of the RF stage preceding the filter
  D. The amplitude of the signals passing through the filter

The *bandwidth and response* of a crystal ladder filter is determined by the frequency of the *individual crystals* within that filter unit. **ANSWER A**

E7C05 Which filter type is described as having ripple in the passband and a sharp cutoff?

A. A Butterworth filter
B. An active LC filter
C. A passive op-amp filter
D. A Chebyshev filter

If you look at the word *"Chebyshev,"* it almost looks like it has a *ripple*, doesn't it? **ANSWER D**

Butterworth

Chebyshev

Elliptical

Comparison of Low-Pass Filter Circuits

E7C06 What are the distinguishing features of an elliptical filter?

A. Gradual passband rolloff with minimal stop-band ripple
B. Extremely flat response over its passband, with gradually rounded stop-band corners
C. Extremely sharp cutoff, with one or more infinitely deep notches in the stop band
D. Gradual passband rolloff with extreme stop-band ripple

The *elliptical filter* has an immediate and extremely *sharp cutoff*, with one or more *deep notches* in the stop band. **ANSWER C**

E4C03 What is the term for the blocking of one FM phone signal by another, stronger FM phone signal?

A. Desensitization
B. Cross-modulation interference
C. Capture effect
D. Frequency discrimination

A unique property of your *FM* receiver is the ability to hear only the strongest incoming FM signal. If a distant station is transmitting, and a strong local station comes on the air, you will only hear the local station. *The stronger signal is "capturing" your receiver.* **ANSWER C**

E4C02 Which of the following is the result of the capture effect in an FM receiver?

A. All signals on a frequency are demodulated
B. None of the signals could be heard
C. The strongest signal received is the only demodulated signal
D. The weakest signal received is the only demodulated signal

When someone breaks into a conversation on FM causing the other signal to completely disappear, this is called *"capture effect,"* where *only the strongest FM signal received is demodulated.* **ANSWER C**

E7C07 What kind of audio filter would you use to attenuate an interfering carrier signal while receiving an SSB transmission?
A. A band-pass filter   C. A Pi-network filter
B. A notch filter   D. An all-pass filter
To *attenuate* and block a *specific* whistle (or *"heterodyne"*) on an SSB receiver, switch on the *notch filter*, and ever so carefully sweep through the signal until it disappears. Tune slowly! A notch filter can require mighty critical adjustment! **ANSWER B**

E7C08 What kind of digital signal processing audio filter might be used to remove unwanted noise from a received SSB signal?
A. An adaptive filter   C. A Hilbert-transform filter
B. A crystal-lattice filter   D. A phase-inverting filter
The *"adaptive filter"* found in digital signal processing (DSP) circuits to *removes unwanted noise* from incoming SSB signals. **ANSWER A**
www.nctclearspeech.com and www.bhinstrumentation.co.uk

E4D05 If a receiver tuned to 146.70 MHz receives an intermodulation-product signal whenever a nearby transmitter transmits on 146.52 MHz, what are the two most likely frequencies for the other interfering signal?
A. 146.34 MHz and 146.61 MHz   C. 146.10 MHz and 147.30 MHz
B. 146.88 MHz and 146.34 MHz   D. 73.35 MHz and 239.40 MHz
To calculate the possible sources of intermodulation interference, we check for the signals that lead to this type of a common problem at base and repeater stations. **ANSWER A**

Finding the Intermodulation Interference Frequencies

There are four possible calculations to find the intermodulation interfering frequencies — two where the frequencies are added and two where the frequencies are subtracted. The calculations where the frequencies are subtracted are the only ones used because only these calculations produce frequencies close enough to cause significant interference. As the question states, the intermodulation product f_{IMD} is received on 146.70 MHz when a signal at 146.52 MHz is transmitted. The calculations when the frequencies are subtracted are:

$$f_{IMD(2)} = 2f_1 - f_2 \qquad\qquad f_{IMD(4)} = 2f_2 - f_1$$

Rearranging,   Rearranging,

$$f_2 = 2f_1 - f_{IMD(2)} \qquad\qquad 2f_2 = f_{IMD(4)} + f_1$$

$$f_2 = 2(146.52) - 146.70 \qquad\qquad f_2 = \frac{f_{IMD(4)} + f_1}{2}$$

$$f_2 = 146.34 \text{ MHz} \qquad\qquad f_2 = \frac{146.70 + 146.52}{2}$$

$$f_2 = 146.61 \text{ MHz}$$

E4D07 Which of the following describes the most significant effect of an off-frequency signal when it is causing cross-modulation interference to a desired signal?
A. A large increase in background noise
B. A reduction in apparent signal strength
C. The desired signal can no longer be heard
D. The off-frequency unwanted signal is heard in addition to the desired signal

You are *listening* to a pal *on the repeater, and now* his signal is joined by *a simultaneous dispatch* of Peter's Perfect Plumbing Service. This is a classic example of *cross-modulation interference* to your friend's signal. **ANSWER D**

E4C05 What does a value of -174 dBm/Hz represent with regard to the noise floor of a receiver?
A. The minimum detectable signal as a function of receive frequency
B. The theoretical noise at the input of a perfect receiver at room temperature
C. The noise figure of a 1 Hz bandwidth receiver
D. The galactic noise contribution to minimum detectable signal

Noise occurs anywhere objects are warmed above absolute zero. If you had a perfect receiver with no internal noise, it would still detect noise when connected to an antenna. *At room temperature, that noise level is about -174 dBm* for every 1 Hz of bandwidth. In addition to the natural noise, man-made noise also occurs, and it is much more prevalent at some frequencies that others. On HF bands, man-made noise is so common that a receiver with a very good noise floor is not nearly as important as it would be for a receiver used at 10 GHz trying to detect an EME signal. **ANSWER B**

E4C06 The thermal noise value of a receiver is -174 dBm/Hz. What is the theoretically best minimum detectable signal for a 400 Hz bandwidth receiver?
A. 174 dBm
B. -164 dBm
C. -155 dBm
D. -148 dBm

The weakest signal a receiver can receive is one that is just above the total of all noise in the receiver. -174 dBm/Hz is the background noise the receiver will see at room temperature. Add the noise caused by the receiver's bandwidth to the noise floor of the receiver and you have the total noise. The receiver described in this question matches the -174 dBm/Hz noise of the background, so it is a theoretically-perfect receiver, one with no noise floor of its own. Thus, the weakest signal it can receive is $-174 + 10 \log (\text{bandwidth}) = \text{noise floor} = -174 + 10 \log (400) + 0 = -174 + 26 \text{ dBm} = -148 \text{ dBm}$. **ANSWER D**

E4C07 What does the MDS of a receiver represent?
A. The meter display sensitivity
B. The minimum discernible signal
C. The multiplex distortion stability
D. The maximum detectable spectrum

The *Minimum Discernable Signal* is tested in the SSB or CW mode, with internal preamps and internal attenuators OUT. Automatic gain control is OFF, and RF gain is full ON. Manufacturers of modern HF equipment have achieved extraordinary low noise floors, with product designs that minimize phase noise. **ANSWER B**

E4C08 How might lowering the noise figure affect receiver performance?
A. It would reduce the signal to noise ratio
B. It would increase signal to noise ratio
C. It would reduce bandwidth
D. It would increase bandwidth

I know I have a great high frequency receiver when I can turn the volume all the way up with no antenna connected, and hear almost nothing coming out of the receiver. Once I add the antenna, even the weak signals will have a good signal to noise ratio. An *increase in signal to noise* ratio is the sign of a quality receiver. Signal to noise ratio can be improved either by raising the signal level or *by lowering the noise figure*. The lower the noise floor of a receiver, the weaker the signals we can detect. **ANSWER B** www.flex-radio.com

E4C09 Which of the following is most likely to be the limiting condition for sensitivity in a modern communications receiver operating at 14 MHz?
A. The noise figure of the RF amplifier
B. Mixer noise
C. Conversion noise
D. Atmospheric noise

Manufacturers of high frequency and VHF/UHF weak signal radios have all developed receiver circuits that offer a high signal to noise ratio. This means that any noise in the RF receiver amplifier transistors is kept to a minimum, along with a minimum of mixer noise and any noise in the IF. However, this question asks what might be the *limiting condition* for weak signal reception in a modern high frequency receiver, operating at 14 MHz, and the nemesis is *atmospheric noise*. If you can hear static crashes from a storm a thousand miles away, you have a hot receiver! And don't blame the receiver if your noisy power lines cause that strong signal to register only S-9. **ANSWER D**

E4C12 What is an undesirable effect of using too wide a filter bandwidth in the IF section of a receiver?
A. Output-offset overshoot
B. Filter ringing
C. Thermal-noise distortion
D. Undesired signals may be heard

Using an AM 10-kHz IF filter for pulling in 2.3 kHz SSB signals would result in *receiving undesired signals* beyond the normal bandwidth of the desired signal. **ANSWER D**

E4C10 Which of the following is a desirable amount of selectivity for an amateur RTTY HF receiver?
A. 100 Hz
B. 300 Hz
C. 6000 Hz
D. 2400 Hz

For *RTTY, 300 Hz* is good selectivity. **ANSWER B**

E4C11 Which of the following is a desirable amount of selectivity for an amateur single-sideband phone receiver?
A. 1 kHz
B. 2.4 kHz
C. 4.2 kHz
D. 4.8 kHz

For *SSB, a 2.4-kHz* filter bandwidth is the most popular for good fidelity audio. **ANSWER B**

Product detector circuit used for SSB.

E4C13 How does a narrow band roofing filter affect receiver performance?
A. It improves sensitivity by reducing front end noise
B. It improves intelligibility by using low Q circuitry to reduce ringing
C. It improves dynamic range by keeping strong signals near the receive frequency out of the IF stages
D. All of these choice are correct

Roofing filters in the IF will minimize contesting receiver "swamping" when you have another ham nearby idly chatting with his buddy, running a kilowatt, well up the band. IF stage roofing filters, like automatically-selected 15 kHz, 6 kHz, and 3 kHz filters, may feature 4-pole, fundamental-mode monolithic crystal filter design to produce an ideal shape factor. The filters usually are positioned after the first mixer and significantly improve the 3rd-order intercept point performance for all stages that follow. I appreciate the performance of roofing filters on 40 meters early in the morning when a nearby shortwave station numbs my receiver. My new rig with *roofing filters* eliminates this problem thanks to an *improvement in the rig's dynamic range.* **ANSWER C**

E4C14 Which of these choices is a desirable amount of selectivity for an amateur VHF FM receiver?
A. 1 kHz
B. 2.4 kHz
C. 4.2 kHz
D. 15 kHz

This question asks about selectivity in a VHF-FM receiver, not SSB. Selectivity of 15 kHz is what you want in your VHF FM receiver. Selectivity allows you to separate adjacent signals from one another. But it doesn't help if the selectivity is narrower than the signal you are trying to detect, because it filters out information from that signal. *VHF FM signals* have a *bandwidth* near *15 kHz*, so your *selectivity should be near 15 kHz* to give your receiver best performance. **ANSWER D**

E4C15 What is the primary source of noise that can be heard from an HF-band receiver with an antenna connected?
A. Detector noise
B. Induction motor noise
C. Receiver front-end noise
D. Atmospheric noise

When you hook up an HF transceiver to your antenna, *most of the noise* received is *atmospheric* noise. **ANSWER D**

E4C04 What is meant by the noise floor of a receiver?

A. The minimum level of noise at the audio output when the RF gain is turned all the way down

B. The equivalent phase noise power generated by the local oscillator

C. The minimum level of noise that will overload the RF amplifier stage

D. The equivalent input noise power when the antenna is replaced with a matched dummy load

For VHF and UHF weak signal work on SSB and CW, you want to operate a receiver with an extremely low noise floor. The GaAsFET transistor is found in quality VHF/UHF transceivers for weak signal work because of its extremely low noise floor that will allow weak signals to be detected above the receiver's internal noise. A *receiver with a good noise* floor will yield nearly *identical noise power when switched between a dummy load and an antenna*, measured 3 dB S + N/N, single tone, at 500 Hz and 2400 Hz. **ANSWER D**

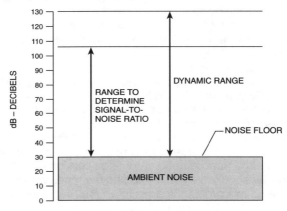

Noise Floor in a Receiver

Source: *Installing and Maintaining Sound Systems,* G. McComb, ©1996, Master Publishing, Inc.

E4D01 What is meant by the blocking dynamic range of a receiver?

A. The difference in dB between the level of an incoming signal which will cause 1 dB of gain compression, and the level of the noise floor

B. The minimum difference in dB between the levels of two FM signals which will cause one signal to block the other

C. The difference in dB between the noise floor and the third order intercept point

D. The minimum difference in dB between two signals which produce third order intermodulation products greater than the noise floor

When you are working a contest on high frequency and tune in to a rare station just above the noise floor, you may hear that station request USA responses to transmit 5 kHz "up." This is contest "split operation," and it leaves the station in the clear without people calling right on top of his ultra weak signal. Powerful stations just a few kilohertz away will sometimes cause the weak station's signal to disappear in the noise because your receiver is saturated with powerful signals nearby on the band. A receiver with good dynamic range will minimize desensitization when nearby signals blast your front end circuitry. *Blocking dynamic range is measured in decibels at your receiver noise floor, with AGC turned off, and a nearby signal that leads to 1 dB of gain compression in the receiver*, causing that weak signal to dip slightly into the noise. Blocking dynamic range tests are more fairly calculated at 100 kHz off from the desired signal. **ANSWER A**

E4D02 Which of the following describes two types of problems caused by poor dynamic range in a communications receiver?
  A. Cross modulation of the desired signal and desensitization from strong adjacent signals
  B. Oscillator instability requiring frequent retuning, and loss of ability to recover the opposite sideband, should it be transmitted
  C. Cross modulation of the desired signal and insufficient audio power to operate the speaker
  D. Oscillator instability and severe audio distortion of all but the strongest received signals

In a *receiver* that *does not have good dynamic range, cross-modulation* of the desired signal can be encountered, and the receiver can *drop in sensitivity* (be desensitized) by strong adjacent frequency signals. **ANSWER A**

E4D09 What is the purpose of the preselector in a communications receiver?
  A. To store often-used frequencies
  B. To provide a range of AGC time constants
  C. To improve rejection of unwanted signals
  D. To allow selection of the optimum RF amplifier device

You ask why those big contest HF transceivers are so large? On the inside, they may maintain high-Q, motor-driven *preselector coils* that can automatically track, or may be manually adjusted, to your desired receive frequency. These preselector coils may achieve a Q of over 300 and provide steep passband filtering not available with smaller fixed components or older external bandpass boxes. The peak of these optional built-in preselector modules may even be adjusted AWAY from your frequency to *provide added isolation* from a specific adjacent frequency transmitting station. The Q is so high that each preselector on each band needs its own micro-motor drive assembly. But for big contesters, the big radio can really cut through the QRM. **ANSWER C**

E4D10 What does a third-order intercept level of 40 dBm mean with respect to receiver performance?
  A. Signals less than 40 dBm will not generate audible third-order intermodulation products
  B. The receiver can tolerate signals up to 40 dB above the noise floor without producing third-order intermodulation products
  C. A pair of 40 dBm signals will theoretically generate the same output on the third order intermodulation frequency as on the input frequency
  D. A pair of 1 mW input signals will produce a third-order intermodulation product which is 40 dB stronger than the input signal

If you input two tones that are fHz apart to the receiver input, the mixer will output not only those two tones shifted down to the intermediate frequency but also third-order intermodulation tones at fHz above and below the original tones. At normal input signal levels, these third-order tones are much weaker than the original two tones. But as you increase the amplitude of the original two tones, *the third-order tones* increase in amplitude three times faster than the original tones. If you continue to increase the input tone signal levels, at some point the *signal strength of the input tones and the third-order tones will be equal.* This is called the third order intercept point. A third-order intercept point of 40 dBm means that, if the input tones were 40 dBm, then the third order tones would also be 40 dBm. The 3rd order IP is not achievable in actual practice, as the receiver will saturate long before it reaches that point. **ANSWER C**

E4D11 Why are third-order intermodulation products within a receiver of particular interest compared to other products?
    A. The third-order product of two signals which are in the band is itself likely to be within the band
    B. The third-order intercept is much higher than other orders
    C. Third-order products are an indication of poor image rejection
    D. Third-order intermodulation produces three products for every input signal
Your new high-frequency transceiver boasts extraordinary receiver sensitivity, ultra-tight selectivity, and a +30 dBm third order intercept point. Third order intermodulation could occur in the receiver IF or RF stages when a pair of contest stations near you are hammering your "front end" just a few kHz away. Improved equipment designs minimize the *third order "phantom signals"* that are non-desirable weak signal products from these other two stations, *strong enough to interfere with the station you are trying to tune* in. Not only are you hammered by two strong signals of interference, but also artifacts of their clean transmitted signals that may sometimes cover up the desired DX station you are trying to tune in. Physically larger inductors in the band pass filter stage may help, along with low-distortion diodes in the band pass frequency switching circuitry. Monolithic roofing filters, more expensive than overtone mode filters, will offer a better shape factor and are less susceptible to intermodulation distortion within your top quality transceiver's RF and IF stages. If you are considering a contest-capable transceiver to feed into your 100-foot-long boom HF antenna, the multi-thousand-dollar high end HF transceivers will offer you the ultimate in the rejection of third order phantom signals with a distortion-free, high-dynamic-range receiver system. **ANSWER A**

E4D12 What is the term for the reduction in receiver sensitivity caused by a strong signal near the received frequency?
    A. Desensitization   C. Cross-modulation interference
    B. Quieting   D. Squelch gain rollback
If signals mysteriously come in strong then abruptly get weak, and then come back strong again, chances are there is someone nearby transmitting on an adjacent frequency, *desensitizing* your receiver. The best way to check for adjacent signals is through the use of a frequency counter. The very best way to check is with a spectrum analyzer. **ANSWER A**

E4D13 Which of the following can cause receiver desensitization?
    A. Audio gain adjusted too low
    B. Strong adjacent-channel signals
    C. Audio bias adjusted too high
    D. Squelch gain adjusted too low
Adjacent frequency signals may overload a receiver's front end *causing the receiver to momentarily lose sensitivity.* **ANSWER B**

E4D14 Which of the following is a way to reduce the likelihood of receiver desensitization?
A. Decrease the RF bandwidth of the receiver
B. Raise the receiver IF frequency
C. Increase the receiver front end gain
D. Switch from fast AGC to slow AGC

If you have a dual-band handheld transceiver, you'll notice that the insides are all enclosed in tiny metal cans. This shielding is necessary to keep the receiver from desensitizing on one band when you are transmitting on another band. Shielding is a good way to *minimize internal desensitization*. Desensitization occurs when nearby signals get into your receiver and cause the gain to be reduced. By *decreasing the RF bandwidth* of the receiver, you reduce the likelihood of nearby signals affecting your receiver. Only signals that are within the passband of the RF are likely to affect your receive. **ANSWER A**

E7E10 What is the process of detection?
A. The extraction of weak signals from noise
B. The recovery of information from a modulated RF signal
C. The modulation of a carrier
D. The mixing of noise with a received signal

Your radio's *detector recovers information* from a modulated RF signal. **ANSWER B**

E7E11 How does a diode detector function?
A. By rectification and filtering of RF signals
B. By breakdown of the Zener voltage
C. By mixing signals with noise in the transition region of the diode
D. By sensing the change of reactance in the diode with respect to frequency

Since a *diode* only conducts for half of the AC signal, it *may be used as a rectifier*. By *filtering out the radio frequency energy* after rectification, detection is accomplished – the modulating signal is what remains. **ANSWER A**

Diode Detector

E7E12 Which of the following types of detector is well suited for demodulating SSB signals?

A. Discriminator
B. Phase detector

C. Product detector
D. Phase comparator

A *product detector* is found in *SSB receivers*. It mixes the incoming signal with a beat frequency oscillator signal. The beat frequency oscillator signal is a locally-generated carrier that is mixed with the incoming signal. **ANSWER C**

E7E06 What circuit is added to an FM receiver to restore attenuated lower audio frequencies?
    A. A de-emphasis network   C. An audio prescaler
    B. A heterodyne suppressor   D. A pre-emphasis network

In order to *restore* proportionally-attenuated *lower audio frequencies*, a *de-emphasis network* is found in the communications receiver. **ANSWER A**

FM De-emphasis Circuit

E7C14 Which of these modes is most affected by non-linear phase response in a receiver IF filter?
    A. Meteor Scatter   C. Digital
    B. Single-Sideband Voice   D. Video

Non-linear phase response within a receiver's IF filter is seldom noticed in CW, SSB, or video modes. Unfortunately, complex *digital modes are most affected by non-linear phase response* where individual data pulses incur unwanted shifts of TIME, disrupting the smooth flow of data within the intermediate frequency filter. Although most filters may incur a small amount of phase distortion, all but data can work through this problem. **ANSWER C**

E4C01 What is the effect of excessive phase noise in the local oscillator section of a receiver?
    A. It limits the receiver ability to receive strong signals
    B. It reduces the receiver sensitivity
    C. It decreases the receiver third-order intermodulation distortion dynamic range
    D. It can cause strong signals on nearby frequencies to interfere with reception of weak signals

The latest amateur transceivers all boast minimum phase noise in the receiver local oscillator. Any worldwide set with *excessive phase noise* in the LO might allow *adjacent frequency signals to interfere* with on-frequency weak signals. **ANSWER D**

E7E07 What is one result of the process of mixing two signals?
    A. The elimination of noise in a wideband receiver by phase comparison
    B. The elimination of noise in a wideband receiver by phase differentiation
    C. The recovery of the intelligence from a modulated RF signal
    D. The creation of new signals at the sum and difference frequencies

The result of *mixing two signals* within your transceiver's mixer stage is to *produce sum and difference frequencies* to end up with the desired single frequency for the design of the circuit. **ANSWER D**

Block Diagram Showing Mixer Function

Source: *Basic Communications Electronics*, Hudson & Luecke, © 1999 Master Publishing, Inc., Niles, IL

E7E08 What are the principal frequencies that appear at the output of a mixer circuit?

A. Two and four times the original frequency
B. The sum, difference and square root of the input frequencies
C. The original frequencies, and the sum and difference frequencies
D. 1.414 and 0.707 times the input frequency

Out of the mixer comes your *original two frequencies, and* the *sum and difference frequencies*. The more elaborate the transceiver, the more mixing stages found in the sets. This helps filter out unwanted signals or phantom signals that could cause interference. **ANSWER C**

Frequency spectrum plot of mixer signals.

Source: *Basic Communications Electronics*, Hudson & Luecke, © 1999 Master Publishing, Inc., Niles, IL

E7E09 What occurs when an excessive amount of signal energy reaches a mixer circuit?
A. Spurious mixer products are generated
B. Mixer blanking occurs
C. Automatic limiting occurs
D. A beat frequency is generated

Some VHF power amplifiers may incorporate a hefty pre-amplifier circuit for use on receiving that boosts incoming signal levels. The pre-amp turned on could generate spurious mixer products as a result of the *high signal level*. The *spurious products* are not really signals that you are trying to receive. If you use a handheld with a power amp, turn the pre-amp off. **ANSWER A**

E7E15 What is meant by "direct conversion" when referring to a software defined receiver?
A. Software is converted from source code to object code during operation of the receiver
B. Incoming RF is converted to the IF frequency by rectification to generate the control voltage for a voltage-controlled oscillator
C. Incoming RF is mixed to "baseband" for analog-to-digital conversion and subsequent processing
D. Software is generated in machine language, avoiding the need for compilers

In a software defined receiver (SDR) the analog to digital conversion begins directly at the input RF stage where *the DSP oscillator translates this signal to baseband*. You can see this on high-end transceiver spectrum analyzers that are continually displaying a wide range of frequencies without any refresh gap on the signal you have selected. What once took multiple stages in the receiver section can now be accomplished by a software defined receiver, working with your home or laptop computer. **ANSWER C** www.flex-radio.com

E7E13 What is a frequency discriminator?
A. An FM generator circuit
B. A circuit for filtering two closely adjacent signals
C. An automatic band-switching circuit
D. A circuit for detecting FM signals

Anytime you see the words *frequency discriminator* you know that you are dealing with an *FM* transceiver. **ANSWER D**

E4E01 Which of the following types of receiver noise can often be reduced by use of a receiver noise blanker?
A. Ignition Noise
B. Broadband "white" noise
C. Heterodyne interference
D. All of these choices are correct

Going mobile with your HF transceiver? A good *noise blanker* will help *minimize ignition noise* from recurring spark plug "pops." A manual repetition rate blanker, or, better yet, an automatic noise blanker will synch with the plug "pops" and cancel them almost completely – along with noise from other sources. However, the noise blanker may result in any signal over S-9 sounding distorted – this is a common problem. **ANSWER A**

E4E02 Which of the following types of receiver noise can often be reduced with a DSP noise filter?
A. Broadband "white" noise
B. Ignition noise
C. Power line noise
D. All of these choices are correct

Most high frequency transceivers now include a digital signal processing filter. This filter will magically subtract broadband white noise, help minimize power line noise, may cancel out a steady frequency heterodyne signal, and help to reduce ignition noise. *All of these* may be addressed with a *DSP noise filter*, but, you know, I always recommend solving the noise problem at the source, rather than trying to mask it, or subtract it, with DSP. **ANSWER D**

E4E03 Which of the following signals might a receiver noise blanker be able to remove from desired signals?
A. Signals which are constant at all IF levels
B. Signals which appear correlated across a wide bandwidth
C. Signals which appear at one IF but not another
D. Signals which have a sharply peaked frequency distribution

The *noise blanker* works best on repetitive, *correlated, wide-bandwidth noise* like sparkplug noise, motor noise, and pesky home QTH light dimmers. **ANSWER B**

E4E07 How can you determine if line-noise interference is being generated within your home?
A. By checking the power-line voltage with a time-domain reflectometer
B. By observing the AC power line waveform with an oscilloscope
C. By turning off the AC power line main circuit breaker and listening on a battery-operated radio
D. By observing the AC power line voltage with a spectrum analyzer

Home-office equipment like FAX machines or telephones with intercom, fish-tank heaters, and ultrasonic bug repellers all can create whistles and rhythmical pulsing sounds on both high-frequency and VHF/UHF station outputs. To find out whether the noise is being generated by your own home electronics, *shut off your AC power mains and continue listening as you run your rig off of a 12-volt battery source*. If the noise instantly disappears, use your 2-meter handi-talkie and start "sniffing" for the noise source when the power is turned on again. Of course, many home appliances will blink 12:00 after you turn the power back on! **ANSWER C**

E4E12 What is one disadvantage of using some automatic DSP notch-filters when attempting to copy CW signals?
A. The DSP filter can remove the desired signal at the same time as it removes interfering signals
B. Any nearby signal passing through the DSP system will always overwhelm the desired signal
C. Received CW signals will appear to be modulated at the DSP clock frequency
D. Ringing in the DSP filter will completely remove the spaces between the CW characters

Digital signal processing (DSP) can relieve your eardrums of constant static roar while waiting for a station to come up on the air. DSP subtracts recurring "hash," allowing only voice, data, and CW tones to pass through to the receiver. The voice may sound slightly pinched with DSP turned on, but you won't hear the static roar between each syllable. A good DSP filter will work magic on CW, as long as the operator is sending at medium to moderate speeds – above 5 wpm. Any *CW signal* sent slower *may be interpreted as an annoying heterodyne* by the DSP circuit, and the circuit will take any continuous steady tone and cancel it – not what you want when copying CW. Just tell the operator to speed up their code sending. The modern DSP notch-filter will recognize the spaces between the dots and dashes, and bring the signal through clearly. **ANSWER A**

E4E13 What might be the cause of a loud "roaring" or "buzzing" AC line type of interference that comes and goes at intervals?
   A. Arcing contacts in a thermostatically controlled device
   B. A defective doorbell or doorbell transformer inside a nearby residence
   C. A malfunctioning illuminated advertising display
   D. All of these answers are correct

With your new, big, directional HF antenna, taking advantage of your new Extra Class privileges, you may pick up noise in one specific direction, likely when you're aimed at the local shopping center. *All of these* answers *can generate a variety of interference* that may come and go at intervals, just like that flashing neon sign down the street. There is no simple filter to cancel out many of these nuisance noise sources, other than aiming your beam to a point where the noise sources are minimized. **ANSWER D**

E4E14 What is one type of electrical interference that might be caused by the operation of a nearby personal computer?
   A. A loud AC hum in the audio output of your station receiver
   B. A clicking noise at intervals of a few seconds
   C. The appearance of unstable modulated or unmodulated signals at specific frequencies
   D. A whining type noise that continually pulses off and on

Personal computers and other digital equipment use square-wave signals called *"clocks"* that run at very high frequencies. These clocks can cause problems for radio receivers because they are composed of all the odd harmonics of the fundamental clock frequency. As you tune your receiver up and down the band, you can expect to find those harmonics. They may be *unstable* because clocks are turned on and off as different operations take place in the computer, and they may appear modulated when they are affected by other signals or operations of the computer. If you suspect interference from a digital device, find a frequency where the interference is happening, and then simply turn off the suspected device. If the interference goes away, you've identified the culprit. To reduce the noise from such devices, try moving them farther away from the receiver, or try adding shielding around the device to reduce the level of interference. **ANSWER C**

E4E10 What is a common characteristic of interference caused by a "touch controlled" electrical device?
   A. The interfering signal sounds like AC hum on an AM receiver or a carrier modulated by 60 Hz FM on a SSB or CW receiver
   B. The interfering signal may drift slowly across the HF spectrum
   C. The interfering signal can be several kHz in width and usually repeats at regular intervals across an HF band
   D. All of these answers are correct

If you or your neighbor has a *touch lamp, or an electronic light dimmer* control, be prepared to hear *pulse noise* created by these circuits. Sometimes the touch lamp interference will *drift*, sometimes it will have a *hum* on it, and it is *usually wide and repeats itself* up the entire HF band. The touch circuit usually radiates the energy directly through the air, so there is no magic filter to quiet the QRN. Buy your neighbor a new type of lamp control, and ban touch lamps from your home QTH! Oh yes, one more thing – don't be surprised when you operate on 40 meters and these turned off lamp circuits switch on with your nearby transmissions! **ANSWER D**

E4E09 What undesirable effect can occur when using an IF type noise blanker?
    A. Received audio in the speech range might have an echo effect
    B. The audio frequency bandwidth of the received signal might be compressed
    C. Nearby signals may appear to be excessively wide even if they meet emission standards
    D. FM signals can no longer be demodulated

For mobile applications, a high frequency transceiver will incorporate an IF noise blanker as well as digital noise reduction (DNR), which is part of the transceiver's digital signal processing. If the IF type noise blanker is variable in pulse repetition rate, all the better! Most are not. Some transceivers may offer blanker on or blanker off with no adjustable amount of noise blanking. Yet others may offer variable noise blanker settings. This is better. It is possible that the *IF noise blanker may cause a very strong signal to sound distorted* when the noise blanker is set to maximum. It may also cause strong signals up to 30 kHz away to begin "chattering" your audio circuit on a frequency that is absolutely open. You may be tempted to tell the offending station up frequency that they are "splattering," but the actual problem is not their transmitter (well within specs), but the fact that you left your noise blanker turned on. Turn off your noise blanker when there are strong signals coming in to your mobile or base transceiver! **ANSWER C**

E4E11 What is the most likely cause if you are hearing combinations of local AM broadcast signals inside one or more of the MF or HF ham bands?
    A. The broadcast station is transmitting an over-modulated signal
    B. Nearby corroded metal joints are mixing and re-radiating the BC signals
    C. You are receiving skywave signals from a distant station
    D. Your station receiver IF amplifier stage is defective

Your modern, high-frequency transceiver employs filter networks, many specifically tuned to minimize powerful, double-sideband local AM broadcast signals coming in on your lower ham bands. But don't blame the AM broadcaster just yet – *corroded contacts* on your tower or aluminum rain gutters might *re-radiate the broadcast (BC) station signals*. This is why many hams with big towers will use multiple insulators in their guy lines to minimize rectification of broadcast band signals due to corroded metal joints. **ANSWER B**

E7H01 What are three major oscillator circuits often used in Amateur Radio equipment?
A. Taft, Pierce and negative feedback
B. Pierce, Fenner and Beane
C. Taft, Hartley and Pierce
D. Colpitts, Hartley and Pierce

Colpitts oscillators have a capacitor just like C in the name. *Hartley* is tapped, and a *Pierce* oscillator uses a crystal. **ANSWER D**

a. Pierce

b. Hartley

c. Colpitts

Three major types of Oscillators

E7H02 What condition must exist for a circuit to oscillate?
    A. It must have at least two stages
    B. It must be neutralized
    C. It must have a positive feedback loop with a gain greater than 1
    D. It must have negative feedback sufficient to cancel the input signal

In order to keep an *oscillator* oscillating, it must have positive feedback sufficient to overcome its natural losses. To keep your kids out there swinging on their swing set, you have to give them a push every so often. That's exactly what *positive feedback* does, but on every cycle. **ANSWER C**

Most oscillator circuits are basically amplifiers with some positive feedback. This example shows *direct* positive feedback.

For an AC amplifier, the output would most likely be nearly a sinewave.

a. Amplifier with Positive Feedback – Oscillator

VOLTAGE WAVEFORMS

SINE WAVE OSCILLATOR

SQUARE WAVE OSCILLATOR

SAWTOOTH WAVE OSCILLATOR

b. Oscillator Waveforms

Oscillators – An oscillator is basically an amplifier with positive feedback from output to input.

Source: *Basic Electronics* © 1994, Master Publishing, Inc., Niles, Illinois

E7H03 How is positive feedback supplied in a Hartley oscillator?
    A. Through a tapped coil
    B. Through a capacitive divider
    C. Through link coupling
    D. Through a neutralizing capacitor

Hartley is always tapped. The *tapped coil* provides inductive coupling for *positive feedback*. Look at the schematic on page 141. **ANSWER A**

E7H04 How is positive feedback supplied in a Colpitts oscillator?
    A. Through a tapped coil
    B. Through link coupling
    C. Through a capacitive divider
    D. Through a neutralizing capacitor

On the *Colpitts* oscillator, we use a *capacitive divider* to provide feedback. Look at the schematic on page 141. **ANSWER C**

E7H05 How is positive feedback supplied in a Pierce oscillator?

A. Through a tapped coil
B. Through link coupling
C. Through a neutralizing capacitor
D. Through a quartz crystal

Every *Pierce oscillator* has a *quartz crystal*, and we use the quartz crystal to obtain positive feedback. Look at the schematic on page 141. **ANSWER D**

E7H06 Which type of oscillator circuits are commonly used in VFOs?

A. Pierce and Zener
B. Colpitts and Hartley
C. Armstrong and deForest
D. Negative feedback and Balanced feedback

Since the *Colpitts oscillator* uses a big capacitor in a variable frequency oscillator (VFO), it's the most common oscillator circuit for older VFO radios. Newer radios, even though they say they have a VFO, are really digitally controlled via an optical reader. They just look like they have a *large capacitor* behind that big tuning dial! **ANSWER B**

E7H07 What is a magnetron oscillator?

A. An oscillator in which the output is fed back to the input by the magnetic field of a transformer
B. A crystal oscillator in which variable frequency is obtained by placing the crystal in a strong magnetic field
C. A UHF or microwave oscillator consisting of a diode vacuum tube with a specially shaped anode, surrounded by an external magnet
D. A reference standard oscillator in which the oscillations are synchronized by magnetic coupling to a rubidium gas tube

When you work with X-band and K-band microwave enthusiasts, you may spot a *vacuum tube surrounded by a big fat horseshoe magnet*. This is the *magnetron oscillator*, giving the electrons leaving the cathode a spin between the electrodes resulting in the tube oscillating. Keep your screwdrivers several feet away from this powerful horseshoe magnet. Always wear protective lenses around this glass tube. And watch out for high voltages! **ANSWER C**

E7H08 What is a Gunn diode oscillator?

A. An oscillator based on the negative resistance properties of properly-doped semiconductors
B. An oscillator based on the argon gas diode
C. A highly stable reference oscillator based on the tee-notch principle
D. A highly stable reference oscillator based on the hot-carrier effect

Years ago, the Gunn diode oscillator was popular with FM 10 GHz full duplex enthusiasts. We still find Gunn diode oscillators beaming harmless microwave energy at your supermarket door entrance, magically sensing the Doppler shift of someone approaching the doorway, driving a circuit to close a contact to engage the door opener. *Gunn diode oscillators are designed around the negative resistance properties of properly-doped semiconductors*. The Gunn diode is usually mounted in the 10 GHz horn feedpoint, in a tuned cavity. **ANSWER A**

E7H09 What type of frequency synthesizer circuit uses a stable voltage-controlled oscillator, programmable divider, phase detector, loop filter and a reference frequency source?
A. A direct digital synthesizer
B. A hybrid synthesizer
C. A phase locked loop synthesizer
D. A diode-switching matrix synthesizer

Almost all new VHF and UHF transceivers use *phase-locked loop synthesizers*. But the latest switch for high frequency manufacturers is to direct digital synthesis for lower phase noise. **ANSWER C**

E7H16 What is a phase-locked loop circuit?
A. An electronic servo loop consisting of a ratio detector, reactance modulator, and voltage-controlled oscillator
B. An electronic circuit also known as a monostable multivibrator
C. An electronic servo loop consisting of a phase detector, a low-pass filter and voltage-controlled oscillator
D. An electronic circuit consisting of a precision push-pull amplifier with a differential input

Few other circuits have changed the course of Amateur Radio equipment as the phase-locked loop (PLL) circuit. There is only one correct answer with the word phase in it, so *look for the word phase when you read phase-locked loop* in the question. **ANSWER C**

Phase-Locked Loop (PLL)

In a phase-locked loop the output frequency of the VCO is locked by phase and frequency to the frequency of the input signal V_{in}.

By using a very accurate crystal controlled source and dividing it down (or multiplying it up), the output frequency, f_{out}, of the PLL will be controlled very accurately and with rigid stability to the input frequency, f_{in}. The phase detector develops an error voltage that is determined by the frequencies and phase of the two inputs. The feedback system wants to reduce the error voltage to zero.

V_D is a voltage proportional to the frequency changes occuring in V_{in}; therefore, the PLL can be used as an FM demodulator.

With divide by N network, f_{out} will be f_{in} multiplied by N.

Channel tuning occurs in the Digital Counter Dividers.

E7H17 Which of these functions can be performed by a phase-locked loop?
A. Wide-band AF and RF power amplification
B. Comparison of two digital input signals, digital pulse counter
C. Photovoltaic conversion, optical coupling
D. Frequency synthesis, FM demodulation

When I built my first external *frequency synthesizer*, I was able to *"synthesize"* *hundreds of channels* with just a couple of crystals. How many of you remember being "rock bound" with an old rig? **ANSWER D**

E7H10 What type of frequency synthesizer circuit uses a phase accumulator, lookup table, digital-to-analog converter and a low-pass anti-alias filter?
A. A direct digital synthesizer
B. A hybrid synthesizer
C. A phase locked loop synthesizer
D. A diode-switching matrix synthesizer

Direct digital synthesis will now allow a single chip to handle multi-loop synthesizer circuits in your radio's local oscillator. Although the DDS does not output a pure sine wave, it offers fractions of a Hertz resolution with an extremely low noise floor. Within the chip is a *phase accumulator, lookup table, digital-to-analog converter, and a low-pass anti-alias filter* with a spectrally clean output. **ANSWER A**

E7H13 Which of these circuits would be classified as a principal component of a direct digital synthesizer (DDS)?
A. Phase splitter   C. Chroma demodulator
B. Hex inverter   D. Phase accumulator

Components within that large scale integrated (LSI) *direct digital synthesis* chip included a crystal oscillator frequency reference, random-access memory, electronic controller, a counter, and a digital-to-analog converter(DAC). One ham radio manufacturer has developed a high spec, ultra-low-noise local oscillator system for their DSS chip that produces a clean first IF signal. The high carrier-to-noise (C/N) ratio of the 200 MHz high-speed digital PLL is the result of a very fast lock time because the local design does not entail the use of a pre-scaler, but rather locks directly on the first local frequency. This reduces spurious emissions and increases close-in blocking performance. The *phase accumulator* is part of the running step where the phase accumulator is instructed to advance a certain amount by each pulse from the frequency reference. This selects each item in the data table in sequence. The DAC converts this sequence of bits to an analog wave form. **ANSWER D**

E7H11 What information is contained in the lookup table of a direct digital frequency synthesizer?
A. The phase relationship between a reference oscillator and the output waveform
B. The amplitude values that represent a sine-wave output
C. The phase relationship between a voltage-controlled oscillator and the output waveform
D. The synthesizer frequency limits and frequency values stored in the radio memories

Within the DDS, a lookup table will *sample* nearest available *voltage levels* in the digital to analog converter (DAC) *that represent a sine-wave output.* **ANSWER B**
Here is what a block diagram of direct-digital-frequency synthesizer (DDS) looks like

The DDS Sub Loop is part of a dual-loop PLL system. The main loop PLL supplies all HF band coverage within 500-kHz steps. The sub-loop PLL uses a DDS system for 500 kHz coverage within 10-Hz steps. The DDS system provides a rapid lockup time and high-quality frequency oscillation. A DC signal (lock voltage) out of the loop filter is applied to the VCO to lock the oscillating frequency.

DDS Sub Loop of a Transmitter Dual-Loop PLL
Courtesy of ICOM America, Inc.

E7H12 What are the major spectral impurity components of direct digital synthesizers?

A. Broadband noise
B. Digital conversion noise
C. Spurs at discrete frequencies
D. Nyquist limit noise

Unwanted components of a DDS output are spurs at discrete frequencies – unwanted emissions. These are easier to filter out than broadband noise. However, filtering these numerous spurious signals generated by the direct digital frequency synthesizer is tricky because they are spread over a wide frequency range. Some signals are called "alias signals." These are usually in multiples on each side of the desired frequency and may extend several MHz above and below the desired frequency. Many times a low pass filter may help mitigate the problem with some of these *spurs at discreet frequencies.* **ANSWER C**

E7H15 What is the capture range of a phase-locked loop circuit?

A. The frequency range over which the circuit can lock
B. The voltage range over which the circuit can lock
C. The input impedance range over which the circuit can lock
D. The range of time it takes the circuit to lock

When a phase-locked loop circuit drops out of lock it has exceeded the frequency range over which the circuit can effectively lock. *The "capture range" is the frequency range over which a PLL circuit will lock.* **ANSWER A**

Modern transcievers, like this small hand-held, use PLLs to lock on to the receiving frequency.

Oscillate & Synthesize This!

E7H19 Why is a phase-locked loop often used as part of a variable frequency synthesizer for receivers and transmitters?

A. It generates FM sidebands
B. It eliminates the need for a voltage controlled oscillator
C. It makes it possible for a VFO to have the same degree of stability as a crystal oscillator
D. It can be used to generate or demodulate SSB signals by quadrature phase synchronization

Today's modern, high-frequency transceiver with digital direct synthesis have rock solid stability thanks to the 24-bit phase accumulator providing over 16 million points and a frequency resolution of about 0.25 Hz when used with a 5 MHz clock. The output frequency of the *PLL voltage controlled oscillator* is locked by phase and frequency to the frequency of the input signal from the DSS. With a continuous feedback loop to the phase detector, that big transceiver's variable frequency oscillator knob now has the *same degree of stability as a temperature compensated crystal oscillator*. **ANSWER C**

E7H18 Why is a stable reference oscillator normally used as part of a phase locked loop (PLL) frequency synthesizer?

A. Any amplitude variations in the reference oscillator signal will prevent the loop from locking to the desired signal
B. Any phase variations in the reference oscillator signal will produce phase noise in the synthesizer output
C. Any phase variations in the reference oscillator signal will produce harmonic distortion in the modulating signal
D. Any amplitude variations in the reference oscillator signal will prevent the loop from changing frequency

The reference oscillator must have little phase variations because *phase variations* will *produce phase noise* in the synthesizer output. Excessive phase noise can degrade transmitter and receiver performance. **ANSWER B**

An oscillator outputs a signal of constant frequency.

Source: *Basic Communications Electronics*, Hudson & Luecke, © 1999 Master Publishing, Inc., Niles, IL

E7H20 What are the major spectral impurity components of phase-locked loop synthesizers?

A. Broadband noise
B. Digital conversion noise
C. Spurs at discrete frequencies
D. Nyquist limit noise

Broadband noise is the nemesis of a *PLL synthesizer*. **ANSWER A**

E7H14 What circuit is often used in conjunction with a direct digital synthesizer (DDS) to expand the available tuning range?

A. Binary expander

B. J-K flip-flop

C. Phase locked loop

D. Compander

It is the job of the *phase locked loop* to take the data from the *DDS* and either divide it down or multiply it up for the desired output frequency, over a large ham radio frequency span. The phase lock loop is controlled very accurately and with rigid stability to the input frequency as the phase detector develops an error voltage that is determined by the frequencies and the phase of the two inputs. The feedback system wants to reduce the error voltage to zero. Many ham transceivers incorporate a high-stability master oscillator, providing +/– 0.5 ppm (-10 degrees C to +50 degrees C), which is required for data operations like PSK and MFSK.
ANSWER C

ELI THE ICE ELMER!

E5A01 What can cause the voltage across reactances in series to be larger than the voltage applied to them?
A. Resonance
B. Capacitance
C. Conductance
D. Resistance

Coils (having inductance) and capacitors (having capacitance) will be at resonance when the capacitive reactance equals the inductive reactance. *At resonance, large voltages greater than the applied voltage can be present* across these components in the circuit. You can see this with a mobile whip antenna – if something were to touch the whip in transmit, you might see quite a spark! **ANSWER A**

Equation for Resonant Frequency	
X_L = Inductive Reactance	At Resonance $X_L = X_C$
$X_L = 2\pi f L$	$2\pi f_r L = \dfrac{1}{2\pi f_r C}$
X_C = Capacitive Reactance	Solving for f_r
$X_C = \dfrac{1}{2\pi f C}$	$f_r{}^2 = \dfrac{1}{(2\pi)^2 LC}$
L = Inductance in henrys	The Resonant Frequency, f_r, is:
C = Capacitance in farads	$f_r = \dfrac{1}{2\pi \sqrt{LC}}$
f = Frequency in hertz	

On-line calculator site:
www.calculatoredge.com/index.htm

E5A02 What is resonance in an electrical circuit?
A. The highest frequency that will pass current
B. The lowest frequency that will pass current
C. The frequency at which the capacitive reactance equals the inductive reactance
D. The frequency at which the reactive impedance equals the resistive impedance

At resonance, X_L (inductive reactance) equals X_C (capacitive reactance). In a mobile series resonant whip antenna, there will be maximum current through the loading coil when the whip is tuned to resonance. On your base station vertical trap antenna or trap beam antenna, parallel resonant circuits offer high impedance, trapping out a specific length of the antenna for a certain frequency. At resonance, the resonant parallel circuit looks like a high impedance to any of your power getting through to the longer length of the antenna system. **ANSWER C**

E5A03 What is the magnitude of the impedance of a series R-L-C circuit at resonance?
A. High, as compared to the circuit resistance
B. Approximately equal to capacitive reactance
C. Approximately equal to inductive reactance
D. Approximately equal to circuit resistance

Did you ever wonder why the serious mobile ham always uses a gigantic loading coil for his series resonant antenna? The bigger the loading coil, the less resistance. *At resonance, the magnitude of the impedance is equal to the circuit resistance.* **ANSWER D**

E5A04 What is the magnitude of the impedance of a circuit with a resistor, an inductor and a capacitor all in parallel, at resonance?
A. Approximately equal to circuit resistance
B. Approximately equal to inductive reactance
C. Low, as compared to the circuit resistance
D. Approximately equal to capacitive reactance

Whether the system is parallel or series R-L-C resonant, the *impedance will always be equal to the circuit resistance.* **ANSWER A**

E5A05 What is the magnitude of the current at the input of a series R-L-C circuit as the frequency goes through resonance?
A. Minimum
B. Maximum
C. R/L
D. L/R

A mobile whip antenna will have *maximum current* in a series R-L-C circuit *at resonance.* One way you can tell whether or not a mobile whip is working properly is to feel the coil after the transmitter has been shut down. If it's warm, there has been current through the coil and up to the whip tip stinger. **ANSWER B**

a. Series   b. Parallel

Series and Parallel Resonant Circuits

E5A06 What is the magnitude of the circulating current within the components of a parallel L-C circuit at resonance?

A. It is at a minimum
B. It is at a maximum
C. It equals 1 divided by the quantity [2 multiplied by Pi, multiplied by the square root of (inductance "L" multiplied by capacitance "C")]
D. It equals 2 multiplied by Pi, multiplied by frequency "F", multiplied by inductance "L"

A parallel circuit at resonance is similar to a tuned trap in a multi-band trap antenna. At resonance, the trap keeps power from going any further to the longer antenna elements. But be assured there is *maximum circulating current* within the parallel R-L-C circuit. Now don't get confused with this question – a parallel circuit has maximum current within it, and minimum current going on to the next stage. That's why they call those parallel resonant circuits "traps." **ANSWER B**

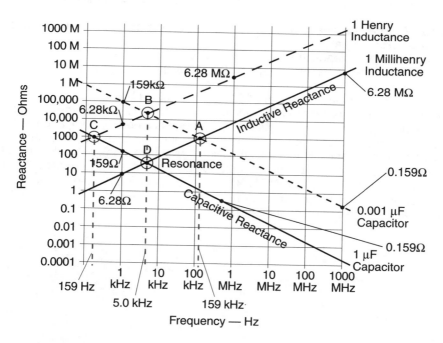

Variation of inductance and capacitive reactance with frequency
(illustration not to exact log-log scale).

Source: *Basic Communications Electronics*, Hudson & Luecke, © 1999 Master Publishing, Inc., Niles, IL

E5A07 What is the magnitude of the current at the input of a parallel R-L-C circuit at resonance?

A. Minimum   C. R/L
B. Maximum   D. L/R

The total *current into* and out of *a parallel RLC circuit at resonance is at a minimum*. On old radios, we would tune a plate control to see the current dip at resonance. **ANSWER A**

E5A08 What is the phase relationship between the current through and the voltage across a series resonant circuit?
   A. The voltage leads the current by 90 degrees
   B. The current leads the voltage by 90 degrees
   C. The voltage and current are in phase
   D. The voltage and current are 180 degrees out of phase

When a circuit is *at resonance, voltage and current are in phase*. If you remember "ELI the ICE man," it will help you visualize the relationship of voltage and current when they are NOT in resonance. **ANSWER C**

 ELI = voltage (E) leads current (I) in an inductive (L) circuit.

ICE = current (I) leads voltage (E) in a capacitive (C) circuit.

At *Resonance*: $X_L = X_C$ = voltage and current in phase (neither is leading the other).

E5A09 What is the phase relationship between the current through and the voltage across a parallel resonant circuit?
   A. The voltage leads the current by 90 degrees
   B. The current leads the voltage by 90 degrees
   C. The voltage and current are in phase
   D. The voltage and current are 180 degrees out of phase

Whether the circuit is series or parallel resonant, at resonance voltage and current are always in phase. When a mobile whip antenna is tuned for resonance, voltage and current are in phase, and your antenna stainless steel stinger receives all of the power from your transceiver, minus the slight resistance in the network. On that big 3-element trap beam you put up for tri-band operation, the traps are actually parallel resonant circuits, and current WITHIN the trap is at maximum, and only that portion of the antenna BEFORE the trap is radiating. Just remember that voltage and current are in phase at resonance. **ANSWER C**

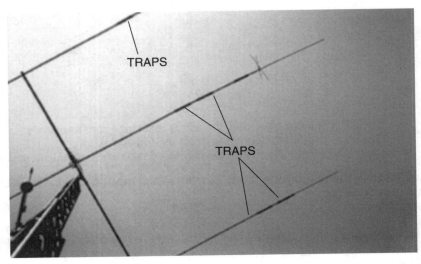

Yagi Antenna with Traps

E5B07 What is the phase angle between the voltage across and the current through a series R-L-C circuit if X_C is 500 ohms, R is 1 kilohm, and X_L is 250 ohms?

    A. 68.2 degrees with the voltage leading the current
    B. 14.0 degrees with the voltage leading the current
    C. 14.0 degrees with the voltage lagging the current
    D. 68.2 degrees with the voltage lagging the current

Here is a question on the phase angle between voltage and current in a series RLC circuit. When an applied voltage produces a current in a series R-L-C circuit, the voltage and current will be out of phase due to the reactance (X_L and X_C) in the circuit. Refer to the schematic below.

Series RLC Circuit Schematic for Phase Angle Calculations

Here is the formula, memorize it:

 $$\text{Tan } \phi = \frac{X}{R}$$ where: ϕ is the phase angle in **degrees**
                                 $X = (X_L - X_C)$ is total reactance in the circuit in **ohms**
                                   R is circuit resistance in **ohms**

Don't panic, it gets easier. Since X_L and X_C are in opposition, we simply subtract one from the other. Now recall ELI the ICE man. Remember him? ELI the ICE man! Say it out loud, "ELI the ICE man." In an inductive (L) circuit, voltage (E) leads current (I) just like in the word "ELI" where E is before I. In a capacitive (C) circuit, current (I) leads voltage (E), just like the word "ICE" where I comes before E. This is an ICE circuit, because X_C is 500 ohms and X_L is only 250 ohms. The total reactance (X) is 500 − 250 = 250. By dividing 1000 (the resistance) into 250 the tangent of ϕ comes out 0.25. We know that a tangent of 0.25 is a *phase angle of 14 degrees, and since the circuit is ICE, voltage lags the current.* (Another way of saying current leads the voltage!) **ANSWER C**

E5B08 What is the phase angle between the voltage across and the current through a series R-L-C circuit if X_C is 100 ohms, R is 100 ohms, and X_L is 75 ohms?

    A. 14 degrees with the voltage lagging the current
    B. 14 degrees with the voltage leading the current
    C. 76 degrees with the voltage leading the current
    D. 76 degrees with the voltage lagging the current

This is more ICE than ELI because X_C is greater than X_L, and the tangent of ϕ of 0.25 gives us a *14-degree* phase angle. Since the circuit is ICE, *voltage* (E) is *lagging current* (I). **ANSWER A**

Vector Addition

Here is more detail. In an ac circuit, when calculating the impedance of the circuit, the reactance and resistance must be added vectorially rather than algebraically. This vector addition can be understood best by looking at the following diagram:

$R = 100$ ohms
$X_L = 100$ ohms
$X_C = 75$ ohms

$X_L = 100$ ohms

Total Reactance $= X = X_L - X_C = 25$ ohms (X_L)

If $X_L > X_C$, circuit is inductive and an ELI circuit

If $X_C > X_L$, circuit is capacitive and an ICE circuit

$\text{Tan } \phi = \dfrac{25}{100} = 0.25$

$\phi = 14°$

$X_C = 75$ ohms

The resistance vector (of a size proportional to its value) is plotted horizontally (along x axis). Any reactance vector (using same scale as for resistance value) is plotted at right angles (90°) to the resistance vector at the tip of the resistance vector (Point A). Inductive reactance (X_L) would be plotted at +90°, while capacitive reactance (X_C) would be plotted at −90°. The total reactance is determined by plotting the X_C vector from the tip (Point B) of the X_L vector. The result is Point C on the X_L vector. The total impedance vector, Z, is drawn from the origin (tail of R vector)

to point C. The triangle formed is a right triangle; therefore, by trigonometry and the Pythagorean theorem:

$$Z = \sqrt{R^2 + (X_L - X_C)^2} = \sqrt{100^2 + 25^2}$$
$$= \sqrt{10625} = 103.08 \text{ ohms}$$

and:

$$\text{Tan } \phi = \frac{X}{R} = \frac{25}{100} = 0.25 \quad \phi = 14°$$

The tangent of the angle ϕ is found by dividing the value of the side opposite (X) vector by the value of the side adjacent (R) vector. ϕ is the phase angle of the impedance.

E5B09 What is the relationship between the current through and the voltage across a capacitor?
    A. Voltage and current are in phase
    B. Voltage and current are 180 degrees out of phase
    C. Voltage leads current by 90 degrees
    D. Current leads voltage by 90 degrees

A *capacitor is an "ICE" circuit where current leads the voltage*, as you see in "ICE" where the letter "I" is leading the letter "E". **ANSWER D**

E5B10 What is the relationship between the current through an inductor and the voltage across an inductor?
    A. Voltage leads current by 90 degrees
    B. Current leads voltage by 90 degrees
    C. Voltage and current are 180 degrees out of phase
    D. Voltage and current are in phase

This is an *"ELI" condition where voltage leads the current* as we see in "ELI" where the letter "E" is ahead of the letter "I". **ANSWER A**

E5B11 What is the phase angle between the voltage across and the current through a series RLC circuit if X_C is 25 ohms, R is 100 ohms, and X_L is 50 ohms?

A. 14 degrees with the voltage lagging the current
B. 14 degrees with the voltage leading the current
C. 76 degrees with the voltage lagging the current
D. 76 degrees with the voltage leading the current

When an applied voltage produces a current in a series R-L-C circuit, the voltage and current will be out of phase due to the reactance (X_L and X_C) in the circuit. Right off the bat, you can zero in on 2 out of 4 answers by looking to see whether voltage is lagging the current, or voltage is leading the current. Voltage lagging is an ICE, more capacitive circuit. Voltage leading the current, ELI, is more inductive. Now let's take a look at this problem where X_C is 25 ohms, and X_L is 50 ohms, and R is 100 ohms. Let's first work on the reactance (X) which is 50 - 25 = 25. Simple subtraction. Easy stuff. We find the tangent by dividing 100 (the resistance) into 25 = 0.25. From our trig table stored in our brain, the tangent of 14 degrees is 0.25. This gives us a memorized *phase angle of 14 degrees, and voltage is leading the current (ELI)*. Since present and past test questions either ended up with .75 or .25, just keep in mind that .75 = 37 degrees, and .25 = 14 degrees. It looks to me that these series R-L-C circuits always end up at 14 degrees with you calculating ELI or ICE. Now that wasn't so tough, was it? **ANSWER B**

E5B12 What is the phase angle between the voltage across and the current through a series RLC circuit if X_C is 75 ohms, R is 100 ohms, and X_L is 50 ohms?

A. 76 degrees with the voltage lagging the current
B. 14 degrees with the voltage leading the current
C. 14 degrees with the voltage lagging the current
D. 76 degrees with the voltage leading the current

Here is another ICE circuit, coming out at *14 degrees. Voltage is lagging current* (ICE). X is 75 - 50 = 25, and tangent of ϕ = 0.25. **ANSWER C**

E5B13 What is the phase angle between the voltage across and the current through a series RLC circuit if X_C is 250 ohms, R is 1 kilohm, and X_L is 500 ohms?

A. 81.47 degrees with the voltage lagging the current
B. 81.47 degrees with the voltage leading the current
C. 14.04 degrees with the voltage lagging the current
D. 14.04 degrees with the voltage leading the current

Here is a Mr. ELI circuit, coming out at *14 degrees, where voltage leads the current*. X is 500 - 250, and the tangent ϕ is 250 ÷ 1000 = 0.25. **ANSWER D**

E5C13 What coordinate system is often used to display the resistive, inductive, and/or capacitive reactance components of an impedance?

A. Maidenhead grid
B. Faraday grid
C. Elliptical coordinates
D. Rectangular coordinates

The *coordinate system to display resistive, inductive, and/or capacitive reactance components of an impedance is rectangular coordinates*. It represents each component reactance or resistance as a vector whose length represents the magnitude of the reactance or resistance. **ANSWER D**

E5C09 When using rectangular coordinates to graph the impedance of a circuit, what does the horizontal axis represent?
A. The voltage or current associated with the resistive component
B. The voltage or current associated with the reactive component
C. The sum of the reactive and resistive components
D. The difference between the resistive and reactive components

The horizontal axis represents the *resistive component* of the impedance. When the impedance is in a circuit and voltage is applied, there will be a current, and the voltage drop across the resistance is plotted on the *horizontal axis*. **ANSWER A**

Representing an AC Quantity

Rectangular Coordinates

A quantity can be represented by points that are measured on an X-Y plane with an X and Y axis perpendicular to each other. The point where the axes cross is the origin, the points on the X and Y axis are called coordinates, and the magnitude is represented by the length of a vector from the origin to the unique point defined by the *rectangular coordinates*.

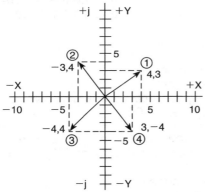

To be able to identify ac quantities and their phase angle, the X axis is called the real axis and the Y axis is called the imaginary axis. There are positive and negative real axis coordinates and positive and negative imaginary axis coordinates. The imaginary axis coordinates have a **j** operator to identify that they are imaginary coordinates.

In rectangular coordinates:
Vector 1 is 4 + j3
Vector 2 is −3 + j4
Vector 3 is −4 − j4
Vector 4 is 3 − j4

Polar Coordinates

A quantity can be represented by a vector starting at an origin, the length of which is the magnitude of the quantity, and rotated from a zero axis through 360°.

The position of the Vector A can be defined by the angle through which it is rotated. When we do so we are defining the ac quantity in *polar coordinates*.

In polar coordinates:

Vector 1 is A∠30°

Vector 2 is A∠120°

Vector 3 is A∠225°

Vector 4 is A∠315°

E5C22 In rectangular coordinates, what is the impedance of a network comprised of a 10-microhenry inductor in series with a 40-ohm resistor at 500 MHz?

A. 40 + j31,400
B. 40 − j31,400
C. 31,400 + j40
D. 31,400 − j40

Don't panic, I promise I won't send you back to high school for algebra. We have a circuit containing both reactance and resistance, giving us impedance, represented by the letter Z. Impedance has both a resistive (R) and reactive part (X_C or X_L). The parts are represented by <u>vectors</u> that are at right angles (perpendicular) to each other. As a result, $Z = \sqrt{R^2 + X^2}$. Each part forms a leg of a right triangle and contributes to the magnitude of the impedance, which is the hypotenuse of the triangle. You determine the magnitude of the impedance by calculating each part, R and X, and then Z. Let's first calculate the inductive reactance X_L of this question's circuit with the formula for inductive reactance:

▶ $X_L = 2\pi f L$ Where: L is inductance in **henrys**
f is frequency in **hertz**
π is equal to 3.14

At 500 MHz,
$X_L = 2 \times 3.14 \times 500 \times 10^{+6} \times 10 \times 10^{-6}$
$X_L = 31,400$

The resistance, R, is given as 40 ohms.
Therefore,

$$Z = \sqrt{40^2 + 31,400^2} = \sqrt{1600 + 985,960,000} = \sqrt{985,961,600}$$
$$Z = 31,400.2 \text{ rounded to } 31,400$$

The examination question asks for the answer in rectangular coordinates. This is great news because it allows us to simplify the problem-solving – even to the point of doing the problem in our head. Here's why – rectangular coordinates consist of the 2 parts of the impedance discussed above – the first part is the resistance, and the second part is the reactance. The reactance is preceded by a (+j) or a (−j), which indicates whether the circuit's reactance is inductive with a (+j), or capacitive with a (-j). The resistance is placed first, followed by the reactance: therefore, the impedance of an inductive circuit is $Z = R + jX_L$, and for a capacitive circuit it is $Z = R - jX_C$. The problem has an inductor in series with a 40-ohm resistor. Since it is an inductor, the reactance is inductive and a (+j) precedes it. Therefore, for this major problem, *the easy answer is 40+j.* Now that wasn't so hard, was it? **ANSWER A**

E5C17 In rectangular coordinates, what is the impedance of a circuit that has an admittance of 5 millisiemens at -30 degrees?

A. 173 - j100 ohms
B. 200 + j100 ohms
C. 173 + j100 ohms
D. 200 - j100 ohms

$Z = 1/5 \times 10^{-3}\underline{/-30°} = 0.2 \times 10^3\underline{/30°} = 200\underline{/30°}.$

Converting polar coordinates to rectangular gives R = 200 cos30° = 173 ohms, and jX = 200 sin30° = 100 ohms. *The impedance in rectangular coordinates is 173 + j100,* answer C. Be careful of answer A. You will be tempted to put a −j in front of the reactance because the admittance is given initially with a −30° angle. **ANSWER C**

E5C10 When using rectangular coordinates to graph the impedance of a circuit, what does the vertical axis represent?
- A. The voltage or current associated with the resistive component
- B. The voltage or current associated with the reactive component
- C. The sum of the reactive and resistive components
- D. The difference between the resistive and reactive components

When graphing rectangular coordinates, the *vertical axis represents the reactive component of the impedance*. When the impedance is in a circuit and voltage is applied, there will be a current, and the voltage across the reactance is plotted perpendicular to the horizontal axis and parallel to the vertical axis. Remember – horizontal is resistive, and vertical is reactive. **ANSWER B**

E5C11 What do the two numbers represent that are used to define a point on a graph using rectangular coordinates?
- A. The magnitude and phase of the point
- B. The sine and cosine values
- C. The coordinate values along the horizontal and vertical axes
- D. The tangent and cotangent values

When we see the *two numbers* defining a point on a *rectangular coordinate graph*, these two numbers are the *coordinate values* along the horizontal and vertical axes, respectively. The horizontal coordinate is usually given first. **ANSWER C**

E5C12 If you plot the impedance of a circuit using the rectangular coordinate system and find the impedance point falls on the right side of the graph on the horizontal line, what do you know about the circuit?
- A. It has to be a direct current circuit
- B. It contains resistance and capacitive reactance
- C. It contains resistance and inductive reactance
- D. It is equivalent to a pure resistance

If you are computing the impedance using rectangular coordinates, and the *impedance point falls to the right side and directly on the horizontal line*, the impedance is equivalent to a *pure resistance*. **ANSWER D**

E5C19 Which point on Figure E5-2 best represents the impedance of a series circuit consisting of a 400 ohm resistor and a 38 picofarad capacitor at 14 MHz?
- A. Point 2
- B. Point 4
- C. Point 5
- D. Point 6

Figure E5-2 is a rectangular-coordinate system with axes at right angles to each other. The points on the plane indicate X and Y coordinate values. In this question, the resistance of *400 ohms* can be found *along the +X axis*; and since the circuit is capacitive, we go down to *300 on the -Y axis and project a line* parallel to the X axis *to intersect at Point 4* a projection from 400 on the +X axis. You can work the problem all the way out, but in this question you can visually spot it at a glance. **ANSWER B**

To check yourself, solve the formula $X_C = 1/2\pi fC$ as follows:

$$X_C = \frac{1}{2\pi fC} = \frac{1}{6.28 \times 14 \times 10^6 \times 38 \times 10^{-12}}$$

$$= \frac{1}{3.341 \times 10^3 \times 10^{-6}} = 0.2993 \times 10^3 = 299.3 \text{ ohms or 300 ohms}$$

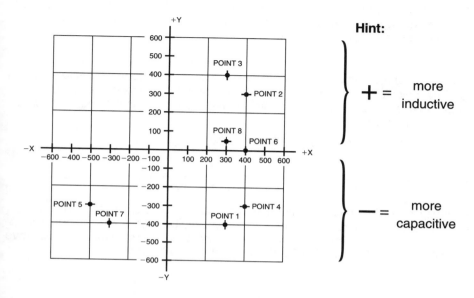

Figure E5-2

E5C20 Which point in Figure E5-2 best represents the impedance of a series circuit consisting of a 300 ohm resistor and an 18 microhenry inductor at 3.505 MHz?

    A. Point 1
    B. Point 3
    C. Point 7
    D. Point 8

The inductive reactance at 3.505 MHz is $X_L = 2\pi \times 3.505 \times 10^6 \times 18 \times 10^{-6} =$ 396.2 or approximately 400 ohms of inductive reactance. Follow the *+X axis* out to *300* for the resistance value. Move up on a line parallel to the *+Y axis* until you intersect the *400 line*. You need to go in a positive Y direction because the circuit is inductive. *Point 3* is the answer. **ANSWER B**

E5C21 Which point on Figure E5-2 best represents the impedance of a series circuit consisting of a 300 ohm resistor and a 19 picofarad capacitor at 21.200 MHz?

    A. Point 1   C. Point 7
    B. Point 3   D. Point 8

The capacitive reactance is $X_C = 1/2\pi f C = 1/6.28 \times 21.2 \times 10^6 \times 19 \times 10^{-12} =$ $1/2.53 \times 10^{-3} = 395$ ohms. We first move to the right along the *+X axis* to the value of the *300-ohm resistor*, and move *DOWN* on a line perpendicular to the X axis (parallel to *the -Y axis) to Point 1* at the intersection with the minus 400 line. 395 ohms is considered as 400 ohms. (If we went up, rather than down, we would be incorrect. Going up the +Y axis would mean the circuit is inductive. 19 picofarads makes the circuit capacitive, so we go down.) **ANSWER A**

E5C23 Which point on Figure E5-2 best represents the impedance of a series circuit consisting of a 300-ohm resistor, a 0.64-microhenry inductor and an 85-picofarad capacitor at 24.900 MHz?

A. Point 1

C. Point 5

B. Point 3

D. Point 8

Figure E5-2 is a rectangular-coordinate system with axes at right angles to each other. The indicated points on the plane show X and Y coordinate values that are possible answers to this question. In this problem we must calculate both inductive and capacitive reactance.

$$X_L = 2\pi \times 24.9 \times 10^6 \times 0.64 \times 10^{-6} = 100 \text{ ohms.}$$

$$X_C = \frac{1}{2\pi \times 24.9 \times 10^6 \times 85 \times 10^{-12}} = \frac{1}{1.33 \times 10^{-2}} = 75 \text{ ohms.}$$

The inductive reactance (100 ohms) minus the capacitive reactance (75 ohms) results in 25 ohms final reactance for this series circuit, which is slightly inductive at 24.9 MHz. Move out to the right to the *300-ohm resistance line on the +X axis.* Move up slightly to the *+Y axis to find Point 8 at 25 ohms.* **ANSWER D**

Figure E5-2

E5C14 What coordinate system is often used to display the phase angle of a circuit containing resistance, inductive and/or capacitive reactance?

A. Maidenhead grids

B. Faraday grid

C. Elliptical coordinate

D. Polar coordinates

To display the impedance of a circuit with its phase angle, you would use a polar coordinate system. *Polar coordinates provides a visual representation of the value of the impedance and its phase angle.* **ANSWER D**

E5C04 In polar coordinates, what is the impedance of a network consisting of a 400-ohm-reactance capacitor in series with a 300-ohm resistor?
- A. 240 ohms at an angle of 36.9 degrees
- B. 240 ohms at an angle of -36.9 degrees
- C. 500 ohms at an angle of 53.1 degrees
- D. 500 ohms at an angle of -53.1 degrees

Here is a series problem which is easily solved by first calculating the magnitude of the impedance which equals the square root of resistance squared plus reactance squared. The square root of 300 squared plus 400 squared is the square root of 250,000 or **500 ohms**. Since the circuit is capacitive, the phase angle will have a minus sign in front of it. Remember again, a right triangle with a 3:4:5 relationship of the sides and hypotenuse is an easy one to determine the hypotenuse value. With sides of 300 and 400, the hypotenuse will be 500, with a phase angle whose tangent is 3/4 or 4/3 depending on the relationship of the sides. In this case it's 4/3 and the *angle is -53.1 degrees*. **ANSWER D**

E   **Complex Numbers (Real and Imaginary) and Operator j**

Recall from algebra that $+2 \times +2 = +4$ and $-2 \times -2 = +4$ $\therefore \sqrt{4}$ has two roots $+2$ or -2. In ac circuit analysis there is a need to take the square root of a negative number. For example, $\sqrt{-4}$ has a root $\sqrt{-1} \times \sqrt{4} = j2$ and $-j2$. The root of a negative number is called an *imaginary number* and this is indicated by writing the operator j in front of the root. j is equal to $\sqrt{-1}$ and is the basic imaginary quantity. Since $j = \sqrt{-1}$, it is interesting to note the following because they will be encountered in ac circuit analysis:

$$j^2 = j \times j = \sqrt{-1} \times \sqrt{-1} = -1$$

$$j^3 = j \times j \times j = j^2 \times j = -1 \times j = -j$$

$$j^4 = j \times j \times j \times j = j^2 \times j^2 = -1 \times -1 = +1$$

$$\frac{1}{j} = \frac{1}{j} \times \frac{j}{j} = \frac{j}{j^2} = \frac{j}{-1} = -j$$

Summary

$$j = \sqrt{-1}$$
$$j^2 = -1$$
$$j^3 = -j$$
$$j^4 = +1$$
$$\frac{1}{j} = -j$$

j Operator as Vector Rotator

Note that an imaginary quantity can be considered as a vector being rotated by the operator j.

Vector starts at 0°.

The j operator, when it multiplies a vector, rotates the vector by 90° counter clockwise.

A second 90° rotation puts the vector at 180°.

A third 90° rotation puts the vector at 270°.

A fourth 90° rotation puts the vector back at 0°.

E5C01 In polar coordinates, what is the impedance of a network consisting of a 100-ohm-reactance inductor in series with a 100-ohm resistor?

    A. 121 ohms at an angle of 35 degrees
    B. 141 ohms at an angle of 45 degrees
    C. 161 ohms at an angle of 55 degrees
    D. 181 ohms at an angle of 65 degrees

This one is relatively easy – impedance equals the square root of the sum of the resistance squared and the inductive reactance squared. Z in polar coordinates is:

$$Z = \sqrt{100^2 + 100^2} \text{ /arctan } 100/100$$

$$Z = \sqrt{20000} \text{ /arctan } 1$$

$$Z = 141.4 \text{ /}+45°$$

You might recognize the square root easier if you work in powers of 10. The magnitude of $Z = \sqrt{(1 \times 10^2)^2 + (1 \times 10^2)^2} = \sqrt{2 \times 10^4} = \sqrt{2} \times 10^2 = 1.414 \times 10^2$. You may recognize the $\sqrt{2}$ as 1.414, so *the answer is 141.4*. From just the magnitude, you could have selected the correct answer, or you might have used the phase angle. A right triangle with equal R and X has a *phase angle of 45°* because, as you probably recall, the tangent of 45° is 1. **ANSWER B**

E5C05 In polar coordinates, what is the impedance of a network consisting of a 400-ohm-reactance inductor in parallel with a 300-ohm resistor?

    A. 240 ohms at an angle of 36.9 degrees
    B. 240 ohms at an angle of -36.9 degrees
    C. 500 ohms at an angle of 53.1 degrees
    D. 500 ohms at an angle of -53.1 degrees

We know right off the bat that the answer is going to be either A or C because an inductive reactance will have a positive polar coordinate angle. To come up with 240 ohms at an angle of +36.9° as the correct impedance, let's start out by defining the two impedances that are in parallel:

$Z_1 = 300 \text{ /}0°$ since it is a resistance in **ohms**
$Z_2 = 400 \text{ /}+90°$ since it is an inductive reactance in **ohms**

$$Z = \frac{Z_1 \times Z_2}{Z_1 + Z_2} \quad \text{or Special Case: } Z = \frac{RX_L \text{ /}+90°}{\sqrt{R^2 + X_L^2} \text{ /arctan} \frac{X_L}{R}}$$

Additions and subtractions are easier in rectangular coordinates, and multiplication and division are easier in polar coordinates.

$$Z = \frac{300 \times 400 \text{ /}0° + 90°}{(300 + j0) + (0 + j400)} = \frac{120,000/+90°}{500 \text{ /arctan } 400/300}$$

$$Z = 240 \text{ /}+90°-53.1°$$

$$Z = 240 \text{ /}36.9° \text{ ohms}$$

The correct answer is A. We used the 3:4:5 ratio, and both rectangular and polar coordinates. **ANSWER A**

E5C02 In polar coordinates, what is the impedance of a network consisting of a 100-ohm-reactance inductor, a 100-ohm-reactance capacitor, and a 100-ohm resistor, all connected in series?

A. 100 ohms at an angle of 90 degrees
B. 10 ohms at an angle of 0 degrees
C. 10 ohms at an angle of 90 degrees
D. 100 ohms at an angle of 0 degrees

Easy one again – since inductive reactance cancels capacitive reactance, in this circuit with both reactances equal, the final reactance is zero, and all we have left is 100 ohms resistance. Since there is no reactance vector, there is no phase difference, so the phase angle is zero degrees. The resistance vector lies on the 0° axis. One of the easiest ways to check this is to put the impedance in rectangular coordinates: Z = 100 +j100 -j100 = 100 +j0, just a *resistance of 100 ohms lying on the zero axis.* **ANSWER D**

E5C03 In polar coordinates, what is the impedance of a network consisting of a 300-ohm-reactance capacitor, a 600-ohm-reactance inductor, and a 400-ohm resistor, all connected in series?

A. 500 ohms at an angle of 37 degrees
B. 900 ohms at an angle of 53 degrees
C. 400 ohms at an angle of 0 degrees
D. 1300 ohms at an angle of 180 degrees

Even though the answer is requested in polar coordinates, it is best to start out using rectangular coordinates. Z = (400 +j600 -j300) = (400 +j300). Remember, in a right triangle with a 3:4:5 relationship, it is easy to determine the value of the hypotenuse. With sides of 300 and 400, the hypotenuse will be 500, with a phase angle whose tangent is 3/4 or 4/3, depending upon the relationship of the sides. With the resistance side of a right triangle at 400 ohms and the reactance side at 300 ohms, you know that the hypotenuse magnitude of the *impedance is Z = 500.* The angle is a positive one with an arctan of (an angle whose tangent is) 300/400, or 0.75. Grab a trig table or scientific calculator for *an angle of 36.8° rounded to 37°.* **ANSWER A**

E5C06 In polar coordinates, what is the impedance of a network consisting of a 100-ohm-reactance capacitor in series with a 100-ohm resistor?

A. 121 ohms at an angle of -25 degrees
B. 191 ohms at an angle of -85 degrees
C. 161 ohms at an angle of -65 degrees
D. 141 ohms at an angle of -45 degrees

R = 100 ohms and $-X_C$ = 100 ohms. Calculate Z = $\sqrt{100^2 + 100^2}$ = $\sqrt{2 \times 10^4}$. This works out to be the square root of 20,000, which is *141 ohms*. The phase angle will be negative so the correct answer D can be selected without going further. However, the arctan is 100/100 or 1, and from this we know that the *angle is 45°.* **ANSWER D**

E5C07 In polar coordinates, what is the impedance of a network comprised of a 100-ohm-reactance capacitor in parallel with a 100-ohm resistor?

A. 31 ohms at an angle of -15 degrees
B. 51 ohms at an angle of -25 degrees
C. 71 ohms at an angle of -45 degrees
D. 91 ohms at an angle of -65 degrees

Polar coordinates again, but you are given X_C so you don't have to calculate it. First calculate impedance:

$$Z = \frac{100 \underline{/0°} \times 100 \underline{/-90°}}{\sqrt{100^2 + 100^2} \underline{/\arctan -1}} = \frac{10000 \underline{/-90°}}{141.4 \underline{/-45°}}$$

$$Z = 70.7 \underline{/-45°}$$

You can determine the correct answer as C just from the impedance magnitude, but since the arctan is 1, you know the phase angle is 45°. **ANSWER C**

E5C08 In polar coordinates, what is the impedance of a network comprised of a 300-ohm-reactance inductor in series with a 400-ohm resistor?
    A. 400 ohms at an angle of 27 degrees
    B. 500 ohms at an angle of 37 degrees
    C. 500 ohms at an angle of 47 degrees
    D. 700 ohms at an angle of 57 degrees
Easy one here – let's find the magnitude of the impedance and see if the correct answer can be determined just from it. The phase angle will be positive because the circuit is inductive. You don't really have to calculate if you recognize that the right triangle sides have a ratio of 3:4:5. Since resistance is 400 ohms, inductive reactance 300 ohms, *Z will have a magnitude of 500 ohms. The angle is 37°.* You don't need to know more than that. **ANSWER B**

$$\text{Tangent } \Theta = \frac{X \text{ Reactance}}{R \text{ Resistance}} = \frac{300}{400} = 0.75$$

E5C15 In polar coordinates, what is the impedance of a circuit of 100 -j100 ohms impedance?
    A. 141 ohms at an angle of -45 degrees
    B. 100 ohms at an angle of 45 degrees
    C. 100 ohms at an angle of -45 degrees
    D. 141 ohms at an angle of 45 degrees
R = 100 ohms and X_I = −j100 ohms.
Calculate
$$Z = \sqrt{100^2 + 100^2} = \sqrt{2 \times 10^4} =$$
$$\sqrt{20,000} = \sqrt{2 \times 10^2} = 141.$$
The circuit is capacitive because of −j100. Since the resistance is 100 ohms and the capacitive reactance is 100 ohms, the angle (Θ) has a tangent of −1; therefore, the angle

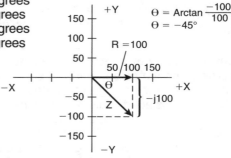

$\Theta = \text{Arctan} \frac{-100}{100} = -1$
$\Theta = -45°$

Vector Diagram for E5C15

is a negative 45°. The *impedance in polar coordinates is 141/−45°.* **ANSWER A**

E5C16 In polar coordinates, what is the impedance of a circuit that has an admittance of 7.09 millisiemens at 45 degrees?
    A. 5.03 × 10(−5) ohms at an angle of 45 degrees
    B. 141 ohms at an angle of -45 degrees
    C. 19,900 ohms at an angle of -45 degrees
    D. 141 ohms at an angle of 45 degrees

Admittance is the reciprocal of impedance. Admittance is 1/Z; therefore, $Z = 1/A = 1/7.09 \times 10^{-3} \underline{/45°} = 141\underline{/-45°}$. Remember, the +45° angle in the denominator becomes minus 45° when divided into 1. **ANSWER B**

E5C18 In polar coordinates, what is the impedance of a series circuit consisting of a resistance of 4 ohms, and an inductive reactance of 4 ohms, and a capacitive reactance of 1 ohm?

    A. 6.4 ohms at an angle of 53 degrees
    B. 5 ohms at an angle of 37 degrees
    C. 5 ohms at an angle of 45 degrees
    D. 10 ohms at an angle of -51 degrees

Start your calculation by using rectangular coordinates. $Z = (4 + j4 - j1) = (4 + j3)$. Since the circuit is more inductive than capacitive, the answer will have positive degrees with nothing in front of the angle, as opposed to a negative sign in front of the angle. And if you remember trigonometry, you will know that a right triangle with a 3:4:5 relationship of the sides and hypotenuse is an easy one to determine the hypotenuse value. With sides 3 and 4, the hypotenuse will be 5, with a phase angle whose tangent is 3/4 or 4/3 depending on the relationship of the sides. You have the 3 and 4, and *answer B has the 5 with no negative sign in front of 37 degrees*. The vector diagram is shown below. **ANSWER B**

To solve for phase angle:
$$\Theta = \text{Arctan} \frac{3}{4} = 0.75$$
$$\Theta = 36.86$$

Vector Diagram for E5C18

E4B17 Which of the following can be used as a relative measurement of the Q for a series-tuned circuit?

    A. The inductance to capacitance ratio
    B. The frequency shift
    C. The bandwidth of the circuit's frequency response
    D. The resonant frequency of the circuit

In a series-tuned circuit, the higher the Q of a large mobile antenna coil, the narrower the bandwidth of frequencies it will pass. Small helical-coil, high-frequency mobile whip antennas have a relatively lower Q, offering good *bandwidth*, but with less efficiency. **ANSWER C**

A large loading coil on a mobil whip helps antennas achieve high Q resonance.

E5A10 What is the half-power bandwidth of a parallel resonant circuit that has a resonant frequency of 1.8 MHz and a Q of 95?

A. 18.9 kHz   C. 94.5 kHz
B. 1.89 kHz   D. 9.45 kHz

Here is a series of questions on the half-power bandwidth of a parallel resonant circuit. There is a good chance one of these question will be asked on your actual Extra Class examination.

Here is the formula:

 Half-power bandwidth $= \dfrac{f_r}{Q}$;   where: f_r is the resonant frequency in **kHz**
                                        Q is a **quality factor** of the circuit

This is a handy formula to allow you to look at a circuit design and see what frequencies are covered in its half-power bandwidth. Since the answers come out in kHz, you will need to *take their stated resonant frequency in MHz and convert it to kHz by moving the decimal point three places to the right* before you solve the problem. Here's how you do it on your calculator: Clear, *1800 ÷ 95 = 18.94 kHz* so the answer is 18.9 kHz. Yikes, take a look at the possible answers and see if you goofed up on moving the decimal point! **ANSWER A**

For tuned circuits the quality factor, Q, is:

Series Resonant Circuit   Parallel Resonant Circuit

$X_L = 2\pi f_r L$

$X_C = \dfrac{1}{2\pi f_r C}$

$X_L = X_C$ at f_r, the resonant frequency

$Q = \dfrac{X_L}{R_S}$ or $\dfrac{X_C}{R_S}$ $Q = \dfrac{R_P}{X_L}$ or $\dfrac{R_P}{X_C}$

For tuned circuits with Q greater than 10:

f_r = Resonant frequency in Hz

BW = Half-power Bandwidth (−3db)

$Q = \dfrac{f_r}{BW}$

$\therefore BW = \dfrac{f_r}{Q}$

Q is the quality factor for a tuned circuit.

Source: *Advanced Class*, 2ED, G. West, © 1992, 1995, Master Publishing Inc., Niles, IL.

E5A11 What is the half-power bandwidth of a parallel resonant circuit that has a resonant frequency of 7.1 MHz and a Q of 150?

A. 157.8 Hz   C. 47.3 kHz

B. 315.6 Hz   D. 23.67 kHz

7.1 MHz is 7100 kHz, divided by 150. Remember for kHz from MHz, move three decimal places to the right. Clear, *7100 ÷ 150 = 47.33*. **ANSWER C**

Half-Power Bandwidth

An amplifier's voltage gain will vary with frequency as shown. At the cutoff frequencies, the voltage gain has dropped to 0.707 of what it is in the mid-band. These frequencies, f_1 and f_2, are sometimes called the half-power frequencies.

If the output voltage is 10 volts across a 100-ohm load when the gain is A at the mid-band, then the power output, P_O, at mid-band is:

$$P_O = \frac{V^2}{R} = \frac{10^2}{100} = \frac{100}{100} = 1 \text{ Watt}$$

At the cutoff frequency, the output voltage will be 0.707 of what it is at the mid-band; therefore, 7.07 volts. The power output is:

$$P_{0.707} = \frac{(7.07)^2}{100} = \frac{50}{100} = 0.5 \text{ Watt}$$

The power output at the cutoff frequency points is one-half the mid-band power. The half-power bandwidth is between the frequencies f_1 and f_2.

Power Ratio in dB

$$P_{dB} = 10 \log_{10} \frac{P_O}{P_{0.707}}$$

$$= 10 \log_{10} \frac{1}{0.5}$$

$$= 10 \log_{10} 2$$

$$= 10 \times 0.301$$

$$= 3 \text{ db}$$

The power output at the 0.707 frequencies is 3 db down from the mid-band power.

E5A12 What is the half-power bandwidth of a parallel resonant circuit that has a resonant frequency of 3.7 MHz and a Q of 118?

A. 436.6 kHz   C. 31.4 kHz

B. 218.3 kHz   D. 15.7 kHz

With this many half-power bandwidth questions in the pool, you can count on at least one being on your upcoming Extra Class Element 4 exam. With this question, go from MHz to kHz, and then divide it by the Q. Clear, enter *3700 ÷ 118 = 31.36*. Round the answer to 31.4. **ANSWER C**

E5A13 What is the half-power bandwidth of a parallel resonant circuit that has a resonant frequency of 14.25 MHz and a Q of 187?

A. 38.1 kHz   C. 1.332 kHz

B. 76.2 kHz   D. 2.665 kHz

Here is your last half-power bandwidth problem. Hopefully by now you have memorized the formula of E5A10. Remember the conversion to kHz so the general steps are: *MHz to kHz, enter the number in the calculator and divide it by the Q. There is your answer, in kHz.* **ANSWER B**

E5A14 What is the resonant frequency of a series RLC circuit if R is 22 ohms, L is 50 microhenrys and C is 40 picofarads?

    A. 44.72 MHz
    B. 22.36 MHz

    C. 3.56 MHz
    D. 1.78 MHz

The schematic diagram shown is a simple series resonant circuit. Don't panic. The following resonance formula will carry you through many questions on series and parallel circuits – one of which may be on your exam. You can throw away the resistance found in the parallel or series diagrams. You won't need it for the resonance formula.

Here is the resonance formula, which you should memorize:

$$f_r = \frac{10^6}{2\pi\sqrt{LC}}$$

where: f_r is resonant frequency in **kHz**
  $2\pi = 6.28$
  L is inductance in **microhenrys**
  C is capacitance in **picofarads**

Series Resonan
Circuit

Your first step is multiplying L × C. For this question, that is 50 × 40 = 2000. Now we need the square root of this, since L and C are under the square root sign. With 2000 showing on your calculator, simply press the square root key. Presto, you should have 44.72. Now multiply by 2π, which is 6.28 × 44.72 = 280.84. This leaves us with 1,000,000 ÷ 280.84. Press your clear button, and enter 1,000,000 ÷ 280.84 = 3560.7463 kHz. Your answer came out in kHz, but they are looking for MHz. No problem here – simply move the decimal point three places to the left, and you get answer C, *3.56MHz*. That's all there is to it! **ANSWER C**

E5A15 What is the resonant frequency of a series RLC circuit if R is 56 ohms, L is 40 microhenrys and C is 200 picofarads?

    A. 3.76 MHz
    B. 1.78 MHz

    C. 11.18 MHz
    D. 22.36 MHz

Use the formula at E5A14. Solve the denominator first, then divide it into 106. Here are the calculator keystrokes using a calculator that has a square root ($\sqrt{}$) key: Clear, 40 × 200 = $\sqrt{}$ × 6.28 = 561.7. Remember 561.7. Clear, *1,000,000 ÷ 561.7 = 1780 kHz = 1.78 MHz.* **ANSWER B**

E5A16 What is the resonant frequency of a parallel RLC circuit if R is 33 ohms, L is 50 microhenrys and C is 10 picofarads?

    A. 23.5 MHz
    B. 23.5 kHz

    C. 7.12 kHz
    D. 7.12 MHz

Use the formula at E5A14. First multiply microhenrys and picofarads, take their square root, multiply by 6.28, and then divide your answer into 1,000,000. Finally, change kHz to MHz. Easy! Here are the keystrokes: Clear, 50 × 10 = $\sqrt{}$ × 6.28 = 140.4. Remember 140.4. Clear, *1,000,000 ÷ 140.4 = 7122 kHz which is 7.12 MHz.* C is not correct, it's in kHz. **ANSWER D**

E5A17 What is the resonant frequency of a parallel RLC circuit if R is 47 ohms, L is 25 microhenrys and C is 10 picofarads?

    A. 10.1 MHz
    B. 63.2 MHz

    C. 10.1 kHz
    D. 63.2 kHz

Use the formula at E5A14. L × C, √ ̄, multiply by 2π, and then divide your answer into 1,000,000. Remember to change kHz to MHz. The keystrokes are: Clear, 25 × 10 = √ ̄ × 6.28 = 99.29. Clear, *1,000,000 ÷ 99.3 = 10070.5 kHz which is 10.1 MHz.* Answer C is not correct. **ANSWER A**

E5B01 What is the term for the time required for the capacitor in an RC circuit to be charged to 63.2% of the supply voltage?
    A. An exponential rate of one   C. One exponential period
    B. One time constant   D. A time factor of one
In an RC circuit, assuming there is no initial charge on the capacitor, *it takes one time constant to charge a capacitor to 63.2 percent of its final supply voltage* value.
ANSWER B

a. Schematics   b.Curves

E5B02 What is the term for the time it takes for a charged capacitor in an RC circuit to discharge to 36.8% of its initial value of stored charge?
    A. One discharge period
    B. An exponential discharge rate of one
    C. A discharge factor of one
    D. One time constant
Consider the filter capacitors in a power supply, where the capacitors discharge when the input power is removed. The time it takes a capacitor in an RC circuit to *discharge to 36.8 percent* of its initial value of stored charge is *one time constant.*
ANSWER D

GOOD TO KNOW, not on the test...

To calculate the percentage of the supply voltage after two time constants in an RC circuit, write down the percent after a single time constant as 63.2 percent. The remaining percent of charge that the capacitor must charge is 36.8 percent. It is found by deducting 63.2 percent from 100 percent. Since 36.8 percent is the final value to which the capacitor will charge after it has charged to 63.2 percent, in the next time constant the capacitor will charge to 63.2 percent of the 36.8 percent. In other words, another percent charge is added to the capacitor in the second time constant equal to:

$36.8\% \times 63.2\% = 23.26\%$ (rounded to 23.3%)

This really needs to be calculated in decimal format as:

$0.368 \times 0.632 = 0.2326$

Percent values are converted to decimals by moving the decimal point two places to the left. Decimal values are converted to percent values by multiplying by 100 (moving decimal point to right two places.)

Since the final percent of charge in two time constants is desired, it is only necessary to add the two percent charges together:

	Percent	Decimal
Charge in first time constant =	63.2%	0.632
Charge in second time constant =	23.3%	0.233
Total charge after two time constants	86.5%	0.865

The process can be continued for the third time constant. Since the capacitor has charged to 86.5 percent in two time constants, if you start from that point the value of the third charge would be another 13.5 percent. Therefore, in the next time constant, the third, the capacitor would charge another:

$13.5\% \times 63.2\% = 8.53\%$ (rounded to 8.5%)

After the third time constant the total charge is:

$86.5\% + 8.5\% = 95\%$

If the process is continued through five time constants, the capacitor charge is 99.3 percent. Therefore, in electronic calculations, the capacitor is considered to be fully charged (or discharged) after five time constants

Time Constants Showing V and I Percentages

E5B03 The capacitor in an RC circuit is discharged to what percentage of the starting voltage after two time constants?
A. 86.5%   C. 36.8%
B. 63.2%   D. 13.5%

This question asks to what percent the capacitor has *discharged after two time constants.* The capacitor discharges the same percent in a time constant as it charges (for the same RC circuit values of course.) However, the question is asking for the amount of charge remaining. At one time constant, the capacitor discharges 63.2%, therefore the percent charge remaining on the capacitor is 36.8% (100%-63.2%). Thus, on discharge, the capacitor discharges another 23.3% in the second time constant. After two time constants the capacitor has discharged by 86.5%; therefore, *the remaining charge is 13.5%* (100%-86.5%). In five time constants the capacitor would have discharged 99.3% of its charge, so 0.7% of charge remains – it is considered to be fully discharged. **ANSWER D**

E5B04 What is the time constant of a circuit having two 220-microfarad capacitors and two 1-megohm resistors all in parallel?
A. 55 seconds   C. 440 seconds
B. 110 seconds   D. 220 seconds

Here is an RC circuit with all components in parallel. It will be easy if you remember that two equal capacitors in parallel have a total capacitance of twice the value of one of the capacitors, and that two equal value resistors in parallel have a total resistance equal to one-half the value of one of the resistors. And more good news – "megs" are being multiplied by "micros" so the powers of ten after the numerical value cancel. Two 220 microfarad capacitors in parallel is a larger 440 microfarad capacitor. Two one-megohm resistors in parallel is a resistance of 0.5 megohms. *Solve for the time constant using the simple formula $T = R \times C$.* So you multiply 0.5×440 ("megs" times "micros") *and you end up with 220 seconds* as the correct answer. The calculator keystrokes are: Clear, $0.5 \times 440 = 220$. **ANSWER D**

E5B05 How long does it take for an initial charge of 20 V DC to decrease to 7.36 V DC in a 0.01-microfarad capacitor when a 2-megohm resistor is connected across it?
A. 0.02 seconds   C. 20 seconds
B. 0.04 seconds   D. 40 seconds

Note from the time-constant chart that a capacitor discharges (or charges) 63.2% in one time constant. Thus, after discharging for one time constant, 36.8% of the charge remains on the capacitor. Therefore, in one time constant the 20 volts will drop down to 36.8% or 7.36 volts ($.368 \times 20 = 7.36$). Write down one time constant = 7.36 volts for later reference. Since 7.36 volts matches the voltage referred to in the question, the time asked for is one time constant. *Use the "megs" times "micros" again to calculate the time constant as $2 \times 0.01 = 0.02$ seconds.* That's the correct answer. **ANSWER A**

GOOD TO KNOW, not on the test...

When a resistor is in parallel with a capacitor, the discharging curve from an initial voltage across the capacitor is as shown. The value of a resistor in ohms times a capacitor in farads is called an RC time constant (in seconds). In one RC time constant, the capacitor will discharge 63% of its initial value, leaving a 37% charge. In 5RC, the capacitor is considered totally discharged.

What value of resistor should be used to prevent the capacitor from discharging too much voltage between peaks of the incoming IF signal of 500 kHz? The capacitor has a value of 0.01 microfarads.

Solution:
The time between peaks (the period) of a 500 kHz input signal is

$$\frac{1}{500 \times 10^3} = \frac{1}{5 \times 10^5} = 2 \times 10^{-6}, \text{ or 2 microseconds.}$$

To make the ripple between peaks (the discharge of the capacitor) small, the RC time constant should be 10 times the period of the input waveform. Therefore:

$$RC = 20 \times 10^{-6}, \text{ and since } C = 0.01 \times 10^{-6}$$

$$R \times 0.01 \times 10^{-6} = 20 \times 10^{-6}$$

$$R = \frac{20 \times 10^{-6}}{0.01 \times 10^{-6}} = \frac{20}{1 \times 10^{-2}} = 20 \times 10^2 = 2 \text{ kilohms}$$

E5B06 How long does it take for an initial charge of 800 V DC to decrease to 294 V DC in a 450-microfarad capacitor when a 1-megohm resistor is connected across it?
- A. 4.50 seconds
- B. 9 seconds
- C. 450 seconds
- D. 900 seconds

Since we're having so much fun, let's go for some new numbers, such as 800 volts DC and a 450 microfarad capacitor with a 1 megohm resistor connected across it. Let's continue the same steps as in the previous questions. Since the voltage across a capacitor drops to 36.8% of its initial value, what will the voltage be across the capacitor in one time constant? *800 × 0.368 = 294.4 volts*. Write down 294 volts = one time constant. That's the voltage for this question so we know the time wanted is one time constant. What's the time constant? *Using "megs" × "micros", the time constant = 1 × 450 = 450 seconds*. **ANSWER C**

E5D01 What is the result of skin effect?
    A. As frequency increases, RF current flows in a thinner layer of the conductor, closer to the surface
    B. As frequency decreases, RF current flows in a thinner layer of the conductor, closer to the surface
    C. Thermal effects on the surface of the conductor increase the impedance
    D. Thermal effects on the surface of the conductor decrease the impedance
If you ever had a chance to inspect an old wireless station, you would have seen that the antenna "plumbing" leading out of the transmitter was usually constructed of hollow copper tubing. *Radio frequency current always travels along the* thinner *outside layer of a conductor*, and as frequency increases, there is almost no current in the center of the conductor. The higher the frequency, the greater the *skin effect*. This is why we use wide copper ground foil to minimize the resistance to AC current that we need to pass to ground. **ANSWER A**

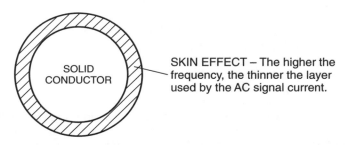

SKIN EFFECT – The higher the frequency, the thinner the layer used by the AC signal current.

SOLID CONDUCTOR

Cross-Section of Wire Conductor Showing Skin Effect

E5D02 Why is the resistance of a conductor different for RF currents than for direct currents?
    A. Because the insulation conducts current at high frequencies
    B. Because of the Heisenburg Effect
    C. Because of skin effect
    D. Because conductors are non-linear devices
The higher the frequency of an *alternating current (AC) signal*, the greater the *skin effect*. For DC, the internal cross-sectional area of a conductor is very important, but for radio frequency signals on the amateur bands, it's not important. **ANSWER C**

E5D03 What device is used to store electrical energy in an electrostatic field?
    A. A battery   C. A capacitor
    B. A transformer   D. An inductor
A *capacitor* is made up of parallel plates separated by a dielectric (non-conductor). When a voltage is placed across a capacitor, *energy is stored in the electrostatic field* developed between the capacitor plates. As a reminder, notice the letters "AC" in the word capacitor, and the letters "ATIC" in the word electrostatic. It should lead you to the correct answer. **ANSWER C**

E5D04 What unit measures electrical energy stored in an electrostatic field?

A. Coulomb

B. Joule

C. Watt

D. Volt

The joule is a measure of energy, or the capacity to do work. The amount of electrical energy stored in an electrostatic field associated with capacitors is expressed in joules. If a *capacitor* is charged with one coulomb of electrons in one second by a voltage of one volt, one joule of energy is stored in the capacitor's electrostatic field. Using energy at a *joule* per second is one watt of electrical power **ANSWER B**

E5D05 What is a magnetic field?

A. Electric current flows through the space around a permanent magnet

B. The region surrounding a magnet through which a magnetic force acts

C. The space between the plates of a charged capacitor, through which a magnetic force acts

D. The force that drives current through a resistor

In marine ham radio installations, we always route our power cables well away from the ship's compass. Do you know why? When you pull current through a conductor, the current produces a *magnetic field as a force around the conductor* – the more current; the stronger the field. The force field can affect the reading of a magnetic compass. **ANSWER B**

E5D06 In what direction is the magnetic field oriented about a conductor in relation to the direction of electron flow?

A. In the same direction as the current

B. In a direction opposite to the current

C. In all directions; omnidirectional

D. In a direction determined by the left-hand rule

If you grab a big straight cable with your left hand, with your thumb pointing in the direction the electrons are flowing in the conductor (opposite from conventional current), your fingers will naturally point in the *direction of the magnetic lines of force*. This is known as the *left-hand rule*. Have you ever been to a junk yard and watched the electromagnet coil magically lift a car off the ground and drop it into a nearby box car? When the coil is energized, it becomes a magnet. As quickly as the energy is cut off, magnetism stops, and the car drops off. **ANSWER D**

Left-Hand Rule

E5D07 What determines the strength of a magnetic field around a conductor?
A. The resistance divided by the current
B. The ratio of the current to the resistance
C. The diameter of the conductor
D. The amount of current

As *increasing current* passes through a conductor, the *strength of the magnetic field* will continue to build. **ANSWER D**

E5D08 What is the term for energy that is stored in an electromagnetic or electrostatic field?
A. Amperes-joules
B. Potential energy
C. Joules-coulombs
D. Kinetic energy

Energy stored in an electromagnetic field in an inductor, or an electrostatic field in a capacitor, is called *potential energy*. **ANSWER B**

E5D09 What is the term for an out-of-phase, nonproductive power associated with inductors and capacitors?
A. Effective power
B. True power
C. Peak envelope power
D. Reactive power

If it is *non-productive*, it is *reactive power* in an AC circuit. The letters AC are found in the word reactive (meaning out-of-phase). It indicates non-productive power produced in circuits containing inductors and capacitors. Since out-of-phase power in inductors will tend to cancel out-of-phase power in capacitors, reactive power is wattless. It is not converted to head and dissipated. It is energy being stored temporarily in a field and then returned to the circuit. It circulates back and forth in a coil's magnetic field and/or a capacitor's electrostatic field. **ANSWER D**

E5D10 In a circuit that has both inductors and capacitors, what happens to reactive power?
A. It is dissipated as heat in the circuit
B. It is repeatedly exchanged between the associated magnetic and electric fields, but is not dissipated
C. It is dissipated as kinetic energy in the circuit
D. It is dissipated in the formation of inductive and capacitive fields

In a circuit that has both capacitors and inductors, the *reactive power* oscillates back and forth between magnetic and electric fields, and *does not get dissipated*. **ANSWER B**

E5D11 How can the true power be determined in an AC circuit where the voltage and current are out of phase?
A. By multiplying the apparent power times the power factor
B. By dividing the reactive power by the power factor
C. By dividing the apparent power by the power factor
D. By multiplying the reactive power times the power factor

If we *multiply apparent power times the power factor* of an AC voltage and current out of phase, we can s. See E5D12 figure. **ANSWER A**

E5D12 What is the power factor of an R-L circuit having a 60 degree phase angle between the voltage and the current?
A. 1.414
B. 0.866
C. 0.5
D. 1.73

If you are using a scientific calculator, you will find *the cosine of 60 degrees*, given in the problem, *comes out 0.5*, answer C. The power factor is cos φ. If you don't have a scientific calculator, you might memorize this table: **ANSWER C**

φ	cos φ
30°	0.866
45°	0.707
60°	0.5

Apparent and True Power

True power is power dissipated as heat, while reactive power of a circuit is stored in inductances or capacitances and then returned to the circuit.

Apparent power is voltage times current without taking into account the phase angle between them. According to right angle trigonometry,

$$cosine \; \phi = \frac{side \; adjacent}{hypotenuse}$$

therefore,

$$cosine \; \phi = \frac{True \; Power}{Apparent \; Power}$$

therefore,

True Power = Apparent Power × Cosine φ

Cosine φ is called the *power factor* (PF) of a circuit.

Since apparent power is E × I,

True Power = E × I × Cos φ

or

True Power = E × I × PF

E5D13 How many watts are consumed in a circuit having a power factor of 0. if the input is 100-V AC at 4 amperes?

A. 400 watts   C. 2000 watts
B. 80 watts   D. 50 watts

This problem is based on the formula:

 True power = E (volts) × I (amps) × PF (power factor).

True power works out to be *100 volts × 4 amps × 0.2, giving us 80 watts*. Easy enough, right? **ANSWER B**

E5D14 How much power is consumed in a circuit consisting of a 100 ohm resistor in series with a 100 ohm inductive reactance drawing 1 ampere?

A. 70.7 Watts   C. 141.4 Watts
B. 100 Watts   D. 200 Watts

Circuits for Resonance for All!

The coil, with 100 ohms inductive reactance, will not factor in this problem, as a purely reactive circuit will not consume power. Ohm's Law, $P = I^2 \times R$, will result in $1 \times 1 = 1$, times R of 100 ohms resistance, equal to *100 watts* of power consumed. **ANSWER B**

$$P = I^2 \times R$$
$$P = (1 \times 1) \times 100$$
$$P = 1 \times 100$$
$$P = 100 \text{ watts}$$

Where: P = Power
I = Amps
R = Resistance in ohms

E5D15 What is reactive power?
A. Wattless, nonproductive power
B. Power consumed in wire resistance in an inductor
C. Power lost because of capacitor leakage
D. Power consumed in circuit Q

The letters AC are found in the word *reactive* (meaning out-of-phase). It indicates *non-productive power* produced in circuits containing inductors and capacitors. Since out-of-phase power in inductors will tend to cancel out-of-phase power in capacitors, reactive power is *wattless*. It is not converted to heat and dissipated. It is energy being stored temporarily in a field and then returned to the circuit. It circulates back and forth in a coil's magnetic field and/or a capacitor's electrostatic field. **ANSWER A**

E5D16 What is the power factor of an RL circuit having a 45 degree phase angle between the voltage and the current?
A. 0.866
B. 1.0
C. 0.5
D. 0.707

Using your scientific calculator, or from memory, remember that *the cosine of 45 degrees is 0.707*. Think of an airplane – the very popular 707 jet aircraft – taking off at an angle of 45 degrees. **ANSWER D**

E5D17 What is the power factor of an RL circuit having a 30 degree phase angle between the voltage and the current?
A. 1.73
B. 0.5
C. 0.866
D. 0.577

At *30 degrees*, the *power factor is 0.866*. If you don't pass your Extra Class exam, you could be 86'd out of the room! **ANSWER C**

E5D18 How many watts are consumed in a circuit having a power factor of 0.6 if the input is 200V AC at 5 amperes?
A. 200 watts
B. 1000 watts
C. 1600 watts
D. 600 watts

Here are 2 simple problems that are based on the formula::

True power = E (volts) × I (amps) × PF (power factor).

Therefore, *200 volts × 5 amps × 0.6 = 600 watts*. Easy, huh? **ANSWER D**

E5D19 How many watts are consumed in a circuit having a power factor of 0.71 if the apparent power is 500 watts?

A. 704 W

B. 355 W

C. 252 W

D. 1.42 mW

Here they have already calculated apparent power at *500 watts. Multiply* apparent power *by power factor 0.71*, and you end up with *355 watts* consumed in the circuit. **ANSWER B**

E4E04 How can conducted and radiated noise caused by an automobile alternator be suppressed?

A. By installing filter capacitors in series with the DC power lead and by installing a blocking capacitor in the field lead

B. By connecting the radio to the battery by the longest possible path and installing a blocking capacitor in both leads

C. By installing a high-pass filter in series with the radio's power lead and a low-pass filter in parallel with the field lead

D. By connecting the radio's power leads directly to the battery and by installing coaxial capacitors in line with the alternator leads

Wire your radio's red and black leads directly to your battery positive and negative terminals using the shortest possible run. Be sure you put a fuse right next to the battery positive pick-off point for safety. Also, it is recommended that you *install coaxial capacitors in the alternator leads.* **ANSWER D**

E4E05 How can noise from an electric motor be suppressed?

A. By installing a ferrite bead on the AC line used to power the motor

B. By installing a brute-force AC-line filter in series with the motor leads

C. By installing a bypass capacitor in series with the motor leads

D. By using a ground-fault current interrupter in the circuit used to power the motor

One way of reducing noise coming up the line from an electric motor is to install an AC-line filter in series with the motor leads. The incorrect answers have got the right components, but the wrong usage. We use RF beads to keep RF off of specific circuits, and we use bypass capacitors in parallel to bypass noise. As for the ground-fault interrupter, this won't help with motor noise. Go with the *brute-force AC-line filter in series.* **ANSWER B**

E6D08 What material property determines the inductance of a toroidal inductor with a 10-turn winding?

A. Core load current

B. Core resistance

C. Core reactivity

D. Core permeability

The key words in the question are *"material property,"* and the material that determines the inductance of a *toroid* is the *core permeability* of the iron donut. **ANSWER D**

Ferrite Toroids
Courtesy of Palomar Engineers

E6D09 What is the usable frequency range of inductors that use toroidal cores, assuming a correct selection of core material for the frequency being used?
A. From a few kHz to no more than 30 MHz
B. From less than 20 Hz to approximately 300 MHz
C. From approximately 1000 Hz to no more than 3000 kHz
D. From about 100 kHz to at least 1000 GHz
If you carefully select the core material, the frequency range of the inductor would span approximately *20 Hz to 300 MHz*. Refer to the charts of core size and core specs when using popular toroidal cores. **ANSWER B**

E6D10 What is one important reason for using powdered-iron toroids rather than ferrite toroids in an inductor?
A. Powdered-iron toroids generally have greater initial permeabilities
B. Powdered-iron toroids generally have better temperature stability
C. Powdered-iron toroids generally require fewer turns to produce a given inductance value
D. Powdered-iron toroids have the highest power handling capacity
Powdered-iron toroid donuts generally have much *better temperature stability* than a straight ferrite toroid. **ANSWER B**

E6D12 What is a primary advantage of using a toroidal core instead of a solenoidal core in an inductor?
A. Toroidal cores contain most of the magnetic field within the core material
B. Toroidal cores make it easier to couple the magnetic energy into other components
C. Toroidal cores exhibit greater hysteresis
D. Toroidal cores have lower Q characteristics
The *toroidal inductor concentrates the magnetic field within the core material*, protecting other nearby components from stray magnetic fields from that inductor. **ANSWER A**

E6D13 How many turns will be required to produce a 1-mH inductor using a ferrite toroidal core that has an inductance index (A_L) value of 523 millihenrys/1000 turns?
A. 2 turns   C. 43 turns
B. 4 turns   D. 229 turns
Here is the formula to calculate the number of turns required to produce a specific inductance where you know the inductance index, A_L, of the material. A_L is determined and published by the core manufacturer and is an index that is the microhenrys of inductance per 1000 turns or millihenrys of inductance per 1000 turns of single layer wire on the core.

$N = 1000 \sqrt{\dfrac{L}{A_L}}$ where: N is number of turns needed
L is inductance in **millihenrys** of core inductor
A_L (A sub L) is inductance index in **mH per 1000 turns**

$N = 1000 \sqrt{\dfrac{1}{523}}$

$N = 1000 \sqrt{0.001912} = 1000 \sqrt{19.12 \times 10^{-4}}$

$N = 1 \times 10^3 \times 4.37 \times 10^{-2}$

$N = 4.37 \times 10^1 = 43.7$

Here's how to work it out on your calculator. Got a calculator, right? Hit the clear button several times. Then enter *1 ÷ 523 =*. The result is *0.001912. Press* √ and the result is *0.0437264. Press* × *1000 = N for the answer 43.7264*. Your closest correct answer is 43. **ANSWER C**

Maximum Number of Turns Using Popular Toroidal Cores

	Core Size				
Wire Size	**T-80**	**T-68**	**T-50**	**T-37**	**T-25**
12	14	9	6	3	
14	18	13	8	5	1
16	24	17	13	7	2
18	32	23	18	10	4
22	53	38	30	19	9
28	108	80	64	42	23
32	171	127	103	68	38

A_Λ — μH per 100 Turns — for Popular Toroidal Cores

CORE SPECS ▶	MIX 6	MIX 10	MIX 12	MIX 0			
Core Size ▼	*μ = 8.5 2-30 MHz	μ = 6.0 10-100 MHz	μ = 4.0 20-200 MHz	μ = 1.0 50-250 MHz	SIZE (INCHES) OD	ID	Ht
T-80	45	32	22	8.5	0.80	0.50	0.25
T-68	47	32	21	7.5	0.68	0.37	0.19
T-50	40	31	18	6.4	0.50	0.30	0.19
T-37	30	25	15	4.9	0.37	0.20	0.13
T-25	27	19	12	4.5	0.25	0.12	0.10
*permeability							

E6D14 How many turns will be required to produce a 5-microhenry inductor using a powdered-iron toroidal core that has an inductance index (A$_L$) value of 40 microhenrys/100 turns?

A. 35 turns
B. 13 turns

C. 79 turns
D. 141 turns

This time we are talking about calculating the number of turns in a powdered-iron toroidal core. What we just worked with on in the last question as a ferrite toroidal core. The tip-off if you miss the wording "powdered-iron" is that we only have 5 microhenrys after a bunch of turns, rather than millihenrys with a ferrite core. Powdered-iron has better temperature stability, but the overall inductance will be dramatically less. Here's your next formula:

$$N = 100 \sqrt{\frac{L}{A_L}}$$

where: N is number of turns
L is inductance in **microhenrys**
A$_L$ (A sub L) is inductance index in **µH per 100 turns**

$$N = 100 \sqrt{\frac{5}{40}}$$

$$N = 100 \sqrt{0.125} = 100 \sqrt{12.5 \times 10^{-2}}$$

$$N = 3.53 \times 10^{-1} \times 10^2 = 3.53 \times 10^1 = 35.3$$

Now that wasn't so hard, was it? The formulas are almost the same, and luckily on both of these problems if you should reverse the formulas in error, they do not have an incorrect answer just waiting for you to get it wrong. **ANSWER A**

E6D18 What is one reason for using ferrite toroids rather than powdered-iron toroids in an inductor?

A. Ferrite toroids generally have lower initial permeabilities
B. Ferrite toroids generally have better temperature stability
C. Ferrite toroids generally require fewer turns to produce a given inductance value
D. Ferrite toroids are easier to use with surface mount technology

Another sound reason to use ferrite toroids rather than powdered-iron toroids is the fact that *ferrite toroids require less turns of wire to produce a given inductance* value. **ANSWER C**

FREE ELECTRONS! JUST THINK... FREE!!!

E6A01 In what application is gallium arsenide used as a semiconductor material in preference to germanium or silicon?
A. In high-current rectifier circuits
B. In high-power audio circuits
C. At microwave frequencies
D. At very low frequency RF circuits

Here's a new word for your amateur radio vocabulary: GaAsFET. The GaAs stands for *gallium arsenide*, and FET stands for field effect transistor. We use the GaAsFET transistor in VHF, UHF, and *microwave receivers*. This transistor offers excellent signal gain with an extremely-low noise figure. **ANSWER C**

E6A02 What type of semiconductor material contains more free electrons than pure germanium or silicon crystals?
A. N-type
B. P-type
C. Bipolar
D. Insulated gate

If there are *more free electrons* orbiting the nucleus, it is an N-type material. **ANSWER A**

You will have one question from this group about semiconductor materials. Remember this phrase, "ANFREE" for an N-type material where antimony atoms or arsenic atoms have been added, and there are more free electrons in an N-type semiconductor. "PIUMH" (pronounced like sneezing) is a P-type material produced by adding either gallIUM or indIUM, producing more "Potholes" than free electrons. Also, anything that PROVIDES is a donor, and an Acceptor impurity will Add holes. Got it? Good reading about semiconductors is found in the latest edition of the American Radio Relay League Handbook for Radio Amateurs.

Bipolar Transistor Basics – PNP and NPN

a. Junction Structure

b. Diode Juction Equivalent

c. PNP Symbol

d. Junction Structure

e. Diode Junction Equivalent

f. NPN Symbol

There are two types of transistors, bipolar and field-effect. A bipolar transistor is a combination of two junctions of semiconductor material built into a semiconductor chip (usually silicon). There are two types – PNP and NPN. Their junction structures are shown in Figure a and d, respectively. For a transistor that produces gain, the emitter-base junction is a forward-biased diode, and the collector-base junction is a reverse-biased diode. The diode equivalents of PNP and NPN transistors are shown in Figure b and e, respectively. However, unlike a reverse-biased diode that does not conduct current (except for a small leakage current), the reverse-biased collector-base junction of a bipolar transistor conducts collector current that is controlled by the current into the base at the base-emitter junction. The normal active

g. NPN Operation

h. PNP Operation

An NPN silicon transistor P base is 0.7 V more positive that its N emitter, and the N collector is several more volts more positive than the emitter. The emitter current is the sum of the base and collector current. The current gain under any DC operating condition is hFE, the ratio of I_C to I_B, and current gains of 50 to 200 are common in modern-day silicon transistors. hFE is actually called "the common-emitter" current gain because the emitter is common in the circuit.

A PNP silicon transistor N base is 0.7 V negative with respect to its emitter in order to have the P emitter more positive than the N base. The P collector is several volts negative from the emitter to keep the collector-base junction reverse biased. As shown in Figure h, the same current equations apply, and the current gain, hFE, is the same. The major difference is in the polarity of the voltages for operation. For NPN common-emitter operation the base and collector voltages are positive with respect to the emitter; while for the PNP the voltages are negative.

Source: *Basic Communications Electronics*, Hudson & Luecke, © 1999 Master Publishing, Inc., Niles, IL

E6A03 What are the majority charge carriers in P-type semiconductor material?

A. Free neutrons
B. Free protons
C. Holes
D. Free electrons

The *charge carriers* are in abundance in *P-type* semiconductor materials, the *holes.* **ANSWER C**

E6A04 What is the name given to an impurity atom that adds holes to a semiconductor crystal structure?

A. Insulator impurity
B. N-type impurity
C. Acceptor impurity
D. Donor impurity

The *impurity atom that adds holes* to a semiconductor crystal structure is called an *acceptor impurity.* **ANSWER C**

E6A05 What is the alpha of a bipolar junction transistor?

A. The change of collector current with respect to base current
B. The change of base current with respect to collector current
C. The change of collector current with respect to emitter current
D. The change of collector current with respect to gate current

In *bipolar* transistors, the term *"alpha"* is the *variation of collector current with respect to emitter current* (CCEC). This is an important consideration when designing a circuit that will utilize a bipolar transistor. **ANSWER C**

a. Characteristic Curves   b. Output Signal

Biasing sets "No-Signal" operating point

E6A06 What is meant by the beta of a bipolar junction transistor?

A. The frequency at which the current gain is reduced to 1
B. The change in collector current with respect to base current
C. The breakdown voltage of the base to collector junction
D. The switching speed of the transistor

The *bipolar junction transistor* could be NPN type, or PNP type, and it is current-operated. The term *"beta"* refers to the change in current gain and is stated as a ratio of the *change in collector current to the applied change in base current.* **ANSWER B**

E6A07 In Figure E6-1, what is the schematic symbol for a PNP transistor?
A. 1   C. 4
B. 2   D. 5

Remember this from your Technician Class examination? Which way is the *arrow* pointing? If it's *pointing in, it is PNP* – "P in." **ANSWER A**

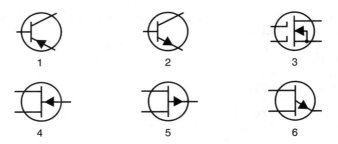

1   2   3

4   5   6

Figure E6-1

E4A10 Which of the following is a useful test for a functioning NPN transistor in an active circuit where the transistor should be biased "on"?
A. Measure base-to-emitter resistance with an ohmmeter; it should be approximately 6 to 7 ohms
B. Measure base-to-emitter resistance with an ohmmeter; it should be approximately 0.6 to 0.7 ohms
C. Measure base-to-emitter voltage with a voltmeter; it should be approximately 6 to 7 volts
D. Measure base-to-emitter voltage with a voltmeter; it should be approximately 0.6 to 0.7 volts

When an NPN transistor is biased "on," the voltage on the base is positive with respect to the emitter. Free electrons can flow from the emitter to the base, and on the collector, assuming the base to collector is reversed bias. A characteristic of a *forward-biased PN junction* is that the *voltage drop* across it is always approximately 0.6 to 0.7V. You don't need to remove the transistor from the circuit for this easy transistor check. **ANSWER D**

E6A08 What term indicates the frequency at which a transistor grounded base current gain has decreased to 0.7 of the gain obtainable at 1 kHz?
A. Corner frequency   C. Beta cutoff frequency
B. Alpha rejection frequency   D. Alpha cutoff frequency

Grounded base is the same as a common base configuration. Common base means alpha. Since *1 kHz* is mentioned in this question, they are referring to the *alpha cutoff frequency* in a transistor. **ANSWER D**

E6A09 What is a depletion-mode FET?
A. An FET that exhibits a current flow between source and drain when no gate voltage is applied
B. An FET that has no current flow between source and drain when no gate voltage is applied
C. An FET without a channel so no current flows with zero gate voltage
D. An FET without a channel so maximum gate current flows

Your handheld battery may become depleted if *depletion-mode FETs* are used in many of the circuits. Even though there is no gate voltage applied, *current still continues to flow*. **ANSWER A**

E6A10 In Figure E6-2, what is the schematic symbol for an N-channel dual-gate MOSFET?
A. 2
B. 4
C. 5
D. 6
Note that the *arrow is pointing iN*, and there are t*wo gates*. **ANSWER B**

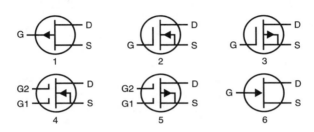

Figure E6-2

E6A11 In Figure E6-2, what is the schematic symbol for a P-channel junction FET?
A. 1
B. 2
C. 3
D. 6
In the *P-channel junction FET*, the *arrow is Pointing out*. For an N-channel junction FET, the arrow is always pointing iN. **ANSWER A**

E6A12 Why do many MOSFET devices have built-in gate-protective Zenner diodes?
A. To provide a voltage reference for the correct amount of reverse-bias gate voltage
B. To protect the substrate from excessive voltages
C. To keep the gate voltage within specifications and prevent the device from overheating
D. To reduce the chance of the gate insulation being punctured by static discharges or excessive voltages

The "front end" transistors of the modern ham transceiver must sometimes sustain major amounts of incoming signals from nearby transmitters, or maybe even a nearby lightning strike. Lightning *static* could destroy a MOSFET if it weren't for the built-in, *gate-protective Zenner diodes*. **ANSWER D**

E6A13 What do the initials CMOS stand for?
A. Common mode oscillating system
B. Complementary mica-oxide silicon
C. Complementary metal-oxide semiconductor
D. Complementary metal-oxide substrate

When we talk about transistorized devices, they are in fact semi-conductors. A *CMOS* is made from layers of *metal-oxide semiconductor* material. **ANSWER C**

E6A14 How does DC input impedance at the gate of a field-effect transistor compare with the DC input impedance of a bipolar transistor?

A. They cannot be compared without first knowing the supply voltage
B. An FET has low input impedance; a bipolar transistor has high input impedance
C. An FET has high input impedance; a bipolar transistor has low input impedance
D. The input impedance of FETs and bipolar transistors is the same

An *FET* is much easier to work with in circuits than the simple bipolar transistor. Its *higher input impedance* is less likely to load down a circuit that it is attached to, and the FET can also handle big swings in signal levels. **ANSWER C**

Pictorial of FET Construction (N-Channel Enhancement)

Unlike bipolar transistors that depend on current into the base to control collector current, field-effect transistor current between source and drain is controlled by a voltage on a gate. The basic structure of an N-channel MOSFET is shown here. Heavily-doped N semiconductor material forms source and drain regions in a P semiconductor material substrate. The region between the source and drain is the gate region, where a thin layer of oxide insulates the P semiconductor substrate underneath from a metal plate that is deposited over the thin oxide. A thick oxide layer over the source and drain regions insulates metal connection pads from the substrate. Holes in this thick oxide layer allow the metal pads to contact the source and drain. There are four common types of MOSFETs: P-channel depletion and enhancement mode devices; and N-channel depletion and enhancement mode devices.

Source: *Basic Communications Electronics*, Hudson & Luecke, © 1999 Master Publishing, Inc., Niles, IL

E6A15 What two elements widely used in semiconductor devices exhibit both metallic and nonmetallic characteristics?

A. Silicon and gold
B. Silicon and germanium
C. Galena and germanium
D. Galena and bismuth

Both *silicon* and *germanium* exhibit a combination of *metallic and non-metallic properties*. Think of silicon rectifiers and germanium diodes. **ANSWER B**

E6A17 What are the majority charge carriers in N-type semiconductor material?

A. Holes
B. Free electrons
C. Free protons
D. Free neutrons

In an *N-type* semiconductor material, there are more *free electrons* than holes. **ANSWER B**

E6A16 What type of semiconductor material contains fewer free electrons than pure germanium or silicon crystals?

A. N-type
B. P-type
C. Superconductor-type
D. Bipolar-type

If there are *more holes than electrons*, it is a *P-type* semiconductor. **ANSWER B**

E6A18 What are the names of the three terminals of a field-effect transistor?

A. Gate 1, gate 2, drain
B. Emitter, base, collector
C. Emitter, base 1, base 2
D. Gate, drain, source

Gosh darn semiconductors! *Gate, drain, source.* Gosh darn field effect transistor, a semiconductor! **ANSWER D**

E6B01 What is the principal characteristic of a Zener diode?

A. A constant current under conditions of varying voltage
B. A constant voltage under conditions of varying current
C. A negative resistance region
D. An internal capacitance that varies with the applied voltage

Always remember that a *Zener diode* is for voltage regulation, for *constant voltage* even though current changes. **ANSWER B**

ANODE   CATHODE

Here is the schematic symbol of a Zener diode. Since a diode only passes energy in one direction, look for that one-way arrow, plus a "Z" indicating it is a Zener diode. Doesn't that vertical line look like a tiny "Z".

Zener Diode

E6B02 What is the principal characteristic of a tunnel diode?

A. A high forward resistance
B. A very high PIV
C. A negative resistance region
D. A high forward current rating

As a *tunnel diode* is conducting current, there is a spot where current increases as the voltage drop across the diode decreases. They call this a *negative resistance region.* **ANSWER C**

E6B03 What is an important characteristic of a Schottky Barrier diode as compared to an ordinary silicon diode when used as a power supply rectifier?

A. Much higher reverse voltage breakdown
B. Controlled reverse avalanche voltage
C. Enhanced carrier retention time
D. Less forward voltage drop

The Schottky Barrier diode is regularly found in solar power and power supply circuits because of its lower forward resistance and a slightly higher peak inverse voltage (PIV) rating. They are slightly more expensive than traditional power supply diodes, but I use them regularly in my mobile and home solar system because the *Schottky diode offers minimal voltage drop* while charging my sealed battery system, and prevents current from flowing out of my battery system and back into the solar panel at night. **ANSWER D**

E6B04 What special type of diode is capable of both amplification and oscillation?

A. Point contact
B. Zener
C. Tunnel
D. Junction

The *tunnel diode* is commonly used in both *amplifier and oscillator circuits*. The negative resistance region is particularly useful in oscillators. **ANSWER C**

E6B05 What type of semiconductor device varies its internal capacitance as the voltage applied to its terminals varies?

A. Varactor diode
B. Tunnel diode
C. Silicon-controlled rectifier
D. Zener diode

We use the *varactor diode* to tune VHF and UHF circuits by *varying the voltage* applied to the varactor diode. **ANSWER A**

E6B06 In Figure E6-3, what is the schematic symbol for a varactor diode?

A. 8
B. 6
C. 2
D. 1

The internal capacitance of a *varactor diode* varies as the voltage applied to its terminals changes. I build microwave equipment with varactor diodes, so be sure to identify the proper symbol. The *symbol* is essentially a *capacitor and a diode combined.* **ANSWER D**

Figure E6-3

E6B11 In Figure E6-3, what is the schematic symbol for a light-emitting diode?

A. 1
B. 5
C. 6
D. 7

The light-emitting diode *(LED)* is a giveaway on the schematic diagram! Look at the *two arrows indicating an illuminating device.* **ANSWER B**

E6B07 What is a common use of a hot-carrier diode?
A. As balanced mixers in FM generation
B. As a variable capacitance in an automatic frequency control circuit
C. As a constant voltage reference in a power supply
D. As a VHF / UHF mixer or detector

When you get involved with *VHF and UHF* equipment, you'll find *hot-carrier diodes* commonly used as *mixers or detectors* of the because of their low noise figure characteristics. **ANSWER D**

E6B08 What limits the maximum forward current rating in a junction diode?
A. Peak inverse voltage   C. Forward voltage
B. Junction temperature   D. Back EMF

Guess what will kill most electronic components? High temperature! The limit of the maximum forward current in a *junction diode* is the *junction temperature*. This is why you'll find these diodes mounted to the chassis of your equipment. The chassis acts as a heat sink to keep the junction temperature from exceeding its maximum limit. **ANSWER B**

E6B09 Which of the following describes a type of semiconductor diode?
A. Metal-semiconductor junction   C. CMOS-field effect
B. Electrolytic rectifier   D. Thermionic emission diode

The two main categories of *semiconductor diodes* are PN junction, and *metal-semiconductor junction*. The semiconductor diode might be found in transistors, power supply rectifier diodes, and photovoltaic panels. **ANSWER A**

E6B10 What is a common use for point contact diodes?
A. As a constant current source   C. As an RF detector
B. As a constant voltage source   D. As a high voltage rectifier

The little *point contact diode*, since it only conducts in one direction, may be used as an *RF detector* in some VHF and UHF equipment. **ANSWER C**

E6B12 How are junction diodes rated?
A. Maximum forward current and capacitance
B. Maximum reverse current and PIV
C. Maximum reverse current and capacitance
D. Maximum forward current and PIV

When choosing a *junction diode*, you'll need to know how much *forward current* will be passing through the diode, and the amount of *peak inverse voltage (PIV)* that the diode must withstand in its non-conducting direction. **ANSWER D**

E6B13 What is one common use for PIN diodes?
A. As a constant current source   C. As an RF switch
B. As a constant voltage source   D. As a high voltage rectifier

PIN diodes may be used in small, handheld transceivers for *RF switching*. This gets away from mechanical relays for switching. **ANSWER C**

E6B14 What type of bias is required for an LED to produce luminescence?
A. Reverse bias   C. Zero bias
B. Forward bias   D. Inductive bias

The *LED* requires *forward bias* in order to *illuminate*. As indicated in symbol 5 of Figure E6-3, the LED is a diode, and it must be forward biased in order to make it give off light. **ANSWER B**

E6C01 What is the recommended power supply voltage for TTL series integrated circuits?

A. 12 volts   C. 5 volts

B. 1.5 volts   D. 13.6 volts

If you ever worked on TTL (transistor-transistor logic) circuits, you know the importance of those 5-volt regulators that always seem to burn up at the wrong time. *TTL circuits run on 5.0 volts.* **ANSWER C**

E6C02 What logic state do the inputs of a TTL device assume if they are left open?

A. A logic-high state

B. A logic-low state

C. The device becomes randomized and
     will not provide consistent high or low-logic states

D. Open inputs on a TTL device are ignored

Here are several key words – *inputs open and high state*. Remember four letters make up the word open, and four letters make up the word high. **ANSWER A**

E6C03 What level of input voltage is a logic "high" in a TTL device operating with a positive 5-volt power supply?

A. 2.0 to 5.5 volts   C. 1.0 to 1.5 volts

B. 1.5 to 3.0 volts   D. -5.0 to -2.0 volts

If the input *voltage is at the high level*, depending on the number of circuits connected at the point, by specification the level will be between *2.0 and 5.5 volts*. **ANSWER A**

E6C04 What level of input voltage is a logic "low" in a TTL device operating with a positive 5-volt power-supply?

A. -2.0 to -5.5 volts   C. 0.0 to 0.8 volts

B. 2.0 to 5.5 volts   D. -0.8 to 0.4 volts

If the input voltage to a *TTL* IC is at the *low level*, it will usually be around *+0.2 volts*. It can be as high as +0.8 volts, but then the noise margin is down to zero. **ANSWER C**

E6C05 Which of the following is an advantage of CMOS logic devices over TTL devices?

A. Differential output capability

B. Lower distortion

C. Immune to damage from static discharge

D. Lower power consumption

The Complimentary Metal Oxide Semiconductor (CMOS) contains both N-channel and P-channel MOSFETs within a single chip. The greatest advantage of the *CMOS* is its *extremely low power consumption* in that new handheld you just bought for the kids. **ANSWER D**

E6C06 Why do CMOS digital integrated circuits have high immunity to noise on the input signal or power supply?

A. Larger bypass capacitors are used in CMOS circuit design

B. The input switching threshold is about two times the power supply voltage

C. The input switching threshold is about one-half the power supply voltage

D. Input signals are stronger

The *CMOS* device is relatively immune to noise because its *switching threshold is one-half the power supply voltage*. As a result, power supply noise transients or input transients much larger than other logic circuit types will not cause a transition in the input state. **ANSWER C**

E6E07 What is the characteristic impedance of circuits in which almost all MMICs are designed to work?

A. 50 ohms
B. 300 ohms
C. 450 ohms
D. 10 ohms

The beauty of the *MMIC* is that it has a *characteristic impedance of 50 ohms*, and this what the microwavers love! **ANSWER A**

E6E08 What is the typical noise figure of a monolithic microwave integrated circuit (MMIC) amplifier?

A. Less than 1 dB
B. Approximately 3.5 to 6 dB
C. Approximately 8 to 10 dB
D. More than 20 dB

The *monolithic microwave integrated circuit* has a *typical noise floor from 3.5 to 6 dB*, but they offer good gain from 8 dB to as high as 24 dB up to 1,000 MHz, so this typical noise figure is acceptable. **ANSWER B**

E6E09 What type of amplifier device consists of a small pill-type package with an input lead, an output lead and 2 ground leads?

A. A junction field-effect transistor (JFET)
B. An operational amplifier integrated circuit (OAIC)
C. An indium arsenide integrated circuit (IAIC)
D. A monolithic microwave integrated circuit (MMIC)

You can spot the *MMIC* device by its input lead, output lead, and 2 ground leads in a *"pill-sized" package*. **ANSWER D**

RF GROUND

RF OUTPUT AND +V_{CC}

RF INPUT (DIAGONAL CUT)

Monolithic Microwave Integrated Circuit
Photo Courtesy of Hewlett Packard Co.

E6E10 What typical construction technique is used when building an amplifier for the microwave bands containing a monolithic microwave integrated circuit (MMIC)?

A. Ground-plane "ugly" construction
B. Microstrip construction
C. Point-to-point construction
D. Wave-soldering construction

Up at microwave frequencies, we use *microstrip construction*, which is *ideal for the MMIC.* **ANSWER B**

E6E11 How is the operating bias voltage normally supplied to the most common type of monolithic microwave integrated circuit (MMIC)?

A. Through a resistor and/or RF choke connected to the amplifier output lead
B. MMICs require no operating bias
C. Through a capacitor and RF choke connected to the amplifier input lead
D. Directly to the bias-voltage (VCC IN) lead

The *operating bias voltage* for the *MMIC* is developed through a *resistor* and RF choke connected to the amplifier output lead. **ANSWER A**

E6E12 What supply voltage do monolithic microwave integrated circuits (MMIC) amplifiers typically require?

A. 1 volt DC
B. 12 volts DC
C. 20 volts DC
D. 120 volts DC

A *MMIC* has a low noise figure, excellent power gain, and at the linear-regulated *12V voltage source,* may draw just 18ma. **ANSWER B**

E6E13 What is the most common package for inexpensive monolithic microwave integrated circuit (MMIC) amplifiers?

A. Beryllium oxide packages
B. Glass packages
C. Plastic packages
D. Ceramic packages

While the military may use ceramic packaging for the *MMIC, plastic packaging* dramatically decreases the expense of a monolithic microwave integrated circuit for use in civilian applications. **ANSWER C**

MY FLIP-FLOP'S TRUTH TABLE TELLS ME YOU'RE GOING TO ACE THE EXAM!

E6C07 In Figure E6-5, what is the schematic symbol for an AND gate?
    A. 1   C. 3
    B. 2   D. 4
AND gate looks like the *letter D*, with two inputs or more, and one output. **ANSWER A**

Figure E6-5

E6C08 (B) In Figure E6-5, what is the schematic symbol for a NAND gate?
    A. 1   C. 3
    B. 2   D. 4
Since the *NAND* gate has a *logic "0" at its output, spot the little tiny "0" on its nose*. It looks like the letter D, the same as the AND gate, except for the small circle at its output. **ANSWER B**

E6C09 In Figure E6-5, what is the schematic symbol for an OR gate?
    A. 2   C. 4
    B. 3   D. 6
The word "OR" starts with an "O", and its input is curved like a portion of the letter "O". The *OR gate symbol* has a *curved input* and a *pointed output*. **ANSWER B**

E6C10 In Figure E6-5, what is the schematic symbol for a NOR gate?

A. 1
B. 2
C. 3
D. 4

Since the *NOR gate* will give us a logic "0" at its output if any inputs are logic "1", look for the little "O" on the nose, and a concave input. It *looks just like an OR gate*, except for the *small circle on its nose*. **ANSWER D**

E6C11 In Figure E6-5, what is the schematic symbol for the NOT operation (inverter)?

A. 2
B. 4
C. 5
D. 6

The *NOT gate* is *triangular in shape* and has a little "O" on its nose. It looks altogether different from any of the other logic gates. You'll probably have one question based on gate symbols. Make up flashcards, and see if you can easily call out which is which. **ANSWER C**

E7A01 What is a bistable circuit?

A. An "AND" gate
B. An "OR" gate
C. A flip-flop
D. A clock

A *bistable circuit* is a *flip-flop*. Bistable stands for two stable states. **ANSWER C**

An IC 555 timer can be used as a bistable, astable, or monostable multivibrator.
This schematic shows it wired as an astable multivibrator.
The resulting astable voltage waveforms at pins 3 and 6 are shown.

Source: *Basic Digital Electronics,* Evans, ©1996, Master Publishing, Inc., Niles, IL

E7A02 How many output level changes are obtained for every two trigger pulses applied to the input of a "T" flip-flop circuit?

A. None
B. One
C. Two
D. Four

Two trigger pulses, two output level changes. The T FF toggles from one state to another for each input pulse. **ANSWER C**

E7A03 Which of the following can divide the frequency of a pulse train by 2?
A. An XOR gate
C. An OR gate
B. A flip-flop
D. A multiplexer
A *flip-flop can* be used to *divide a pulse train* (the frequency of an AC signal).
ANSWER B

E7A04 How many flip-flops are required to divide a signal frequency by 4?
A. 1
C. 4
B. 2
D. 8
Since a flip-flop has two stable states, you will need *two flip-flops to divide a signal frequency by four.* **ANSWER B**

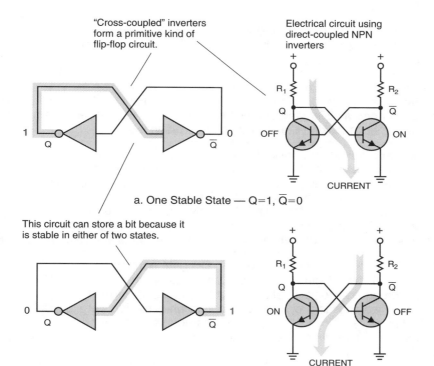

"Cross-coupled" inverters form a primitive kind of flip-flop circuit.

Electrical circuit using direct-coupled NPN inverters

a. One Stable State — Q=1, Q̄=0

This circuit can store a bit because it is stable in either of two states.

b. Second Stable State — Q=0, Q̄=1

Basic concept of the flip-flop, also called a
bistable element or a static memory element.
Source: *Basic Electronics* © 1994, Master Publishing, Inc., Niles, Illinois

---

E7A05 Which of the following is a circuit that continuously alternates between two unstable states without an external clock?
A. Monostable multivibrator
C. T Flip-Flop
B. J-K Flip-Flop
D. Astable Multivibrator
An *astable multivibrator* continuously switches back and forth between *two unstable states without an external clock.* **ANSWER D**

E7A06 What is a characteristic of a monostable multivibrator?
A. It switches momentarily to the opposite binary state and then returns, after a set time, to its original state
B. It is a clock that produces a continuous square wave oscillating between 1 and 0
C. It stores one bit of data in either a 0 or 1 state
D. It maintains a constant output voltage, regardless of variations in the input voltage

This type of *multivibrator may momentarily be monostable* (MO MO). It stays in an original state until triggered to its other state, where it remains for a time usually determined by external components, after which it *returns to the original state*. **ANSWER A**

E7A07 What logical operation does an AND gate perform?
A. It produces a logic "0" at its output only if all inputs are logic "1"
B. It produces a logic "1" at its output only if all inputs are logic "1"
C. It produces a logic "1" at its output if only one input is a logic "1"
D. It produces a logic "1" at its output if all inputs are logic "0"

The *AND gate* has two or more inputs with a single output, and *produces a logic "1" at its output only if all inputs are logic "1"*. Remember AND, all, and the number 1 and the number 1 looking like the letters ALL. **ANSWER B**

E7A08 What logical operation does a NAND gate perform?
A. It produces a logic "0" at its output only when all inputs are logic "0"
B. It produces a logic "1" at its output only when all inputs are logic "1"
C. It produces a logic "0" at its output if some but not all of its inputs are logic "1"
D. It produces a logic "0" at its output only when all inputs are logic "1"

The word *NAND* reminds me of the word "naw", meaning no or nothing. The NAND gate *produces a logic "0" at its output only when all inputs are logic "1"*. **ANSWER D**

E7A09 What logical operation does an OR gate perform?
A. It produces a logic "1" at its output if any or all inputs are logic "1"
B. It produces a logic "0" at its output if all inputs are logic "1"
C. It only produces a logic "0" at its output when all inputs are logic "1"
D. It produces a logic "1" at its output if all inputs are logic "0"

The *OR gate* will *produce a logic "1"* at its output *if any* input is, *or all inputs are, a logic "1"*. **ANSWER A**

E7A10 What logical operation does a NOR gate perform?
A. It produces a logic "0" at its output only if all inputs are logic "0"
B. It produces a logic "1" at its output only if all inputs are logic "1"
C. It produces a logic "0" at its output if any or all inputs are logic "1"
D. It produces a logic "1" at its output only when none of its inputs are logic "0"

The *NOR gate* produces a *logic "0"* at its output *if any or all inputs are logic "1"*. With OR gate and NOR gate, spot that word any. **ANSWER C**

E7A11 What is a truth table?
A. A table of logic symbols that indicate the high logic states of an op-amp
B. A diagram showing logic states when the digital device's output is true
C. A list of inputs and corresponding outputs for a digital device
D. A table of logic symbols that indicates the low logic states of an op-amp

Logically Speaking of Counters

We use a *"truth table"* in digital circuitry to *characterize a digital device's function.* If you buy the owner's technical manual on a piece of Amateur Radio gear, you will usually find a page describing the truth table of digital devices used in the equipment. **ANSWER C**

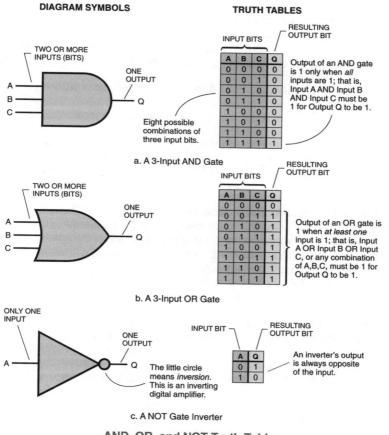

DIAGRAM SYMBOLS

TRUTH TABLES

a. A 3-Input AND Gate

A	B	C	Q
0	0	0	0
0	0	1	0
0	1	0	0
0	1	1	0
1	0	0	0
1	0	1	0
1	1	0	0
1	1	1	1

Output of an AND gate is 1 only when *all* inputs are 1; that is, Input A AND Input B AND Input C must be 1 for Output Q to be 1.

Eight possible combinations of three input bits.

b. A 3-Input OR Gate

A	B	C	Q
0	0	0	0
0	0	1	1
0	1	0	1
0	1	1	1
1	0	0	1
1	0	1	1
1	1	0	1
1	1	1	1

Output of an OR gate is 1 when *at least one* input is 1; that is, Input A OR Input B OR Input C, or any combination of A,B,C, must be 1 for Output Q to be 1.

c. A NOT Gate Inverter

A	Q
0	1
1	0

The little circle means *inversion.* This is an inverting digital amplifier.

An inverter's output is always opposite of the input.

AND, OR, and NOT Truth Tables

Source: *Basic Electronics* © 1994, Master Publishing, Inc., Niles, Illinois

---

E7A12 What is the name for logic which represents a logic "1" as a high voltage?

A. Reverse Logic
B. Assertive Logic
C. Negative logic
D. Positive Logic

In a *positive-logic* circuit, the *logic "1" is a high level*, or the most positive level. Think of the four letters in high and the four letters in plus (for positive). **ANSWER D**

E7A13 What is the name for logic which represents a logic "0" as a high voltage?

A. Reverse Logic
B. Assertive Logic
C. Negative logic
D. Positive Logic

With the inverting digital amplifier, the NOT gate inverter with an input bit of 1, will result in the inverter's output always opposite, a *"0" as a high voltage*. The letter N is a good way to remember *NOT and negative logic.* **ANSWER C**

E7F01 What is the purpose of a prescaler circuit?
A. It converts the output of a JK flip-flop to that of an RS flip-flop
B. It multiplies a higher frequency signal so a low-frequency counter can display the operating frequency
C. It prevents oscillation in a low-frequency counter circuit
D. It divides a higher frequency signal so a low-frequency counter can display the operating frequency

You will find a *prescaler* in frequency counters to *divide down HF and VHF signals* so they can be counted and *displayed on a low-frequency counter.* **ANSWER D**

E7F02 Which of the following would be used to reduce a signal's frequency by a factor of ten?
A. A preamp
B. A prescaler
C. A marker generator
D. A flip-flop

A prescaler has a decade counter that may alter a frequency by a factor of 10. *Prescaler* circuits in frequency counters may *reduce a signal's frequency by a factor of 10* to be displayed within the range of the counter's crystal-controlled circuit. **ANSWER B**

E7F03 What is the function of a decade counter digital IC?
A. It produces one output pulse for every ten input pulses
B. It decodes a decimal number for display on a seven-segment LED display
C. It produces ten output pulses for every input pulse
D. It adds two decimal numbers together

A *decade counter* digital IC gives *one output* pulse *for every 10 input pulses.* **ANSWER A**

E7F04 What additional circuitry must be added to a 100-kHz crystal-controlled marker generator so as to provide markers at 50 and 25 kHz?
A. An emitter-follower
B. Two frequency multipliers
C. Two flip-flops
D. A voltage divider

We would use two flip-flops to take a 100-kHz signal and *provide markers at 50 kHz and 25 kHz.* **ANSWER C**

E7F05 Which of the following circuits can be combined to produce a 100 kHz fundamental signal with harmonics at 100 kHz intervals?
A. A 10 MHz oscillator and a flip-flop
B. A 1 MHz oscillator and a decade counter
C. A 1 MHz oscillator and a flip-flop
D. A 100 kHz oscillator and a phase detector

The *decade counter* will develop 100 kHz signals with harmonics at 100kHz intervals from a *1 MHz oscillator.* **ANSWER B**

E7F06 Which of these choices best describes a crystal marker generator?
A. A low-stability oscillator that sweeps through a band of frequencies
B. An oscillator often used in aircraft to determine the craft's location relative to the inner and outer markers at airports
C. A crystal-controlled oscillator with an output frequency and amplitude that can be varied over a wide range
D. A crystal-controlled oscillator that generates a series of reference signals at known frequency intervals

The *crystal marker generator* is based on a high-stability, crystal-controlled oscillator that will *generate a series of reference signals at known frequency intervals*. The greater the marker generator's crystal stability, the more accurate the frequency intervals. Most reference crystals are temperature compensated, so leave that test gear plugged-in so that the internal oven can bring the crystal up to its optimum running temperature. **ANSWER D**

E7F07 Which type of circuit would be a good choice for generating a series of harmonically related receiver calibration signals?
    A. A Wein-bridge oscillator followed by a class-A amplifier
    B. A Foster-Seeley discriminator
    C. A phase-shift oscillator
    D. A crystal oscillator followed by a frequency divider

The *crystal controlled oscillator*, developing square waves, will develop harmonics that would then be distributed up the band by a *frequency divider*, creating harmonically-related receiver calibration signals. And to calibrate the calibrater, tune to WWV at 10 MHz as a good over-the-air reference signal, or work with a GPS or Loran derived time base. **ANSWER D**

E7F08 What is one purpose of a marker generator?
    A. To add audio markers to an oscilloscope
    B. To provide a frequency reference for a phase locked loop
    C. To provide a means of calibrating a receiver's frequency settings
    D. To add time signals to a transmitted signal

The purpose of a *marker generator* is to provide a means of *calibrating receivers*, as well as showing a calibration mark on monitor scopes and spectrum analyzers. For this question and answer, just look for "calibrating a receiver." **ANSWER C**

E7F09 What determines the accuracy of a frequency counter?
    A. The accuracy of the time base
    B. The speed of the logic devices used
    C. Accuracy of the AC input frequency to the power supply
    D. Proper balancing of the mixer diodes

When shopping for a *frequency counter*, check out the frequency *time base accuracy*. The stability of the counter will depend on the internal crystal reference, and you should regularly check your crystal reference when calibrating transmit equipment for digital operation with no frequency error greater than 5 Hz. **ANSWER A**

E7F10 How does a conventional frequency counter determine the frequency of a signal?
    A. It counts the total number of pulses in a circuit
    B. It monitors a WWV reference signal for comparison with the measured signal
    C. It counts the number of input pulses occurring within a specific period of time
    D. It converts the phase of the measured signal to a voltage which is
        proportional to the frequency

There are several manufacturers of excellent amateur radio frequency counters – accurate enough to also be used in the commercial radio service. A *frequency counter counts the number of input pulses in a specific period of time*. You can usually set the sample rate by pushing a button on the front of the counter. **ANSWER C**

E7F11 What is the purpose of a frequency counter?

A. To provide a digital representation of the frequency of a signal
B. To generate a series of reference signals at known frequency intervals
C. To display all frequency components of a transmitted signal
D. To provide a signal source at a very accurate frequency

The frequency counter is a near-field receiver capable of indicating the frequency of a near-field "strongest input" signal that is within the counter's frequency range. Most counters will easily cover from low frequency all the way through 2 GHz ultra-high frequency. The actual purpose of the *frequency counter* is to present a *digital readout of the transmit frequency* you are measuring, or of the frequency of a specific stage within your transceiver when doing maintenance. **ANSWER A**

Frequency Counter
Courtesy of OptoElectronics

E7F12 What alternate method of determining frequency, other than by directly counting input pulses, is used by some frequency counters?

A. GPS averaging
B. Period measurement
C. Prescaling
D. D/A conversion

Traditional frequency counters are based on a fixed crystal and multiple prescale stages to count frequencies from DC to GHz. An alternate method to counting input pulses is to *measure the sample frequency in time*, called the *period of the cycle*. **ANSWER B**

E7F13 What is an advantage of a period-measuring frequency counter over a direct-count type?

A. It can run on battery power for remote measurements
B. It does not require an expensive high-precision time base
C. It provides improved resolution of signals within a comparable time period
D. It can directly measure the modulation index of an FM transmitter

A common frequency counter calculates the number of cycles per second (Hertz) of the near field frequency it is measuring. These low-cost counters are amazingly precise as they average out the readout from internal counters. In the *period-measuring frequency counter*, which is an expensive proposition, the RF wave is divided up into 360 degrees for a *more precise time measurement*. Phase difference comparisons take place in the reference oscillator, leading to improved signal frequency resolution within a comparable time period. This takes place inside many GPS receivers where signals are measured down to 10 to the minus 15th second, the femto second! **ANSWER C**

E7G14 What is an operational amplifier?

A. A high-gain, direct-coupled differential amplifier whose characteristics are determined by components external to the amplifier

B. A high-gain, direct-coupled audio amplifier whose characteristics are determined by components external to the amplifier

C. An amplifier used to increase the average output of frequency modulated amateur signals to the legal limit

D. A program subroutine that calculates the gain of an RF amplifier

The operational amplifier *(op amp)* is a direct-coupled differential amplifier that offers high gain and high input impedance. The *"differential"* wording refers to the op-amp input design where the output is determined by the difference voltage between the two inputs. Different op-amp circuits and characteristics are determined by the *external components* connected to the amplifier. **ANSWER A**

E7G01 What determines the gain and frequency characteristics of an op-amp RC active filter?

A. The values of capacitors and resistors built into the op-amp

B. The values of capacitors and resistors external to the op-amp

C. The input voltage and frequency of the op-amp's DC power supply

D. The output voltage and smoothness of the op-amp's DC power supply

One of the nice features of an *op-amp* is that it will operate as an *RC filter* – resistors (R) and capacitors (C) are in a circuit *outside the op-amp*. They are not built into the op-amp – they are external. **ANSWER B**

Operational Amplifier Basics

Ideal Operational Amplifier

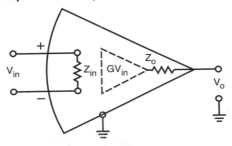

Z_{in} = Infinity

G = Gain = Infinity

Z_o = Zero

Bandwith = Infinity

V_o has no offset
(V_o=0 when V_{in}=0)

IC Operational Ampliifer

Even though IC operational amplifiers do not meet all the ideal specifications, G and Z_{in} are very large. Because G is very large, any small input voltage would drive the output into saturation (for practical supply voltages); therefore, normal operational amplifier operation is with feedback to set the gain. Here's an example for an inverting amplifier:

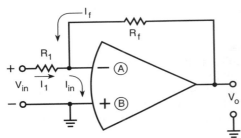

Since Z_{in} is very large, I_{in} = 0

$\therefore I_1 + I_f = 0$

$I_1 = \dfrac{V_{in}}{R_1}$

$I_f = \dfrac{V_o}{R_f}$

$\therefore \dfrac{V_{in}}{R_1} + \dfrac{V_o}{R_f} = 0$

$\dfrac{V_o}{R_f} = -\dfrac{V_{in}}{R_1}$

$\therefore \dfrac{V_o}{V_{in}} = -\dfrac{R_f}{R_1}$

Ⓐ **Inverting Input** — An input voltage that is more positive on this input will cause the output voltage to be less positive.

Ⓑ **Non-Inverting Input** — An input voltage that is more positive on this input will cause the output voltage to be more positive.

The gain of an *inverting IC operational amplifier* is:

▶ $G = -\dfrac{R_f}{R_1}$

The minus sign means the output is out of phase with the input.

E7G02 What causes ringing in a filter?

    A. The slew rate of the filter
    B. The bandwidth of the filter
    C. The frequency and phase response of the filter
    D. The gain of the filter

Choosing the optimum *frequency and phase response* of an extremely tight filter will allow you to narrow reception for such weak signal work as Earth-Moon-Earth reception on VHF and UHF. The change from mechanical filters to digital signal processing filters can mitigate *filter ringing*, as both frequency and phase response are digitally variable. **ANSWER C**

E7G03 What are the advantages of using an op-amp instead of LC elements in an audio filter?
   A. Op-amps are more rugged and can withstand more abuse than can LC elements
   B. Op-amps are fixed at one frequency
   C. Op-amps are available in more varieties than are LC elements
   D. Op-amps exhibit gain rather than insertion loss

That wonderful *op-amp* exhibits *high gain with negligible insertion loss* because its input impedance is also high. **ANSWER D**

E7G04 Which of the following capacitor types is best suited for use in high-stability op-amp RC active filter circuits?
   A. Electrolytic
   B. Disc ceramic
   C. Polystyrene
   D. Paper dielectric

The tiny *op-amp filter* should use *polystyrene capacitors* because they are very stable and will not vary when the circuit begins to heat up. **ANSWER C**

E7G05 How can unwanted ringing and audio instability be prevented in a multi-section op-amp RC audio filter circuit?
   A. Restrict both gain and Q
   B. Restrict gain, but increase Q
   C. Restrict Q, but increase gain
   D. Increase both gain and Q

In order *to keep an op-amp from going into oscillation*, both the *gain and the Q are restricted* and set by the feedback circuit. **ANSWER A**

E7G06 What steps are typically followed when selecting the external components for an op-amp RC active filter?
   A. Standard capacitor values are chosen first, the resistances are calculated, and resistors of the nearest standard value are used
   B. Standard resistor values are chosen first, the capacitances are calculated, and capacitors of the nearest standard value are used
   C. Standard resistor and capacitor values are used, the circuit is tested, and additional resistors are added to make any needed adjustments
   D. Standard resistor and capacitor values are used, the circuit is tested, and additional capacitors are added to make any needed adjustments

When designing an *RC active filter* for a specific frequency range and selectivity, always *choose a readily-available capacitor* value on which to base your op-amp filter calculations. *Then calculate resistance* and work around a standard resistance value, if possible, that won't require you to develop complex series/parallel resistor circuits. Obtaining specific values of resistors by using standard values in parallel and series combinations is much easier to do than finding special values of capacitors. **ANSWER A**

E7G07 Which of the following is the most appropriate use of an op-amp RC active filter?
   A. As a high-pass filter used to block RFI at the input to receivers
   B. As a low-pass filter used between a transmitter and a transmission line
   C. For smoothing power-supply output
   D. As an audio receiving filter

You will find the *op-amp RC active filter in the audio section* of your new transceiver's receiver. As you spend more dollars for that new Extra Class reward radio, filter options become greater, with more filter schemes included with that new, high-priced transceiver. **ANSWER D**

E7G08 Which of the following is a type of active op-amp filter circuit?
A. Regenerative feedback resonator
B. Helical resonator
C. Gilbert cell
D. Sallen-Key

The *active op-amp filter* may be the Sallen-Key design, which is a two-pole cascading stage filter with an extremely steep attenuation curve between pass band and stop band. You can design this filter as low pass or high pass by changing resistor and capacitor combinations. Look up the *Sallen-Key* active op-amp filter on the computer, and enjoy its many uses in your homebrew equipment. **ANSWER D**

E7G09 What voltage gain can be expected from the circuit in Figure E7-4 when R1 is 10 ohms and RF is 470 ohms?
A. 0.21
B. 94
C. 47
D. 24

Take a look at this operational amplifier basics chart, and remember the gain formula of an inverting IC op amp:

   $G = -R_F \div R_1 = R_F/R_1.$

The minus sign means the output is out of phase with the input. $R_F = 470$ ohms; $R_1 = 10$ ohms. Divide 10 into 470, coming out 47. On a calculator, the keystrokes are: Clear, *470 ÷ 10 = 47*. Not really a brain-buster, was it? **ANSWER C**

Figure E7-4

E7G10 How does the gain of a theoretically ideal operational amplifier vary with frequency?
A. It increases linearly with increasing frequency
B. It decreases linearly with increasing frequency
C. It decreases logarithmically with increasing frequency
D. It does not vary with frequency

The gain on an *ideal op amp should not vary with frequency*. **ANSWER D**

E7G11 What will be the voltage of the circuit shown in Figure E7-4 if R1 is 1000 ohms, RF is 10,000 ohms, and 0.23 volts is applied to the input?
A. 0.23 volts
B. 2.3 volts
C. -0.23 volts
D. -2.3 volts

This time we work the formula: $V_{OUT}/V_{IN} = -R_F/R_1$, when $R_1 = 1000$, and $R_F = 10,000$, the gain of the op amp is $V_{OUT}/V_{IN} = -10$. As a result, the *output = -10 × V_{IN} = -10 × 0.23 = -2.3 volts*. **ANSWER D**

E7G12 What voltage gain can be expected from the circuit in Figure E7-4 when R1 is 1800 ohms and RF is 68 kilohms?

A. 1
C. 38
B. 0.03
D. 76

Now we're back to the gain of an inverting IC operational amplifier. *Simply divide 1,800 ohms into 68,000 ohms.* Your calculator keystrokes are: clear, 68000 ÷ 1800 = 37.777, with your correct answer of *38* rounded off. Simple, huh? **ANSWER C**

E7G13 What voltage gain can be expected from the circuit in Figure E7-4 when R1 is 3300 ohms and RF is 47 kilohms?

A. 28
C. 7
B. 14
D. 0.07

One more time, an easy one – *divide* the small number *(3,300) into* the large number *(47,000)*, and you end up with *14.24*, with the correct answer of 14. **ANSWER B**

E7G15 What is meant by the term "op-amp input-offset voltage"?

A. The output voltage of the op-amp minus its input voltage
B. The difference between the output voltage of the op-amp and the input voltage required in the immediately following stage
C. The potential between the amplifier input terminals of the op-amp in a closed-loop condition
D. The potential between the amplifier input terminals of the op-amp in an open-loop condition

If the op amp has been constructed properly, you should see almost no *voltage between the amplifier input terminals* when the feedback loop is closed. **ANSWER C**

E7G16 What is the typical input impedance of an integrated circuit op-amp?

A. 100 ohms
C. Very low
B. 1000 ohms
D. Very high

Remember that the *input impedance* to the ideal op amp is *always Hi iN.* **ANSWER D**

E7G17 What is the typical output impedance of an integrated circuit op-amp?

A. Very low
C. 100 ohms
B. Very high
D. 1000 ohms

Remember that the *output impedance* of the ideal op amp is always *low out.* **ANSWER A**

E6F01 What is photoconductivity?

A. The conversion of photon energy to electromotive energy
B. The increased conductivity of an illuminated semiconductor
C. The conversion of electromotive energy to photon energy
D. The decreased conductivity of an illuminated semiconductor

The *photocell* has high resistance when no light shines on it, and a *varying resistance when light shines on it*. It can be used in an ON or OFF state as a simple beam alarm across a doorway, or may be found in almost all modern SLR cameras as a sensitive light meter to judge the amount of light present. **ANSWER B**

E6F02 What happens to the conductivity of a photoconductive material when light shines on it?

A. It increases
C. It stays the same
B. It decreases
D. It becomes unstable

In the dark, a *photocell* has high resistance. When you *shine light on it*, the *conductivity increases* as the resistance decreases. **ANSWER A**

E6F04 Which of the following is an optoisolator?
A. An LED and a phototransistor
B. A P-N junction that develops an excess positive charge when exposed to light
C. An LED and a capacitor
D. A P-N junction that develops an excess negative charge when exposed to light

Another name for an optocoupler is an optoisolator. An *LED shines through a window at a phototransistor in an optoisolator*. **ANSWER A**

E6F03 What is the most common configuration for an optocoupler?
A. A lens and a photomultiplier
B. A frequency modulated helium-neon laser
C. An amplitude modulated helium-neon laser
D. An LED and a phototransistor

Optocouplers are found in many modern, high-frequency transceivers. When you spin the dial to tune, you are not turning a giant capacitor, but rather interrupting a *light beam on a phototransistor*. **ANSWER D**

E6F05 What is an optical shaft encoder?
A. An array of neon or LED indicators whose light transmission path is controlled by a rotating wheel
B. An array of optocouplers whose light transmission path is controlled by a rotating wheel
C. An array of neon or LED indicators mounted on a rotating wheel in a coded pattern
D. An array of optocouplers mounted on a rotating wheel in a coded pattern

When you *spin the big knob* of your new high-frequency transceiver it is connected to an *optical shaft encoder* that determines the tuned frequency. **ANSWER B**

Optocoupler Used for Shaft Encoder

E6F06 What characteristic of a crystalline solid will photoconductivity change?
    A. The capacitance   C. The specific gravity
    B. The inductance   D. The resistance
The resistance of the crystalline solid varies when light shines on it because of the photoconductive effect. **ANSWER D**

Resistance Variation of a Photodiode			
Light Incidence	**Current I**	**Resistance**	**Test Conditions**
Dark	5 nA	2000 MΩ	$V_R = 10$ V *$E_e = 0$
Light	15 µA	666.7 kΩ	$V_R = 10$ V $E_e = 250$ µW/cm² at 940 nm
*Irradiance (E_e) is the radiant power per unit area incident on surface			

E6F07 Which material will exhibit the greatest photoconductive effect when illuminated by visible light?
    A. Potassium nitrate   C. Cadmium sulfide
    B. Lead sulfide   D. Sodium chloride
Cadmium sulfide offers the greatest photoconductive effect when light shines on it. *Photocells* used in amateur radio optical encoders may *contain cadmium sulfide*. **ANSWER C**

b. Schematic Diagram

c. Diode with Top Removed   d. Photodiode Schematic Symbol

A photodiode is like an ordinary p-n junction diode with a window to admit light. The light greatly increases reverse leakage current.

Source: *Basic Electronics* © 1994, Master Publishing, Inc., Niles, Illinois

E6F08 Which material will exhibit the greatest photoconductive effect when illuminated by infrared light?
    A. Potassium nitrate   C. Cadmium sulfide
    B. Lead sulfide   D. Sodium chloride
Lead sulfide is used for infrared light systems. Remember this – *lead for infrared*, and cadmium for visible. **ANSWER B**

E6F09 Which of the following materials is affected the most by photoconductivity?

A. A crystalline semiconductor

B. An ordinary metal

C. A heavy metal

D. A liquid semiconductor

The *crystalline semiconductor* is found inside the optical shaft encoder mechanism, and might also be found outside your ham shack as part of your solar-charging system. The light-emitting diode is normally the light source inside your tuning dial optocoupler. **ANSWER A**

E6F10 What characteristic of optoisolators is often used in power supplies?

A. They have low impedance between the light source and the phototransistor

B. They have very high impedance between the light source and the phototransistor

C. They have low impedance between the light source and the LED

D. They have very high impedance between the light source and the LED

The *optoisolator* offers *isolation* between the light-emitting diode and phototransistor. The light-emitting diode is in the secondary, connected to the output terminals, and the phototransistor might be in a circuit at AC line potential. **ANSWER B**

Optical Coupling

Source: *Basic Communications Electronics*, Hudson & Luecke, © 1999 Master Publishing, Inc., Niles, IL

E6F11 What characteristic of optoisolators makes them suitable for use with a triac to form the solid-state equivalent of a mechanical relay for a 120 V AC household circuit?

A. Optoisolators provide a low impedance link between a control circuit and a power circuit

B. Optoisolators provide impedance matching between the control circuit and power circuit

C. Optoisolators provide a very high degree of electrical isolation between a control circuit and a power circuit

D. Optoisolators eliminate (isolate) the effects of reflected light in the control circuit

The chief advantage of the *optoisolator* at household voltages is to provide a *very high degree of electrical isolation* between the control circuit and the house power circuit. Look for the answer "isolation" to agree with the optoisolator device. **ANSWER C**

E6F12 Which of the following types of photovoltaic cell has the highest efficiency?
A. Silicon
B. Silver iodide
C. Selenium
D. Gallium arsenide

Sad to say, no major breakthrough in solar panel efficiency has been made. You pay about $100 for every amp at 12 volts. Typical efficiency is 15 %, but it has been pushed to nearly 20 % through the use of *Gallium Arsenide* semiconductor materials – slightly more expensive per panel, but *yielding more milliamps out*. Solar panels last between 8 and 10 years, and some experts indicate the panel offers greatest output after it has been out in the sun for a year or two. If the panel heats up in the tropical zones with the sun overhead, the heat will actually decrease its output. **ANSWER D**

E6F14 Which of the following is the approximate open-circuit voltage produced by a fully-illuminated silicon-photovoltaic cell?
A. 0.1 V
B. 0.5 V
C. 1.5 V
D. 12 V

That new *solar panel* you purchased for your Field Day ham radio battery likely has an output of 17 volts with no load. Add it to a fresh battery and it drops down to about 12 or 13 volts under load. But in this question they ask about a single cell, and each *cell is rated at 0.5 volts*. CELL, not panel voltage. **ANSWER B**

E6F15 What absorbs the energy from light falling on a photovoltaic cell?
A. Protons
B. Photons
C. Electrons
D. Holes

Photon energy from sunlight is absorbed by the electrons in the photovoltaic cell, creating voltage output from sunlight. When sunlight photons strike the panel, an *electron will absorb the energy* and develop a new energy level, *creating the photovoltaic process*. **ANSWER C**

E6F13 What is the most common type of photovoltaic cell used for electrical power generation?
A. Selenium
B. Silicon
C. Cadmium Sulfide
D. Copper oxide

The *solar cell* is made up of *silicon wafers*, which offer relatively high voltage output and durability for the many years it will be out in the sunlight. **ANSWER B**

Solar Panel array for
Charging Storage Batteries

Schematic of Solar Panel
for Charging Storage Battery

E4A01 How does a spectrum analyzer differ from a conventional oscilloscope?

    A. A spectrum analyzer measures ionospheric reflection; an oscilloscope displays electrical signals

    B. A spectrum analyzer displays the peak amplitude of signals; an oscilloscope displays the average amplitude of signals

    C. A spectrum analyzer displays signals in the frequency domain; an oscilloscope displays signals in the time domain

    D. A spectrum analyzer displays radio frequencies; an oscilloscope displays audio frequencies

The *spectrum analyzer* displays the strength of signals at particular frequencies according to frequency (in the *frequency domain*) along a horizontal axis. A signal can be locked in and centered in the middle of the screen with 25 kHz to the left and 25 kHz to the right for a close examination of any off-frequency spurs it might have. A simple oscilloscope cannot display the signal in the frequency domain – it displays the signals on a time axis (in the time domain) going from left to right. With your output signal displayed on a spectrum analyzer, you may adjust your transmitter output network for minimum spurious signals. **ANSWER C**

Spectrum Analyzer
Courtesy of Hewlett-Packard Company

E4A02 Which of the following parameters would a typical spectrum analyzer display on the horizontal axis?
A. SWR
B. Q
C. Time
D. Frequency

The *spectrum analyzer* displays a portion of the frequency spectrum and shows you the amplitude of signals within that spectrum. The *horizontal axis* represents the *frequency* of the signals, while the vertical axis represents their amplitudes. **ANSWER D**

E4A03 Which of the following parameters would a typical spectrum analyzer display on the vertical axis?
A. Amplitude
B. Duration
C. SWR
D. Q

The *vertical axis* of the *spectrum analyzer* displays the *amplitude* of the signal. **ANSWER A**

E4A04 Which of the following test instruments is used to display spurious signals from a radio transmitter?
A. A spectrum analyzer
B. A wattmeter
C. A logic analyzer
D. A time-domain reflectometer

You can check for *spurious signals* using a *spectrum analyzer*. **ANSWER A**

E4A05 Which of the following test instruments is used to display intermodulation distortion products in an SSB transmission?
A. A wattmeter
B. A spectrum analyzer
C. A logic analyzer
D. A time-domain reflectometer

Only the *spectrum analyzer* allows you to see your output versus frequency by displaying it in the frequency domain. This allows you to *check for* harmonics that cause *distortion in your SSB transmitter*. **ANSWER B**

E4A06 Which of the following could be determined with a spectrum analyzer?
A. The degree of isolation between the input and output ports of a 2 meter duplexer
B. Whether a crystal is operating on its fundamental or overtone frequency
C. The spectral output of a transmitter
D. All of these choices are correct

As an Extra Class operator, the *spectrum analyzer* may become your ultimate best radio service monitor. The spectrum analyzer allows you to view the purity of your transmitted signal. The spectrum analyzer also can show fundamental and overtone crystal response, and you could use it for tuning up the input and output ports of a VHF or UHF duplexer. It *can do all of these things!* With the addition of an attenuator to protect the spectrum analyzer from overload, isolation of the transmit frequency in the receive port of a duplexer can be determined. **ANSWER D**

E4A11 Which of the following test instruments can be used to indicate pulse conditions in a digital logic circuit?
A. A logic probe
B. An ohmmeter
C. An electroscope
D. A Wheatstone bridge

An oscilloscope is always your best piece of test equipment – but the *logic probe* is a close second because of all the electronic functions now being performed *digitally*. **ANSWER A**

Logic Probe
Courtesy of RadioShack

E4A12 Which of the following procedures is an important precaution to follow when connecting a spectrum analyzer to a transmitter output?
 A. Use high quality double shielded coaxial cables to reduce signal losses
 B. Attenuate the transmitter output going to the spectrum analyzer
 C. Match the antenna to the load
 D. All of these choices are correct

Never transmit directly into a *spectrum analyzer*. You'll blow it up, for sure. Your *transmitter signal must be attenuated* to just a fraction of a watt in order to protect the spectrum analyzer input. I make it a practice to NEVER direct couple to a spectrum analyzer. Rather, I use a little pigtail and "sniff" my transmit RF. **ANSWER B**

E4B03 What is an advantage of using a bridge circuit to measure impedance?
 A. It provides an excellent match under all conditions
 B. It is relatively immune to drift in the signal generator source
 C. The measurement is based on obtaining a null in voltage, which can be done very precisely
 D. It can display results directly in Smith chart format

Multiband, high-frequency antenna traps, containing both coil inductive reactance and outer sleeve capacitive reactance, can be tuned to a specific frequency that will stop the RF signal from going further out the element. A portable impedance-measuring bridge circuit will show a much more precise dip, or null, in voltage, as opposed to many other methods of impedance measurement. Try to loosely couple the impedance *bridge circuit* so the pronounced *dip* is as *precisely on frequency* as possible. **ANSWER C**

E4B02 Which of the following factors most affects the accuracy of a frequency counter?
 A. Input attenuator accuracy
 B. Time base accuracy
 C. Decade divider accuracy
 D. Temperature coefficient of the logic

Everyone should have *frequency counter* in their ham shack. Be sure to get one that has excellent *time base*. **ANSWER B**

E4B06 If a frequency counter with a specified accuracy of +/- 10 ppm reads 146,520,000 Hz, what is the most the actual frequency being measured could differ from the reading?
A. 146.52 Hz
B. 10 Hz
C. 146.52 kHz
D. 1465.20 Hz

Keystroke the following on your calculator: Clear *146.52 × 10 = 1465.2 Hz.* You are *multiplying the frequency in MHz by the time base accuracy of 10 ppm.* **ANSWER D**

Frequency Counter
Courtesy of OptoElectronics

E4B04 If a frequency counter with a specified accuracy of +/- 1.0 ppm reads 146,520,000 Hz, what is the most the actual frequency being measured could differ from the reading?
A. 165.2 Hz
B. 14.652 kHz
C. 146.52 Hz
D. 1.4652 MHz

You may have a question on your test regarding the error readout on a frequency counter with a specific part per million (ppm) time base. It's easy to solve these problems with a simple calculator. Since they're asking parts per million, first conver the frequency given in Hz to MHz. You do this simply by moving the decimal point 6 places to the left. Now multiply the frequency in MHz times the parts per million time base accuracy (in this case 1 ppm). This will give you the error they are looking for in the answer. Try this on your calculator: Clear *146.52 × 1 = 146.52 Hz.* **ANSWER C**

Counter Readout Error   f = Frequency in **MHz** being measured
Readout Error = f × a   a = Counter accuracy in **parts per million**

E4B05 If a frequency counter with a specified accuracy of +/- 0.1 ppm reads 146,520,000 Hz, what is the most the actual frequency being measured could differ from the reading?
A. 14.652 Hz
B. 0.1 MHz
C. 1.4652 Hz
D. 1.4652 kHz

Hertz to MHz will give you a frequency of 146.52. Multiple that by 0.1 parts per million, and see if your calculator reads 14.652 Hz. The keystrokes are: Clear *146.52 × 0.1 = 14.652.* **ANSWER A**

E4B01 Which of the following is a characteristic of a good harmonic frequency marker?
A. Wide tuning range
B. Frequency stability
C. Linear output amplifier
D. All of the above

Is that garage sale transceiver smack dab on frequency? If it is a newer piece of ham radio high frequency equipment, tune in to general coverage and dial in WWV at 10 or 15 MHz. Go for the finest tuning speed, which usually brings up a 10 Hertz trailing 0 or, better yet, a 1 Hertz 0. Now switch between upper sideband and lower sideband while listening to the WWV voice and once-a-second tones and you should hear no change in tone frequency. If you are in a screen room, you will not be able to hear the stable WWV *frequency standard for calibration*, so you will need an alternate *stable* frequency – one with good harmonic frequency outputs. A good way to go in this situation is to use the ultra-stable frequency standard of a GPS-based calibration generator. **ANSWER B**

E4B07 How much power is being absorbed by the load when a directional power meter connected between a transmitter and a terminating load reads 100 watts forward power and 25 watts reflected power?

A. 100 watts
C. 25 watts
B. 125 watts
D. 75 watts

Here's a great question that points out the importance of working your antenna system for maximum power transfer, minimum SWR, and a better signal on the air than simply using an antenna tuner to make up for manually working over the antenna elements for better antenna resonance. *If 25 watts are reflected from 100 watts initially delivered to the load (the antenna), only 75 watts are truly being absorbed by the antenna.* The tuner won't help; it is just fooling your transceiver into thinking everything is ok with your antenna system! The reflected 25 watts does not represent lost power, except for line loss attenuation over and above the matched attenuation of the feedline. What is being absorbed by the load and radiated will be 75 watts, with those extra 25 watts circulating in the feedline between the transmitter and the load. Good reading is *Maxell's Reflections II.* **ANSWER D**

E4B08 Which of the following is good practice when using an oscilloscope probe?

A. Keep the ground connection of the probe as short as possible
B. Never use a high impedance probe to measure a low impedance circuit
C. Never use a DC-coupled probe to measure an AC circuit
D. All of these choices are correct

When working on radio equipment *using an oscilloscope probe*, we want the probe's ground lead to be kept as short as possible and clipped to the ground chassis near where you are testing. The *short ground lead* will minimize stray pickup from other stages of the radio. **ANSWER A**

VERTICAL   HORIZONTAL   TRIGGER
AMPLIFIER   AMPLIFIER   CIRCUIT
CONTROLS   CONTROLS   CONTROLS

TIME/DIV
TIME BASE
GENERATOR
CONTROLS

AC

SOURCE

INPUT
SIGNAL

A Typical Oscilloscope showing an AC Waveform

Source: *Basic Electronics* © 1994, Master Publishing, Inc., Niles, Illinois

E4B09 Which of the following is a characteristic of a good DC voltmeter?
A. High reluctance input
B. Low reluctance input
C. High impedance input
D. Low impedance input

Your modern high-frequency or VHF/UHF transceiver has circuits so sensitive that they will quit oscillating if you attempt to measure DC voltage with an inexpensive, low-impedance *multimeter. High impedance input* – usually greater than 25 k ohms per volt – may help to prevent loading or changing the characteristics of the circuit. An excellent example is your digital multimeter with an input impedance of 10 meg-ohms. **ANSWER C**

E4B10 What is indicated if the current reading on an RF ammeter placed in series with the antenna feedline of a transmitter increases as the transmitter is tuned to resonance?
A. There is possibly a short to ground in the feedline
B. The transmitter is not properly neutralized
C. There is an impedance mismatch between the antenna and feedline
D. There is more power going into the antenna

When I am working aboard boats testing the output of a long-wire antenna tuner I insert a series thermocouple RF ammeter to monitor RF output levels. This lets me confirm that the tuner is operating properly when I change bands, and *see RF power* increase up to an amp *going into the long-wire antenna*. Another good indicator of RF output to the antenna circuit is the common fluorescent tube. If the tube glows on CW dots when held within an inch of the antenna radiating element on high frequency, it is a good indication that there is plenty of RF to work the world. **ANSWER D**

E4B13 What is the significance of voltmeter sensitivity expressed in ohms per volt?
A. The full scale reading of the voltmeter multiplied by its ohms per volt rating will provide the input impedance of the voltmeter
B. When used as a galvanometer, the reading in volts multiplied by the ohms/volt will determine the power drawn by the device under test
C. When used as an ohmmeter, the reading in ohms divided by the ohms/volt will determine the voltage applied to the circuit
D. When used as an ammeter, the full scale reading in amps divided by ohms/volt will determine the size of shunt needed

When measuring anything in a circuit, it is important that the measuring instrument cause as little change to the circuit as possible. Since a voltmeter is placed across a circuit (connected between two points in that circuit), it acts as a resistance in parallel with that part of the circuit. In order to cause the least change, the meter should be as high a resistance as possible. *By multiplying the ohms per volt rating times the maximum voltage on a given scale of the meter, you can determine the equivalent resistance your meter will look like to the circuit.* **ANSWER A**

E4B14 How is the compensation of an oscilloscope probe typically adjusted?

A. A square wave is observed and the probe is adjusted until the horizontal portions of the displayed wave is as nearly flat as possible

B. A high frequency sine wave is observed, and the probe is adjusted for maximum amplitude

C. A frequency standard is observed, and the probe is adjusted until the deflection time is accurate

D. A DC voltage standard is observed, and the probe is adjusted until the displayed voltage is accurate

If you regularly use an oscilloscope when working on your ham radio equipment, and you just purchased a new probe, use your *square wave* generator and adjust the oscilloscope for the horizontal portion of the displayed wave *to be as flat as possible*. **ANSWER A**

E4B15 What happens if a dip-meter is too tightly coupled to a tuned circuit being checked?

A. Harmonics are generated

B. A less accurate reading results

C. Cross modulation occurs

D. Intermodulation distortion occurs

If you *put your dip-meter right on top of a coil, you will have a less accurate reading* – only get close enough to see a smooth dip on your readout. On the SWR analyzer type of dip-meters, everything is done for you automatically inside the box. All you need to do is to screw on the antenna cable and sweep the frequency dial to see where the antenna is resonant. **ANSWER B**

E4B16 Which of these factors limits the accuracy of a D'Arsonval-type meter?

A. Its magnetic flux density

B. Coil impedance

C. Deflection rate

D. Electromagnet current

Ham sets are now being produced without the traditional needle movement meter. I'm sad to see them go, but the new colored LED readouts replace the traditional mechanical meter movement. Because the traditional mechanical meter was prone to vibration failure, the jeweled needle movement could go out of calibration. In addition, the mechanical movement has a *lower coil impedance* that limits its spontaneous accuracy. **ANSWER B**

D'Arsonval-type Meter

E4B11Which of the following describes a method to measure intermodulation distortion in an SSB transmitter?

A. Modulate the transmitter with two non-harmonically related radio frequencies and observe the RF output with a spectrum analyzer

B. Modulate the transmitter with two non-harmonically related audio frequencies and observe the RF output with a spectrum analyzer

C. Modulate the transmitter with two harmonically related audio frequencies and observe the RF output with a peak reading wattmeter

D. Modulate the transmitter with two harmonically related audio frequencies and observe the RF output with a logic analyzer

When looking at your signal on a spectrum analyzer, a whistle into the microphone is not a good test of transmit linearity. *Two non-harmonically related tones* from a 2 tone generator is a much better way to observe the RF output on your new $10,000 spectrum analyzer. **ANSWER B**

E9A16 What is meant by the radiation resistance of an antenna?
A. The combined losses of the antenna elements and feed line
B. The specific impedance of the antenna
C. The value of a resistance that would dissipate the same amount of power as that radiated from an antenna
D. The resistance in the atmosphere that an antenna must overcome to be able to radiate a signal

Radiation resistance is an important term because it compares the power radiated from an antenna to the equivalent resistance that would dissipate the same amount of power as heat. The higher the radiation resistance of an antenna, the better its performance. Don't confuse radiation resistance with simple DC resistance – they are exactly opposite. Radiation resistance *is the equivalent resistance that would dissipate the same amount of power as that radiated from the antenna.* **ANSWER C**

E9A05 Which of the following factors determine the radiation resistance of an antenna?
A. Transmission-line length and antenna height
B. Antenna height and conductor length/diameter ratio, and location of nearby conductive objects
C. It is a physical constant and is the same for all antennas
D. Sunspot activity and time of day

Radiation resistance of a mobile *antenna* may be severely compromised if the antenna is *mounted too low*. The *location* of the antenna *with respect to nearby objects*, as well as the *length-to-diameter ratio of the conductors*, is very important. **ANSWER B**

E9A06 What is the term for the ratio of the radiation resistance of an antenna to the total resistance of the system?
A. Effective radiated power
B. Radiation conversion loss
C. Antenna efficiency
D. Beamwidth

The ratio of the radiation resistance of an antenna to the total resistance of the system times 100 is the formula used to calculate *antenna efficiency*. **ANSWER C**

E9A07 What is included in the total resistance of an antenna system?
A. Radiation resistance plus space impedance
B. Radiation resistance plus transmission resistance
C. Transmission-line resistance plus radiation resistance
D. Radiation resistance plus ohmic resistance

To calculate the *total resistance* of an antenna system, *add radiation resistance plus all ohmic resistances* within the coils and conductors. **ANSWER D**

E9A11 How is antenna efficiency calculated?
A. (radiation resistance / transmission resistance) × 100%
B. (radiation resistance / total resistance) × 100%
C. (total resistance / radiation resistance) × 100%
D. (effective radiated power / transmitter output) × 100%

The efficiency of your *antenna* is an important consideration when you plan to upgrade your antenna system. *Efficiency equals the radiation resistance divided by the total resistance, multiplied by 100 percent.* You want to keep your ohmic resistance as low as possible to make your antenna more efficient. Generally, bigger antenna elements have greater radiation resistance, lower ohmic resistance, higher efficiency, and increased bandwidth. Bigger is always better! **ANSWER B**

E9B01 What determines the free-space polarization of an antenna?
A. The orientation of its magnetic field (H Field)
B. The orientation of its free-space characteristic impedance
C. The orientation of its electric field (E Field)
D. Its elevation pattern

Keep in mind that it is *the electric lines of force that determine the polarization of an antenna*. This is called the orientation of the electric field, E Field. **ANSWER C**

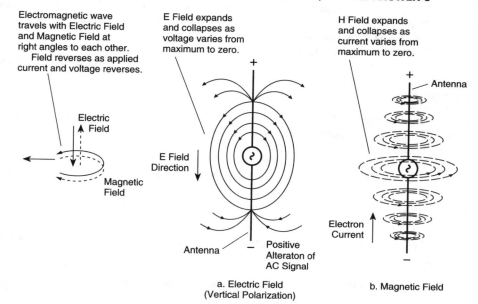

a. Electric Field
(Vertical Polarization)

b. Magnetic Field

Propagating Electromagnetic Waves

Source: *Antennas – Selection and Installation*, A.J. Evans, Copyright ©1986 Master Publishing, Inc., Niles, Illinois

E9A12 How can the efficiency of an HF quarter-wave grounded vertical antenna be improved?

A. By installing a good radial system
B. By isolating the coax shield from ground
C. By shortening the vertical
D. By reducing the diameter of the radiating element

Most *vertical* antennas are *one-quarter wavelength* long, and use a mirror image counterpoise to compare to that of a halfwave antenna. A *good ground radial system* will give your signal more punch, lower the noise floor, lower your take-off angle, and give you good DX. **ANSWER A**

E9A13 Which is the most important factor that determines ground losses for a ground-mounted vertical antenna operating in the 3-30 MHz range?

A. The standing-wave ratio
B. Base current
C. Soil conductivity
D. Base impedance

Dirt is ground, right? Likely not – dry *soil* is not nearly as effective a *conductor* as 4 quarter wavelength radials per band on that new HF vertical antenna in your back yard. Unless you live in a marsh, you'll probably increase antenna performance by mounting it up on the roof, and creating your own ground plane radial system. Looking to really increase your 5 band trap vertical performance on HF? Replace those quarter wavelength ground wires with 3 inch wide copper foil strips, 4 per band, each a quarter wavelength long. **ANSWER C**

E9C15 What strongly affects the shape of the far-field, low-angle elevation pattern of a vertically polarized antenna?
  A. The conductivity and dielectric constant of the soil in the area of the antenna
  B. The radiation resistance of the antenna and matching network
  C. The SWR on the transmission line
  D. The transmitter output power

Vertically polarized antennas work best when mounted above an enormous ground plane, such as sea water. The *conductivity and dielectric constant of the soil* will strongly *affect the shape of the far-field, low-angle radiation pattern.* **ANSWER A**

E9C12 How is the far-field elevation pattern of a vertically polarized antenna affected by being mounted over seawater versus rocky ground?
  A. The low-angle radiation decreases
  B. The high-angle radiation increases
  C. Both the high- and low-angle radiation decrease
  D. The low-angle radiation increases

Here we go – *mount it over salt water* and achieve a *low-angle radiation increase.* This gives you longer-range skywave signals. **ANSWER D**

E9C17 What is the main effect of placing a vertical antenna over an imperfect ground?
  A. It causes increased SWR
  B. It changes the impedance angle of the matching network
  C. It reduces low-angle radiation
  D. It reduces losses in the radiating portion of the antenna

When I outfit boaters with their high frequency antenna systems, I always couple the antenna ground system to sea water. Nothing beats a direct contact to conductive sea water for the antenna ground, lowering the takeoff angle for maximum DX. *Mounting a vertical antenna on your roof, relying only on the metal vent pipe as the ground plane, will produce multiple near-vertical radiation angles, and can reduce the DX low-angle radiation* capability you were hoping to achieve. Any vertical antenna needs a major ground system below it if you plan to work more than the lower 48! **ANSWER C**

E9D14 Which of the following types of conductor would be best for minimizing losses in a station's RF ground system?
  A. A resistive wire, such as a spark-plug wire
  B. A thin, flat copper strap several inches wide
  C. A cable with 6 or 7 18-gauge conductors in parallel
  D. A single 12 or 10 gauge stainless steel wire

What happens when you pass RF through a coil? The coil has inductive reactance, and at certain frequencies the impedance will be high. For ground systems to be effective, we want to minimize any wire runs that will look like a coil and create unwanted impedance. *Copper ground foil is our choice for good grounding* techniques, and it is available in 25 foot, 50 foot, and custom-length rolls from your local ham radio dealer or a copper foil manufacturer. Three inch wide foil is my favorite for minimum inductive reactance. **ANSWER B**

E9D15 Which of these choices would provide the best RF ground for your station?
   A. A 50-ohm resistor connected to ground
   B. A connection to a metal water pipe
   C. A connection to 3 or 4 interconnected ground rods driven into the Earth
   D. A connection to 3 or 4 interconnected ground rods via a series RF choke

A good earth ground to your new $10,000 Extra Class-Reward transceiver should be *copper foil connected to three or four ground rods, driven in to the earth.* Follow manufacturer suggestions on how to ground your tower, too. **ANSWER C**

E9C01 What is the radiation pattern of two 1/4-wavelength vertical antennas spaced 1/2-wavelength apart and fed 180 degrees out of phase?
   A. A cardioid
   B. Omnidirectional
   C. A figure-8 broadside to the axis of the array
   D. A figure-8 oriented along the axis of the array

Two quarter-wave vertical antennas spaced *one-half wavelength apart* and *fed 180 degrees out of phase* results in a *figure-8 radiation pattern* with best radiation *in line with the antennas.* **ANSWER D**

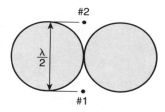

| a. Two λ/4 Verticals Fed 180° Out of Phase (Figure 8 End-Fire In-Line) | b. Two λ/4 Verticals Fed 90° Out of Phase (Cardioid) | c. Two λ/4 Verticals Fed In Phase (Figure 8 Broadside) |

Antenna Radiation Patterns

E9C02 What is the radiation pattern of two 1/4-wavelength vertical antennas spaced 1/4-wavelength apart and fed 90 degrees out of phase?
   A. A cardioid
   B. A figure-8 end-fire along the axis of the array
   C. A figure-8 broadside to the axis of the array
   D. Omnidirectional

Remember when we talked about RDF antennas for direction finding? *Two quarter-wave verticals* spaced *one-quarter wavelength apart* and *fed 90 degrees out of phase* results in *a cardioid pattern*. This is called "unidirectional." **ANSWER A**

E9C03 What is the radiation pattern of two 1/4-wavelength vertical antennas spaced 1/2-wavelength apart and fed in phase?
   A. Omnidirectional
   B. A cardioid
   C. A Figure-8 broadside to the axis of the array
   D. A Figure-8 end-fire along the axis of the array

Two quarter-waves spaced one-half wavelength apart and fed in phase will also result in a *figure-8 pattern*, but maximum gain will be *broadside to the antennas*. **ANSWER C**

E9A08 What is a folded dipole antenna?
 A. A dipole one-quarter wavelength long
 B. A type of ground-plane antenna
 C. A dipole constructed from one wavelength of wire forming a very thin loop
 D. A hypothetical antenna used in theoretical discussions to replace the radiation resistance

The folded dipole is a fun one to build out of television twin-lead cable. As shown in the diagram, the twin-lead *folded dipole is constructed by using a half-wavelength piece of twin lead to formula loop that is one full wavelength long*. Scrape the insulation from the wire ends and twist the wires together on each end. In the center of one of the leads in the twin-lead, cut the lead and scrape some of the insulation off to expose bare wires on the end of each quarter-wave piece. Feed these wires with standard 300-ohm twin-lead, or connect a balun transformer to the bare wires to permit 50-ohm or 75-ohm coax cable to feed the folded dipole. **ANSWER C**

Folded Dipole Antenna Made from 300-Ohm Twin-Lead

E9D10 What is the approximate feed-point impedance at the center of a folded dipole antenna?
 A. 300 ohms   C. 50 ohms
 B. 72 ohms   D. 450 ohms

The *impedance at the center of a folded dipole* may be a whopping *300 ohms*. You'll need an impedance-matching transformer to feed it with 50-ohm coax; however, ordinary TV twin-lead would match very well. **ANSWER A**

E9A04 Why would one need to know the feed point impedance of an antenna?
 A. To match impedances for maximum power transfer from a feed line
 B. To measure the near-field radiation density from a transmitting antenna
 C. To calculate the front-to-side ratio of the antenna
 D. To calculate the front-to-back ratio of the antenna

When the antenna (the load) has the *same characteristic impedance* as the feedline *maximum power will be transferred*. A mismatch may result in high SWR, transmit power feedback, and potential transmitter heat-up. Most coaxial cable presents a 50-ohm impedance. **ANSWER A**

E9A01 Which of the following describes an isotropic Antenna?
 A. A grounded antenna used to measure earth conductivity
 B. A horizontal antenna used to compare Yagi antennas
 C. A theoretical antenna used as a reference for antenna gain
 D. A spacecraft antenna used to direct signals toward the earth

An *isotropic radiator* is simply theoretical; and in every April 1st issue of many magazines, advertisers try to sell "isotropic radiators" to the unsuspecting ham! We use it as a *theoretical reference to calculate the gain* or loss of real antenna systems. **ANSWER C**

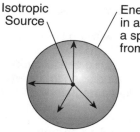

Isotropic Source

Energy radiates equally in all directions forming a sphere of radiation from the point source.

Isotropic Radiator Pattern

E9A03 Which of the following antennas has no gain in any direction?
A. Quarter-wave vertical
B. Yagi
C. Half-wave dipole
D. Isotropic antenna

It is the theoretical *isotropic radiator*, on paper, that has equal signal dispersion in all directions, and *no gain* in any direction. **ANSWER D**

E9A02 How much gain does a 1/2-wavelength dipole have compared to an isotropic antenna?
A. 1.55 dB
B. 2.15 dB
C. 3.05 dB
D. 4.30 dB

The *halfwave dipole* will have approximately *2.1 dB gain* over the theoretical isotropic radiator. **ANSWER B**

E9A14 How much gain does an antenna have over a 1/2-wavelength dipole when it has 6 dB gain over an isotropic antenna?
A. 3.85 dB
B. 6.0 dB
C. 8.15 dB
D. 2.79 dB

The halfwave dipole has about 2.15 dB gain over an isotropic radiator. If an antenna under measurement has 6 dB gain over an isotropic radiator, *6 dB - 2.15 dB = about 3.85 dB gain over the dipole.* **ANSWER A**

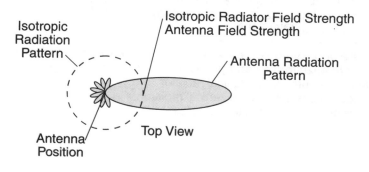

Isotropic Radiation Pattern

Isotropic Radiator Field Strength
Antenna Field Strength

Antenna Radiation Pattern

Antenna Position

Top View

"Gain" of an antenna.

E9A15 How much gain does an antenna have over a 1/2-wavelength dipole when it has 12 dB gain over an isotropic antenna?
- A. 6.17 dB
- B. 9.85 dB
- C. 12.5 dB
- D. 14.15 dB

Here is a bigger antenna that has 12 dB gain over an isotropic radiator, so *12 dB gain - 2.15 dB = about 9.85 dB over the dipole.* **ANSWER B**

E9D11 Why is a loading coil often used with an HF mobile antenna?
- A. To improve reception
- B. To lower the losses
- C. To lower the Q
- D. To cancel capacitive reactance

Since X_L must equal X_C in order for a whip antenna to achieve resonance, we need to add a *loading coil* on an antenna for lower frequency operation *to tune out capacitive reactance.* **ANSWER D**

E9D08 What happens to the bandwidth of an antenna as it is shortened through the use of loading coils?
- A. It is increased
- B. It is decreased
- C. No change occurs
- D. It becomes flat

When you *shorten a vertical antenna with a loading coil, bandwidth decreases*, and losses increase. **ANSWER B**

E9A10 What is meant by antenna bandwidth?
- A. Antenna length divided by the number of elements
- B. The frequency range over which an antenna satisfies a performance requirement
- C. The angle between the half-power radiation points
- D. The angle formed between two imaginary lines drawn through the element ends

If you operate on the lower bands, such as 40 meters, antenna bandwidth is an important consideration. *Bandwidth is the frequency range over which you can expect your antenna to perform well.* Small antennas on 40 meters don't have a very wide bandwidth. Monster antennas for 40 meters have good bandwidth. **ANSWER B**

E9D06 Why should an HF mobile antenna loading coil have a high ratio of reactance to resistance?
- A. To swamp out harmonics
- B. To maximize losses
- C. To minimize losses
- D. To minimize the Q

When you see those giant open-air coils halfway up the mast on a mobile whip antenna, you are looking at *high Q coils which minimize losses*. The bigger the coil, the lower the losses. **ANSWER C**

E9D05 For a shortened vertical antenna, where should a loading coil be placed to minimize losses and produce the most effective performance?
- A. Near the center of the vertical radiator
- B. As low as possible on the vertical radiator
- C. As close to the transmitter as possible
- D. At a voltage node

Antennas

To minimize coil losses and to increase performance of a loaded vertical antenna, *the loading coil should be near the center of the vertical radiator*, not at the base. **ANSWER A** www.hiqantennas.com

Mobile Antenna Loading Coils

E9D09 What is an advantage of using top loading in a shortened HF vertical antenna?

A. Lower Q

B. Greater structural strength

C. Higher losses

D. Improved radiation efficiency

We use *top loading* and helical loading on a shortened HF vertical antenna to *improve radiation efficiency*. With this in mind, it's easy to understand why a little 96-inch CB whip antenna with an automatic antenna tuner inside the trunk of your vehicle will not perform as well as a resonant center-loaded, helical-loaded, or top-loaded vertical antenna. **ANSWER D**

E9D13 What happens at the base feed-point of a fixed-length HF mobile antenna as the frequency of operation is lowered?

A. The resistance decreases and the capacitive reactance decreases

B. The resistance decreases and the capacitive reactance increases

C. The resistance increases and the capacitive reactance decreases

D. The resistance increases and the capacitive reactance increases

As *we operate lower on the bands*, the base *feedpoint resistance decreases* (lower decreases), and the *capacitive reactance (X_C) increases*. You can visualize the correct answer by thinking the lower you operate in frequency, the more coil (inductive reactance, X_L) you will need to offset and equal the added capacitive reactance, which increases. **ANSWER B**

E9D12 What is an advantage of using a trapped antenna?

A. It has high directivity in the higher-frequency bands

B. It has high gain

C. It minimizes harmonic radiation

D. It may be used for multi-band operation

The *trap antenna* may be used for multiband operation, from a single feed line. There are trap dipoles, trap verticals, and trap beam antennas for *multiband operation*. **ANSWER D**

E9D07 What is a disadvantage of using a multiband trapped antenna?
    A. It might radiate harmonics
    B. It can only be used for single-band operation
    C. It is too sharply directional at lower frequencies
    D. It must be neutralized

Trap antennas have one big disadvantage – on older equipment, they can radiate harmonics. Since ham bands may be harmonically related, it's easy to see that the second harmonic of 7 MHz can radiate from a trap antenna quite nicely because the antenna also has perfect resonance on 14 MHz. So watch out for *harmonics on a trap antenna*. **ANSWER A**

E9B09 How can the approximate beamwidth of a directional antenna be determined?
    A. Note the two points where the signal strength of the antenna is 3 dB less than maximum and compute the angular difference
    B. Measure the ratio of the signal strengths of the radiated power lobes from the front and rear of the antenna
    C. Draw two imaginary lines through the ends of the elements and measure the angle between the lines
    D. Measure the ratio of the signal strengths of the radiated power lobes from the front and side of the antenna

On directional antennas, beamwidth is an important consideration. *Beamwidth is* always described by the *angle between the two points where the signal strength is down 3 dB from the maximum signal point*. The "tighter" your beam pattern, the smaller the beamwidth. **ANSWER A**

E9B10 What type of computer program technique is commonly used for modeling antennas?
    A. Graphical analysis
    B. Method of Moments
    C. Mutual impedance analysis
    D. Calculus differentiation with respect to physical properties

The American Radio Relay League has a computer program called *"Method of Moments,"* and this is a great way for *modeling a proposed antenna* on the computer screen. **ANSWER B**

E9B14 What does the abbreviation NEC stand for when applied to antenna modeling programs?
    A. Next Element Comparison
    B. Numerical Electromagnetics Code
    C. National Electrical Code
    D. Numeric Electrical Computation

NEC-based antenna modeling stands for *Numerical Electromagnetics Code*. NEC simulates the electromagnetic response of antennas and metal structures. Jerry Burke and A. Poggio wrote the NEC/MOM family of programs at Lawrence Livermore Labs in 1981, under contract to the U.S. Navy. NEC2 was later released to the public and is now available on most computing platforms. To learn more about NEC, visit: www.nec2.org **ANSWER B**

E9B13 Which of the following is a disadvantage of NEC-based antenna modeling programs?
A. They can only be used for simple wire antennas
B. They are not capable of generating both vertical and horizontal polarization patterns
C. Computing time increases as the number of wire segments is increased
D. All of these answers are correct

If you decide to build your own antennas, GREAT – this is what ham radio is all about! The NEC (Numerical Electromagnetics Code) modeling programs are terrific, but *the more wire segments you add, the longer it will take for the program to compute* your results. **ANSWER C**

E9B12 What is a disadvantage of decreasing the number of wire segments in an antenna model below the guideline of 10 segments per half-wavelength?
A. Ground conductivity will not be accurately modeled
B. The resulting design will favor radiation of harmonic energy
C. The computed feed-point impedance may be incorrect
D. The antenna will become mechanically unstable

When modeling antennas on a computer, we always stay above 10 segments per half wavelength so we don't cause the *feedpoint impedance* to be *miscalculated using less than the recommended 10 segments per half wavelength.* **ANSWER C**

E9B15 What type of information can be obtained by submitting the details of a proposed new antenna to a modeling program?
A. SWR vs. frequency charts
B. Polar plots of the far-field elevation and azimuth patterns
C. Antenna gain
D. All of these answers are correct

Modern *antenna programs will show SWR* plots at a certain frequency, *polar plots, antenna gain, feedpoint impedance*, and you can even tweak your proposed antenna by adding in the diameter of those cool-looking polished copper tube elements! **ANSWER D**

E0A01 What, if any, are the differences between the radiation produced by radioactive materials and the electromagnetic energy radiated by an antenna?
A. There is no significant difference between the two types of radiation
B. Only radiation produced by radioactivity can injure human beings
C. RF radiation does not have sufficient energy to break apart atoms and molecules; radiation from radioactive sources does
D. Radiation from an antenna will damage unexposed photographic film, ordinary radioactive materials do not cause this problem

Radioactive radiation, like they use at hospitals for cancer treatment, *breaks apart atoms and molecules* in certain cells, and is usually administered in precise areas of the body. RF radiation is what comes out of microwave transmitters and your microwave oven, only heating molecules. **ANSWER C**

E0A09 Which insulating material commonly used as a thermal conductor for some types of electronic devices is extremely toxic if broken or crushed and the particles are accidentally inhaled?

A. Mica
B. Zinc oxide
C. Beryllium Oxide
D. Uranium Hexaflouride

Be careful around large antennas that may contain beryllium oxide on the metal internal contactors. These antennas are terrific performers and are safe but, if ever you decide to take one apart, remember that *beryllium oxide is extremely toxic if inhaled.* **ANSWER C**

E9B11 What is the principle of a Method of Moments analysis?

A. A wire is modeled as a series of segments, each having a distinct value of current
B. A wire is modeled as a single sine-wave current generator
C. A wire is modeled as a series of points, each having a distinct location in space
D. A wire is modeled as a series of segments, each having a distinct value of voltage across it

Using Method of Moments *(MOM)* software, a wire is modeled as a series of segments, *each segment having a distinct value of antenna current.* **ANSWER A**

E9A09 What is meant by antenna gain?

A. The numerical ratio relating the radiated signal strength of an antenna in the direction of maximum radiation to that of a reference antenna
B. The numerical ratio of the signal in the forward direction to that in the opposite direction
C. The ratio of the amount of power radiated by an antenna compared to the transmitter output power
D. The final amplifier gain minus the transmission-line losses (including any phasing lines present)

We normally rate *antenna gain* figures in dB. This is the *numerical ratio relating the radiated signal strength of your antenna to that of another antenna* down the street. Generally, the ham with the higher gain antenna will always get better signal reports. **ANSWER A**

E0A07 What is the "far-field" zone of an antenna?

A. The area of the ionosphere where radiated power is not refracted
B. The area where radiated power dissipates over a specified time period
C. The area where radiated field strengths are obstructed by objects of reflection
D. The area where the shape of the antenna pattern is independent of distance

The far field zone of an antenna is where the antenna pattern remains constant, independent of distance. This is generally a safe area when calculating MPE. **ANSWER D**

E9B02 In the antenna radiation pattern shown in Figure E9-1, what is the 3-dB beamwidth?

A. 75 degrees

B. 50 degrees

C. 25 degrees

D. 30 degrees

Looking carefully at the diagram in Figure E9-1, notice that the main lobe of the pattern intersects the 3 dB points at approximately plus and minus 25 degrees. Hence, the *3-dB beamwidth is approximately 50 degrees.* **ANSWER B**

FREE-SPACE PATTERN

14.200 MHz

Figure E9-1

E9B03 In the antenna radiation pattern shown in Figure E9-1, what is the front-to-back ratio?

A. 36 dB

B. 18 dB

C. 24 dB

D. 14 dB

If you look carefully at Figure E9-1, the *rear lobe is about -18 dB down from the front lobe.* **ANSWER B**

E9B04 In the antenna radiation pattern shown in Figure E9-1, what is the front-to-side ratio?

A. 12 dB

B. 14 dB

C. 18 dB

D. 24 dB

Study Figure E9-1 carefully, and go with 14 dB as the *front-to-side ratio.* Looking at the figure, this is not an exact measurement, so just stick *14 dB* in your brain before the test. Figure E9-1 will look exactly like it does here in the book when your VE team gives it to you as part of your test papers at your upcoming Extra Class exam. **ANSWER B**

FRONT LOBES

REAR LOBES

3 dB

BEAM DIRECTION

FOR FIGURE E9-1 THIS USEFUL BEAMWIDTH IS 50°

3 dB

Directional Radiation Pattern of a Yagi Beam

E9B05 What may occur when a directional antenna is operated at different frequencies within the band for which it was designed?
A. Feed-point impedance may become negative
B. The E-field and H-field patterns may reverse
C. Element spacing limits could be exceeded
D. The gain may exhibit significant variations

Building your own homebrew Yagi can teach some fundamental Yagi antenna concepts:

Close element spacing will yield narrow bandwidth response.

Directivity sharpness depends on parasitic-element tuning for maximum gain.

Boom length, not number of directors, influences gain the most.

A Yagi antenna with closely-spaced reflector and director elements may indeed maximize gain, but *overall gain may have significant variations* if your Yagi design is tuned to the bottom of the band and you begin to operate SSB at the top of the band, several hundred kHz away from your homebrew design. **ANSWER D**

E9B06 What usually occurs if a Yagi antenna is designed solely for maximum forward gain?
A. The front-to-back ratio increases
B. The front-to-back ratio decreases
C. The frequency response is widened over the whole frequency band
D. The SWR is reduced

On that brand new Yagi antenna you are computer modeling, the term "front to back ratio" is the ratio of the power radiated in the main lobe to the power being radiated in the opposite direction. As you work your computer antenna modeling program, you will quickly discover that *maximum forward gain will decrease the front to back ratio*. This is why some antenna experts will sacrifice a half db of forward gain to improve one or two nulls off the back of the beam. **ANSWER B**

E9B07 If the boom of a Yagi antenna is lengthened and the elements are properly retuned, what usually occurs?
A. The gain increases
B. The SWR decreases
C. The front-to-back ratio increases
D. The gain bandwidth decreases rapidly

Longer boom, more gain! **ANSWER A**

E9B08 How does the total amount of radiation emitted by a directional (gain) antenna compare with the total amount of radiation emitted from an isotropic antenna, assuming each is driven by the same amount of power?
A. The total amount of radiation from the directional antenna is increased by the gain of the antenna
B. The total amount of radiation from the directional antenna is stronger by its front to back ratio
C. There is no difference between the two antennas
D. The radiation from the isotropic antenna is 2.15 dB stronger than that from the directional antenna

This is a good question to get you thinking about the isotropic antenna – an antenna that radiates equally well in all directions. If you were to pump 100 watts into this theoretical antenna, you would get 100 watts out, unity gain, in every direction, including up and down. Now you switch to the beam antenna and presto, those 100 watts are focused in one direction, with minimum up and minimum down radiation.

By taking energy in all directions and concentrating it in just one direction with a beam, you have improved your signal on transmit and receive. But the total amount of radiation emitted is that same 100 watts at the feedpoint, so there is no magical new power created in the beam, and thus *there is no difference between the two antennas*. A *100 watt* light bulb hanging by a wire and a 100 watt bulb with a polished reflector *is still 100 watts*, right? Sure, but one bulb looks brighter, with the same amount of power, thanks to the reflector! **ANSWER C**

E3C07 How does the radiation pattern of a 3-element, horizontally polarized beam antenna vary with height above ground?
    A. The main lobe takeoff angle increases with increasing height
    B. The main lobe takeoff angle decreases with increasing height
    C. The horizontal beam width increases with height
    D. The horizontal beam width decreases with height

When you put up a 3-element Yagi antenna, the high frequency Yagi is usually mounted horizontally and the antenna should be mounted at least one-half wavelength above the ground on the lowest band of operation. Most 3-element Yagis feature tri-band operation for 10 meters, 15 meters and 20 meters. 20-meter band operation would like to see the antenna at a half wavelength off the earth, or about 32 feet in the air. *Anything lower than a half wavelength* from the operating frequency *dramatically raises the main lobe takeoff angle*, and the higher the takeoff angle, the shorter the skip distance. You want to get your beam up at least one-half wavelength above the earth for a nice low takeoff angle for long-range DX. **ANSWER B**

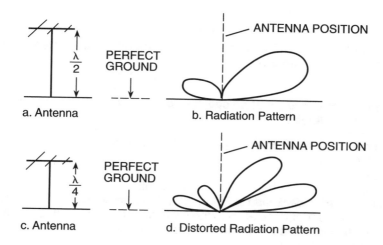

Radiation of 3-Element Yagi for Different Antenna Heights

E3C10 How does the performance of a horizontally polarized antenna mounted on the side of a hill compare with the same antenna mounted on flat ground?
    A. The main lobe takeoff angle increases in the downhill direction
    B. The main lobe takeoff angle decreases in the downhill direction
    C. The horizontal beam width decreases in the downhill direction
    D. The horizontal beam width increases in the uphill direction

If you live on the East coast, build your home and radio shack on a hill that slopes down to the ocean. Your beam will now have a main lobe whose takeoff angle decreases toward the ocean, giving you a dynamite signal to Europe. Here on the West coast, I am up on some headlands, with the ocean just down the way, giving me a good shot to Asia with the *lower takeoff angle in the downhill direction*. **ANSWER B**

E9C08 What type of antenna pattern over real ground is shown in Figure E9-2?

A. Elevation
B. Azimuth
C. Radiation resistance
D. Polarization

Figure E9-2 shows the *takeoff elevation* patterns of an antenna over a real ground source. **ANSWER A**

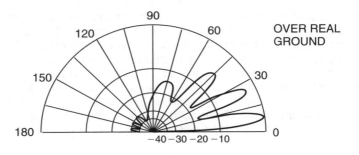

Figure E9-2

E9C09 What is the elevation angle of peak response in the antenna radiation pattern shown in Figure E9-2?

A. 45 degrees
B. 75 degrees
C. 7.5 degrees
D. 25 degrees

The main zero dB lobe is about 7.5 degrees up, with two other significant lobes at higher elevations. **ANSWER C**

E9C10 What is the front-to-back ratio of the radiation pattern shown in Figure E9-2?

A. 15 dB
B. 28 dB
C. 3 dB
D. 24 dB

The antenna *front-to-back ratio* in Figure E9-2 looks to be *about 28 to 30 dB*. This is the ratio of forward "front" radiation to the slight amount of unwanted radiation in the reverse direction from the back of the antenna. This ratio is the same for transmit as well as receive. **ANSWER B**

E9C11 How many elevation lobes appear in the forward direction of the antenna radiation pattern shown in Figure E9-2?

A. 4
B. 3
C. 1
D. 7

There are three big lobes, and one smaller lobe in the forward direction. **ANSWER A**

E9C14 How would the electric field be oriented for a Yagi with three elements mounted parallel to the ground?
A. Vertically
B. Horizontally
C. Right-hand elliptically
D. Left-hand elliptically

When we talk about antenna polarization, we always refer to the electric field. With its elements mounted parallel to the ground, this *Yagi is horizontally polarized*.
ANSWER B

E9D02 What is one way to produce circular polarization when using linearly polarized antennas?
A. Stack two Yagis, fed 90 degrees out of phase, to form an array with the respective elements in parallel planes
B. Stack two Yagis, fed in phase, to form an array with the respective elements in parallel planes
C. Arrange two Yagis perpendicular to each other with the driven elements at the same point on the boom and fed 90 degrees out of phase
D. Arrange two Yagis collinear to each other, with the driven elements fed 180 degrees out of phase

To get *circular polarization* out of a pair of Yagis, arrange the *Yagis perpendicular to each other*, with the driven elements in the same plane, and *fed 90 degrees out of phase*. **ANSWER C**

E9E01 What system matches a high-impedance transmission line to a lower impedance antenna by connecting the line to the driven element in two places spaced a fraction of a wavelength each side of element center?
    A. The gamma matching system
    B. The delta matching system
    C. The omega matching system
    D. The stub matching system
The *delta matching system* is a popular way *to change the impedance of the transmission line to the impedance of the antenna input.* **ANSWER B**

E9E02 What is the name of an antenna matching system that matches an unbalanced feed line to an antenna by feeding the driven element both at the center of the element and at a fraction of a wavelength to one side of center?
    A. The gamma match
    B. The delta match
    C. The omega match
    D. The stub match
A *gamma match* is used with coax cable that forms an *unbalanced feed system* going to a tube that acts as a capacitor in series with the connection point. **ANSWER A**

E9E03 What is the name of the matching system that uses a short perpendicular section of transmission line connected to the feed line near the antenna?

A. The gamma match
B. The delta match
C. The omega match
D. The stub match

When a short *section of transmission line* is connected to the antenna feed line near the antenna, it is called *stub matching*. Perhaps you used to cut a stub to cancel out interference in your TV receiver. **ANSWER D**

Impedance Matching Stubs

Quarter wavelength ($\frac{\lambda}{4}$) stubs

(or multiples of odd numbers of $\frac{\lambda}{4}$ s)

Less than $\frac{1}{4} \lambda$ stub

SHORT — Very High Resistance (Essentially **Open**) Like a Parallel Resonant Circuit — $\frac{1}{4}\lambda$

SHORT — INDUCTIVE [1] REACTANCE — Less than $\frac{\lambda}{4}$

OPEN — Very Low Resistance (Essentially a **Short**) Like a Series Resonant Circuit

OPEN — CAPACITIVE [2] REACTANCE

Half-wavelength ($\frac{\lambda}{2}$) stubs

(or multiples of $\frac{\lambda}{2}$ s)

Greater than $\frac{\lambda}{4}$, less than $\frac{\lambda}{2}$

Think of it as two $\frac{\lambda}{4}$ stubs in series.

Think of it as a $\frac{\lambda}{4}$ stub plus one less than $\frac{\lambda}{4}$.

SHORT OPEN SHORT — $\frac{\lambda}{4}$ $\frac{\lambda}{4}$

SHORT OPEN — CAPACITIVE REACTANCE — $\frac{\lambda}{4}$ Less than $\frac{\lambda}{4}$

OPEN SHORT OPEN

OPEN SHORT — INDUCTIVE REACTANCE

Notes
1. Since a short at end makes the diagram look like a long wire, this should remind the reader that impedance is an inductive reactance.
2. Since an open at end makes the diagram look like two parallel plates, this should remind the reader that impedance is a capacitive reactance.

E9E04 What is the purpose of the series capacitor in a gamma-type antenna matching network?

A. To provide DC isolation between the feed-line and the antenna
B. To compensate for the inductive reactance of the matching network
C. To provide a rejection notch to prevent the radiation of harmonics
D. To transform the antenna impedance to a higher value

In the *gamma match* antenna network, *capacitance* is sometimes achieved by a metal tube surrounding the coax cable center conductor. The gamma match *compensates for the inductive reactance* of the matching network, bringing feedpoint impedance near 50 Ohms to accept the direct coaxial cable connection. Be sure to coat the exposed coax cable connector with vulcanizing tape to keep moisture out. **ANSWER B**

E9E05 How must the driven element in a 3-element Yagi be tuned to use a hairpin matching system?

A. The driven element reactance must be capacitive
B. The driven element reactance must be inductive
C. The driven element resonance must be lower than the operating frequency
D. The driven element radiation resistance must be higher than the characteristic impedance of the transmission line

For the *hairpin matching system* to work well, the *driven element reactance must be capacitive, X_C.* **ANSWER A**

E9E06 What is the equivalent lumped-constant network for a hairpin matching system on a 3-element Yagi?

A. Pi network
B. Pi-L network
C. L network
D. Parallel-resonant tank

We would use an *L-network* to match a 3-element Yagi *for a hairpin matching system.* **ANSWER C**

E9E07 What parameter best describes the interactions at the load end of a mismatched transmission line?

A. Characteristic impedance
B. Reflection coefficient
C. Velocity factor
D. Dielectric Constant

A *mismatched* transmission line will give you *reflections.* **ANSWER B**

Impedance Mismatch Causes Reflected Wave

E9E08 Which of the following measurements describes a mismatched transmission line?

A. An SWR less than 1:1
B. A reflection coefficient greater than 1
C. A dielectric constant greater than 1
D. An SWR greater than 1:1

If the *SWR is greater than 1:1*, this describes a *mismatched* transmission line. See photo for SWR Bridge. **ANSWER D**

SWR Bridge

E9E09 Which of these matching systems is an effective method of connecting a 50-ohm coaxial cable feed-line to a grounded tower so it can be used as a vertical antenna?

A. Double-bazooka match
B. Hairpin match
C. Gamma match
D. All of these answers are correct

I have a grounded tower that I can use on 160 meters, running the cable about halfway up, into a *gamma match, that turns the tower into a halfwave antenna*! The outer braid taps the metal tower leg and I run the center conductor, extended, parallel to the same tower leg, and then making a sharp turn and connect it to the same leg, allowing for the impedance to match the transmission line. If you were to look at it with an ohm meter, it would look like a direct short – but if you work from an antenna book, your gamma match and a manual tuner can get you down to the band of choice. **ANSWER C**

E9E10 Which of these choices is an effective way to match an antenna with a 100-ohm terminal impedance to a 50-ohm coaxial cable feed-line?

A. Connect a 1/4-wavelength open stub of 300-ohm twin-lead in parallel with the coaxial feed-line where it connects to the antenna
B. Insert a 1/2 wavelength piece of 300-ohm twin-lead in series between the antenna terminals and the 50-ohm feed cable
C. Insert a 1/4-wavelength piece of 75-ohm coaxial cable transmission line in series between the antenna terminals and the 50-ohm feed cable
D. Connect 1/2 wavelength shorted stub of 75-ohm cable in parallel with the 50-ohm cable where it attaches to the antenna

n VHF and UHF antenna stacking, we many times end up with the combined antenna system presenting an impedance of 100 ohms, rather than 50 ohms, to feed the coax. *Calculate one quarter wavelength*, including coax velocity factor for your 75 ohm matching network (usually .66), *and insert it between the antenna terminals and the 50 ohm coax leading down to the ham shack.* **ANSWER C**

E9E11 What is an effective way of matching a feed-line to a VHF or UHF antenna when the impedances of both the antenna and feed-line are unknown?

    A. Use a 50-ohm 1:1 balun between the antenna and feed-line
    B. Use the "universal stub" matching technique
    C. Connect a series-resonant LC network across the antenna feed terminals
    D. Connect a parallel-resonant LC network across the antenna feed terminals

The *universal stub* takes unwanted reactance out of the driven portion of the antenna system, without actually computing impedances up the tower. You'll need to use your trusty portable SWR analyzer as you adjust the stiff bare wire shorting elements normally connected to the driven element. **ANSWER B**

E9E12 What is the primary purpose of a "phasing line" when used with an antenna having multiple driven elements?

    A. It ensures that each driven element operates in concert with the others to create the desired antenna pattern
    B. It prevents reflected power from traveling back down the feed-line and causing harmonic radiation from the transmitter
    C. It allows single-band antennas to operate on other bands
    D. It makes sure the antenna has a low-angle radiation pattern

As an Extra Class operator, you likely will choose an exotic, multiband beam antenna to exercise your new privileges. Multiband antennas have a variety of methods to phase most elements for the desired beam pattern. *"Trapless" designs may use rigid phasing lines to ensure each driven element operates in concert with all of the other elements on the antenna for the desired antenna pattern.* **ANSWER A**

Coaxial cable

E9E13 What is the purpose of a "Wilkinson divider"?
A. It divides the operating frequency of a transmitter signal so it can be used on a lower frequency band
B. It is used to feed high-impedance antennas from a low-impedance source
C. It divides power equally among multiple loads while preventing changes in one load from disturbing power flow to the others
D. It is used to feed low-impedance loads from a high-impedance source

With many high frequency antennas now incorporating multiple-band, driven elements, all off one feedline, the *Wilkinson divider distributes the antenna input power equally* to the multiple driven elements *while preventing one driven element from disturbing another.* **ANSWER C**

E9F08 What is the term for the ratio of the actual speed at which a signal travels through a transmission line to the speed of light in a vacuum?
A. Velocity factor
B. Characteristic impedance
C. Surge impedance
D. Standing wave ratio

Comparing the velocity of radio signals through a piece of feed line to the speed of light in a vacuum is called the *velocity factor* of the feed line. **ANSWER A**

E9F01 What is the velocity factor of a transmission line?
A. The ratio of the characteristic impedance of the line to the terminating impedance
B. The index of shielding for coaxial cable
C. The velocity of the wave in the transmission line multiplied by the velocity of light in a vacuum
D. The velocity of the wave in the transmission line divided by the velocity of light in a vacuum

In free space, radio waves travel at 300 million meters per second. But in coaxial cable transmission lines, and other types of feed lines, the radio waves move slower. *Velocity factor is the velocity of the radio wave on the transmission line divided by the velocity in free space.* **ANSWER D**

E9F02 What determines the velocity factor in a transmission line?
A. The termination impedance
B. The line length
C. Dielectric materials used in the line
D. The center conductor resistivity

There are some great low-loss coaxial cable types out there in radio land with different dielectrics separating the center conductor and the outside shield. It is the *type of dielectric* used that *determines the velocity factor.* **ANSWER C**

E9F04 What is the typical velocity factor for a coaxial cable with solid polyethylene dielectric?
A. 2.70
B. 0.66
C. 0.30
D. 0.10

Most coax cable has a velocity factory of 0.66. This is not stated on the outside jacket, and may not even be known by the dealer selling the coax. You can contact the manufacturer or distributor directly to find out the actual velocity factor. **ANSWER**

E9F03 Why is the physical length of a coaxial cable transmission line shorter than its electrical length?
- A. Skin effect is less pronounced in the coaxial cable
- B. The characteristic impedance is higher in a parallel feed line
- C. The surge impedance is higher in a parallel feed line
- D. Electrical signals move more slowly in a coaxial cable than in air

Radio frequency energy moves slightly *slower inside coaxial cable* than it does in free space. **ANSWER D**

E9F05 What is the physical length of a coaxial transmission line that is electrically one-quarter wavelength long at 14.1 MHz? (Assume a velocity factor of 0.66.)

A. 20 meters	C. 3.5 meters
B. 2.3 meters	D. 0.2 meters

When you work on antenna phasing harnesses, you will need to calculate the velocity factor for a piece of coax in order to know where to place the connectors. You must be accurate down to a fraction of an inch! You can calculate the physical length of a coax cable which is electrically one-quarter wavelength long using the formula:

$$L \text{ (in feet)} = \frac{984 \lambda V}{f}$$

Where: L is antenna length in **feet**
λ is wavelength in **meters**
V is **velocity factor**
f is frequency in **MHz**

For this problem, multiply 984 × 0.25, because the coax is one quarter wavelength. Then multiply the result by 0.66, the velocity factor. Remember, 0.66 is the velocity factor for coax. We are assuming that value for these problems. Divide the total by 14.1, the frequency in MHz. The length comes out to about 11.51 feet. The answer needs to be in meters, so divide 11.5 by 3 (there are about 3 feet to a meter). The result is 3.83, but the *3.5 meters* in answer C is the closest. (To calculate coax in meters, simply substitute 300 for 984. This will eliminate one step in the conversion!) **ANSWER C**

Proper coax cable length is important to maximize phased antenna performance.

E9F06 What is the physical length of a parallel conductor feed line that is electrically one-half wavelength long at 14.10 MHz? (Assume a velocity factor of 0.95.)

A. 15 meters   C. 10 meters
B. 20 meters   D. 71 meters

In this problem, the parallel conductor feed line one-half wavelength long at 14.10 MHz, with a velocity factor of .95, is calculated by multiplying *984 × 0.5 × 0.95 and dividing by 14.10,* the frequency in MHz. *Convert feet to meters, and you end up with 10 meters.* **ANSWER C**

E9F07 What characteristic will 450-ohm ladder line have at 50 MHz, as compared to 0.195-inch-diameter coaxial cable (such as RG-58)?

A. Lower loss   C. Smaller reflection coefficient
B. Higher SWR   D. Lower velocity factor

Going to 450-ohm ladder line on the 6-meter band is one way to reduce losses over typical RG-58 coax cable and keep your expenses to a minimum. They both cost about the same. RG-58 should be relegated to test leads, never used for antenna feedline runs. The loss is simply too high. *450 ohm ladder line will have much lower loss at 50 MHz than small RG-58 coax.* **ANSWER A**

Ladder Line   Coax

Outer Insulation

Copper Braid Shield
Inner Conductor
Polyethylene Dielectric

E9F09 What would be the physical length of a typical coaxial transmission line that is electrically one-quarter wavelength long at 7.2 MHz? (Assume a velocity factor of 0.66)

A. 10 meters   C. 24 meters
B. 6.9 meters   D. 50 meters

The coax cable is again one-quarter wavelength, so multiple 984 × 0.25, and the result by 0.66, the velocity factor. We again will assume this value. You must know it. Now divide these three multiplied figures by the frequency, 7.2 MHz, and you end up with 22.55 feet of coax. Dividing by 3 to get approximate length of 7.5 meters, leads you to *6.9 meters.* (See formula at E9F05) **ANSWER B**

E9F10 What kind of impedance does a 1/8-wavelength transmission line present to a generator when the line is shorted at the far end?

A. A capacitive reactance
B. The same as the characteristic impedance of the line
C. An inductive reactance
D. The same as the input impedance to the final generator stage

If a *1/8 wavelength transmission line is shorted out at the far end, it will look like an inductive reactance* at the generator. **ANSWER C**

E9F11 What kind of impedance does a 1/8-wavelength transmission line present to a generator when the line is open at the far end?
A. The same as the characteristic impedance of the line
B. An inductive reactance
C. A capacitive reactance
D. The same as the input impedance of the final generator stage

If that *1/8 wavelength transmission line is open at the far end*, it will look like a *capacitive reactance* at the generator. **ANSWER C**

E9F12 What kind of impedance does a 1/4-wavelength transmission line present to a generator when the line is open at the far end?
A. A very high impedance
B. A very low impedance
C. The same as the characteristic impedance of the line
D. The same as the input impedance to the final generator stage

If the far end of a *quarter-wavelength transmission line is open*, it will look like a *very low impedance* at the generator. **ANSWER B**

E9F13 What kind of impedance does a 1/4-wavelength transmission line present to a generator when the line is shorted at the far end?
A. A very high impedance
B. A very low impedance
C. The same as the characteristic impedance of the transmission line
D. The same as the generator output impedance

On a *quarter-wavelength transmission line, shorting it at the far end* will look like a *very high impedance* at the generator. **ANSWER A**

E9F14 What kind of impedance does a 1/2-wavelength transmission line present to a generator when the line is shorted at the far end?
A. A very high impedance
B. A very low impedance
C. The same as the characteristic impedance of the line
D. The same as the output impedance of the generator

If a *half-wavelength transmission line is shorted at the far end*, it will have a *very low impedance*, essentially a short. **ANSWER B**

E9F15 What kind of impedance does a 1/2-wavelength transmission line present to a generator when the line is open at the far end?
A. A very high impedance
B. A very low impedance
C. The same as the characteristic impedance of the line
D. The same as the output impedance of the generator

If that *half-wavelength transmission line is open at the far end*, it will have a *very high impedance*, essentially an open circuit. **ANSWER A**

Why is Characteristic Impedance So Important?

Let's look at this Figure to help us understand why the characteristic impedance, Z_0, of a transmission line is so important for the efficient transfer of energy. Figure a shows a transmitter coupled to an antenna with a transmission line that has a characteristic impedance of Z_0. The transmitter's output impedance is Z_T and the antenna input impedance is Z_A, the load impedance that the antenna presents to the transmission line.

a. Typical Transmission Line for Coupling Transmitter Power to Antenna

b. Open Circuit at Antenna — $Z_A = \infty$

Standing Wave Ratio (SWR) $= \dfrac{E_{max}}{E_{min}} =$ very large

c. Short Circuit at Antenna — $Z_A = 0$

Standing Wave Ratio (SWR) $= \dfrac{E_{max}}{E_{min}} =$ very large

d. Load $Z_A = \dfrac{Z_0}{3}$ at Antenna

Standing Wave Ratio (SWR) $= \dfrac{E_{max}}{E_{min}} = 3$

Voltage and Current constant along the line so that $\dfrac{V}{I} = Z_0$

e. Load $Z_A = Z_0$ at Antenna

No Reflected Wave

Standing Wave Ratio (SWR) $= \dfrac{E_{max}}{E_{min}} = 1$

All energy in incident wave is delivered and absorbed in load at antenna.

Let's assume that Z_A is infinity — in other words, the load on the transmission line at the antenna is an open circuit. Figure b is a diagram of the interconnection and shows the voltages and currents that exist on the transmission line. Since Z_A is an open circuit, the current at the end of the line is zero and the voltage is maximum. Since the wave of energy sent from the transmitter has no load to absorb the energy, it is reflected back to the transmitter. The voltage and current waveforms shown are the combined resultant of the wave from the transmitter (called the incident wave) and the reflected wave from the load end. In this case, the total wave is reflected back and no signal is transmitted.

Standing-Wave Ratio

The ratio of the maximum amplitude, E_{max}, of the resultant voltage waveform on the line to the minimum amplitude, E_{min}, is called the Standing-Wave Ratio, SWR, or more correctly the Voltage Standing-Wave Ratio, VSWR. In the case of an open load, since there is no energy absorbed at the load and all energy delivered is absorbed as losses in the line or absorbed by the transmitter's output resistance, the VSWR is very high (in the order of 20 or greater). VSWR is a measure of how well energy is being transferred over a transmission line to the load. VSWRs below 1.5 indicate quite efficient transfer of energy (VSWR = 1 is perfect), and VSWRs above 2 begin to indicate poor matching.

Now let's look at Figure c. Here the Z_A is a short circuit. That means the voltage is zero at the end of the line and the current is maximum. Again, no energy is absorbed by the load. It is all reflected back down the line. The voltage and current waveforms vary in minimums and maximums every quarter wavelength, as in the open-circuit case, but are 180° out of phase from the open-circuit case. The standing-wave ratio again is very large and no energy is transferred.

A Matched Case — ZA = Z0

Figure e is the case where all the energy in the incident wave is absorbed by the load. There is no reflected wave because $Z_A = Z_0$. The antenna load is matched to the characteristic impedance of the transmission line and maximum transfer of power from the transmitter to the antenna occurs. The standing-wave ratio is 1 because the voltage and current in the line are constant and are such that they equal Z_0 everywhere along the line. Thus, we see how important it is to match the load impedance to the transmission line Z_0. With $Z_A = Z_0$, there will be some small losses in the transmission line, but if there is a mismatch, energy will be reflected from the load back to the transmitter and large losses on the line will be dissipated as heat.

Source: *Basic Communications Electronics*, Hudson & Luecke, © 1999 Master Publishing, Inc., Niles, IL

E9F16 What is the primary difference between foam-dielectric coaxial cable as opposed to solid-dielectric cable, assuming all other parameters are the same?
A. Reduced safe operating voltage limits
B. Reduced losses per unit of length
C. Higher velocity factor
D. All of these answers are correct

When wiring your new ham station's antenna system, go with the best coaxial cable money can buy. On high frequency bands, coax cable losses are significantly less than operating on VHF and UHF. Popular RG-8 foam coax, on the 15 meter band, represents only 0.7 db loss per 100 feet. Foam coax is lighter weight than solid dielectric cable, but foam dielectric reduces safe operating voltage limits and has a slightly-higher velocity factor than solid dielectric. Recently, land mobile rated (LMR) coax cables, about the same size as RG-8, exhibit wonderful qualities of being lightweight, have a non-contaminating jacket to resist sunlight cracks, exhibit a common 0.66 velocity factor, and have slightly less attenuation on high frequency bands. It handles a little bit like a cold garden hose but, nonetheless, LMR type coax has plenty of benefits. *For this question, all of the answers are correct for the difference between foam dielectric coax and solid-dielectric coax.* **ANSWER D**

Coax Cable Type, Size and Loss per 100 Feet			
Coax Type	Size	Loss at HF 100 MHz	Loss at UHF 400 MHz
RG-6	Large	2.3 dB	4.7 dB
RG-59	Medium	2.9 dB	5.9 dB
RG-58U	Small	4.3 dB	9.4 dB
RG-8X	Medium	3.7 dB	8.0 dB
RG-8U	Large	1.9 dB	4.1 dB
RG-213	Large	1.9 dB	4.5 dB
Hardline	Large, Rigid	0.5 dB	1.5 dB

E4A07 Which of the following is an advantage of using an antenna analyzer vs. a SWR bridge to measure antenna SWR?
A. Antenna analyzers automatically tune your antenna for resonance
B. Antenna analyzers typically do not need an external RF source
C. Antenna analyzers typically display a time-varying representation of the modulation envelope
D. All of these answers are correct

Likely no other ham radio accessory product has offered ham radio experimenters a bigger breakthrough in measuring antenna and feedline SWR than the *antenna analyzer*. Credit goes to MFJ Corporation for their antenna analyzer – an inexpensive, battery-operated micro VFO transmitter that also has a built-in SWR bridge capable of spanning from 2 MHz through UHF. This allows you to check the antenna feedpoint impedance and resonance up on the roof, rather than going back to the ham shack and putting a big test signal out on the air. Since the *micro transmitter is built in* to the analyzer, *you don't need an actual radio transmitter to test your antenna system.* **ANSWER B**

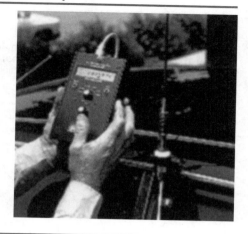

SWR Analyzer
Courtesy of MFJ Enterprises, Inc.

E4B12 How should a portable SWR analyzer be connected when measuring antenna resonance and feedpoint impedance?
A. Loosely couple the analyzer near the antenna base
B. Connect the analyzer via a high-impedance transformer to the antenna
C. Connect the antenna and a dummy load to the analyzer
D. Connect the antenna feedline directly to the analyzer's connector

When I am working on a rooftop mounted high-frequency antenna, I carry my trusty, portable *SWR antenna* analyzer and a *short jumper coax cable that feeds my analyzer directly to the antenna input.* The SWR antenna analyzer contains a signal generator that takes the place of the transmitter when testing an antenna or feedline, so it should be directly connected inline. **ANSWER D**

Frequency counter and SWR indicator
Courtesy of MFJ

E9G01 Which of the following can be calculated using a Smith chart?
A. Impedance along transmission lines
B. Radiation resistance
C. Antenna radiation pattern
D. Radio propagation

The *Smith Chart* (see chart at 252) is an invaluable graph for *calculating the impedance along Amateur Radio transmission lines.* Many times you will see a completed Smith Chart, generated by a computer, illustrating the resonance of a commercial-quality VHF or UHF collinear base station and repeater antenna. **ANSWER A**

Smith Chart—Finding Antenna Impedance

Finding Antenna Impedance, Z_A, when Fed with Known Length of Transmission Line (λ in Wavelengths) of Given Impedance, Z_O.
(Impedance and wavelength of transmission line are at the frequency of transmission)

Outer Wavelength Scales –
Clockwise – toward
generator
Counter clockwise –
toward the load

Point **A** = 1.5 − J0.6

C = 0.30λ

Plus (+)
X_L Values

Prime
Center

Z_{in}

Toward
Generator λ

SWR
Circles

Open
R = ∞
X = ∞

R Axis

Short
R = 0
X = 0

λ Toward
Load

Minus (−)
X_C Values

Z_A

D = 0.22λ

Constant R
Circles

Point **E** = 1.75 − J0.48

SWR Value

100 10 5 4 3 2 1.5 1.0

B = 1.85

Known Values: $Z_O = 50\Omega$, $\lambda_Z = 0.42\lambda$

Steps

1. Connect transmission line to antenna.
2. Measure the input impedance Z_{in} to transmission line. (Example 75 + J30)
3. Normalize Z_{in} by dividing by Z_O.

$$Z_{in} = \frac{75}{50} + J\frac{30}{50} = 1.5 + J0.6$$

4. Plot 1.5 + J0.6 on chart (point A is at intersection of a resistance circle of 1.5 and a positive reactance curve of 0.6)
5. Draw SWR circle with prime center as center and radius through A. Project tangent to SWR circle at point where circle intersects the resistance axis down to linear scale and read value of SWR (Point B = 1.85).
6. Draw a line (radial line) from prime center through Z_{in} at A and project to wavelength scale. Use "toward load" scale because you are going from Z_{in} at generator to the load presented by Antenna. (Point C = 0.30λ)

7. To find the load impedance line on the wavelength (towards load) scale, add the transmission line length to Point C value. (Point D = 0.42 + .30 = 0.72λ)
8. Since the wavelength scales are only plotted for 0.5λ, the values repeat every 0.5λ. Therefore, subtract 0.5 for 0.72 to arrive at 0.22. (Point D = 0.22 toward load)
9. Draw another radial line from prime center to Point D. The intersection with the SWR circle is the load impedance of the antenna. (Point E = 1.75 − J0.48). You may have to interpolate between lines.
10. This is still a normalized value so multiply by $Z_O = 50\Omega$ to obtain true value or antenna impedance. $Z_A = 50$ (1.75 − J0.48) = 87.5 − J24. Which is an impedance of 87.5 ohms of resistance and 24 ohms of capacitive reactance.

E4A08 Which of the following instruments would be best for measuring the SWR of a beam antenna?
    A. A spectrum analyzer   C. An ohmmeter
    B. A Q meter   D. An antenna analyzer

I always take my *portable antenna analyzer* when I go out for any ham radio station checkout. If I'm at the top of a sailboat mast, or up a tower, or down inside a boat's lazarette, my portable analyzer checks everything from automatic antenna tuners, marine VHF antennas, and the big 3-element beam up 90 feet in the air. **ANSWER D**

The AntennaSmith is an automatic antenna impedance analyzer. Built-in software allows you to instantly see the effect of an adjustment or a change made to your antenna system. No computer connection is required to see all the graphs – even the Smith chart – and the unit can run on battery power for use in the field.

E9G02 What type of coordinate system is used in a Smith chart?
    A. Voltage circles and current arcs
    B. Resistance circles and reactance arcs
    C. Voltage lines and current chords
    D. Resistance lines and reactance chords

If you look carefully at a *Smith Chart*, you will see *two circles – resistance circles centered on a resistance axis –* all tangent to an open circuit point (infinity resistance and infinity reactance), and portions of reactance circles fanning out from the resistance axis and passing through the same open circuit point. Inductive reactance curves are plotted positively from the resistance axis, and capacitive reactance curves negatively. **ANSWER B**

E9G03 Which of the following is often determined using a Smith chart?
    A. Beam headings and radiation patterns
    B. Satellite azimuth and elevation bearings
    C. Impedance and SWR values in transmission lines
    D. Trigonometric functions

Commercial-quality coaxial cable, coiled on a 500-foot spool, may also contain a *Smith Chart* that has been computer-generated to *show impedance and SWR value*. **ANSWER C**

E9G04 What are the two families of circles and arcs that make up a Smith chart?
A. Resistance and voltage
B. Reactance and voltage
C. Resistance and reactance
D. Voltage and impedance

Resistance and reactance values comprise the "two families of circles" on the Smith Chart. Circles for positive inductive reactance are to the right of the resistance axis in the figure below; circles for negative capacitance reactance are to the left of the resistance axis. **ANSWER C**

E9G05 What type of chart is shown in Figure E9-3?
A. Smith chart
B. Free-space radiation directivity chart
C. Elevation angle radiation pattern chart
D. Azimuth angle radiation pattern chart

The *Smith chart* is an excellent way of visualizing the contours of resistance or reactance. The chart is used for circuit analysis and provides a graphic presentation for this purpose. **ANSWER A**

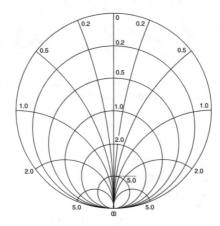

Figure E9-3

E9G06 On the Smith chart shown in Figure E9-3, what is the name for the large outer circle on which the reactance arcs terminate?
A. Prime axis   C. Impedance axis
B. Reactance axis   D. Polar axis

The *large outer circle is the reactance axis*. Within the reactance axis are curved reactance circles that are tangent to the resistance axis. Where the reactance circle intersects with the reactance axis, you will see an assigned value of reactance. Inductive reactance will be to the right, and capacitive reactance will be to the left. **ANSWER B**

E9G07 On the Smith chart shown in Figure E9-3, what is the only straight line shown?

A. The reactance axis
B. The current axis

C. The voltage axis
D. The resistance axis

On a *Smith chart, the straight line* is always the *resistance axis*. **ANSWER D**

E9G08 What is the process of normalization with regard to a Smith chart?

A. Reassigning resistance values with regard to the reactance axis
B. Reassigning reactance values with regard to the resistance axis
C. Reassigning impedance values with regard to the prime center
D. Reassigning prime center with regard to the reactance axis

In order that the Smith chart coordinate system apply to all types of transmission lines, the coordinates are "customized" to a particular transmission line by dividing test measurements by the characteristic impedance of the transmission line. This *process of reassigning resistance and reactance values with regard to the prime center is called "normalizing."* **ANSWER C**

E9G09 What third family of circles is often added to a Smith chart during the process of solving problems?

A. Standing-wave ratio circles
B. Antenna-length circles

C. Coaxial-length circles
D. Radiation-pattern circles

When a computer analyzes an antenna design, it will draw a *third family of circles on the Smith chart for standing-wave ratios*. **ANSWER A**

E9G10 What do the arcs on a Smith chart represent?

A. Frequency
B. SWR

C. Points with constant resistance
D. Points with constant reactance

The arcs (curved lines) on a Smith chart *are portions of reactance circles*. Remember that the large outer circle bounding the coordinate portion of the chart is the reactance axis. **ANSWER D**

E9G11 How are the wavelength scales on a Smith chart calibrated?

A. In fractions of transmission line electrical frequency
B. In fractions of transmission line electrical wavelength
C. In fractions of antenna electrical wavelength
D. In fractions of antenna electrical frequency

The *wavelength scales* on the Smith chart are calibrated in *portions of transmission line electrical wavelength*. **ANSWER B**

E9C04 Which of the following describes a basic rhombic antenna?

A. Unidirectional; four-sided, each side one quarter-wavelength long; terminated in a resistance equal to its characteristic impedance
B. Bidirectional; four-sided, each side one or more wavelengths long; open at the end opposite the transmission line connection
C. Four-sided; an LC network at each corner except for the transmission connection
D. Four-sided, each side of a different physical length

The *resonant rhombic antenna* is a *bidirectional* antenna where *each side is equal to one wavelength*. It is open at one end, with the transmission line connected to the other end. You better have a lot of wire for a resonant rhombic on 80 meters! **ANSWER B**

E9C05 What are the main advantages of a terminated rhombic antenna?
A. Wide frequency range, high gain and high front-to-back ratio
B. High front-to-back ratio, compact size and high gain
C. Unidirectional radiation pattern, high gain and compact size
D. Bidirectional radiation pattern, high gain and wide frequency range

A *terminated rhombic* antenna with the right terminating resistor will offer *wide frequency range, high gain, and high front-to-back ratio*. This is what you want. **ANSWER A**

E9C06 What are the disadvantages of a terminated rhombic antenna for the HF bands?
A. The antenna has a very narrow operating bandwidth
B. The antenna produces a circularly polarized signal
C. The antenna requires a large physical area and 4 separate supports
D. The antenna is more sensitive to man-made static than any other type

The big *disadvantage for the terminated rhombic* antenna for high frequency is the *very large area* it will occupy, and the necessity for a minimum of 4 sturdy supports for proper installation. You better have plenty of real estate! **ANSWER C**

Non-Resonant Rhombic Antenna

FEEDPOINT

EACH LEG = 1λ

HEIGHT ABOVE GROUND = $\frac{1}{2}\lambda$

The non-resonant rhombic antenna will use a non-inductive resistor to terminate the opposite end from the feedpoint. Feedpoint impedance is typically 600-900 ohms. The terminating non-inductive resistor should be around 800 ohms. The non-resonant rhombic radiates in a substantially uni-directional path toward the terminating resistor. But like its brother, the non-resonant rhombic requires plenty of real estate plus multiple poles to keep each leg absolutely straight.

E9C07 What is the effect of a terminating resistor on a rhombic antenna?
A. It reflects the standing waves on the antenna elements back to the transmitte
B. It changes the radiation pattern from bidirectional to unidirectional
C. It changes the radiation pattern from horizontal to vertical polarization
D. It decreases the ground loss

A *terminating resistor* at the opposite end of the rhombic from the feedline *changes* the *radiation pattern* from essentially bidirectional *to unidirectional.* **ANSWER B**

Decibels

It is important to know about decibels because they are used extensively in electronics. Look at the derivation for decibels and note it is a measure of the ratio of two powers, P_1 and P_2. Remember the power changes for different dB values. Also, since 6 dB is a four times change, 16 dB (6 dB + 10 dB) will be a $4 \times 10 = 40$ times change, and 26 dB (6 dB + 20 dB) will be a $4 \times 100 = 400$ times change. Thus, any dB value from 10 dB and above can be evaluted by using the power change of 1 dB to 9 dB and multiplying it by the 10 dB, 20 dB, 30 dB, 40 dB, 50 dB, 60 dB, etc. change. Thus, 57 dB (7 dB + 50 dB) will be a $5 \times 100,000 = 500,000$ times change.

dB	Power Change $\dfrac{P_1}{P_2}$		dB	Power Change $\dfrac{P_1}{P_2}$	
1 dB	1 ¼X	Power change	8 dB	6 ¼X	Power change
2 dB	1 ½X	Power change	9 dB	8X	Power change
3 dB	2X	Power change	10 dB	10X	Power change
4 dB	2 ½X	Power change	20 dB	100X	Power change
5 dB	3X	Power change	30 dB	1000X	Power change
6 dB	4X	Power change	40 dB	10,000X	Power change
7 dB	5X	Power change	50 dB	100,000X	Power change
			60 dB	1,000,000X	Power change

Derivation:

If $dB = 10 \log_{10} \dfrac{P_1}{P_2}$

then what power ratio is 60 dB?

$$60 = 10 \log_{10} \dfrac{P_1}{P_2}$$

$$\dfrac{60}{10} = \log_{10} \dfrac{P_1}{P_2}$$

$$6 = \log_{10} \dfrac{P_1}{P_2}$$

Remember: logarithm of a number is the exponent to which the base must be raised to get the number.

$$\therefore 10^6 = \dfrac{P_1}{P_2}$$

$$1,000,000 = \dfrac{P_1}{P_2}$$

Or $P_1 = 1,000,000 \, P_2$

60 dB means P_1 is one million times P_2

E9H04 What term describes station output (including the transmitter, antenna and everything in between), when considering transmitter power and system gains and losses?
A. Power factor
B. Half-power bandwidth
C. Effective radiated power
D. Apparent power

It's important to always calculate *effective radiated power* when you set up your ham station. This table shows you the dB's you could lose with cheap coax cable, and the valuable dB's you can gain by using a quality collinear VHF or UHF antenna. **ANSWER C**

E9H01 What is the effective radiated power of a repeater station with 150 watts transmitter power output, 2-dB feed line loss, 2.2-dB duplexer loss and 7-dBd antenna gain?
A. 1977 watts
B. 78.7 watts
C. 420 watts
D. 286 watts

Our total loss is about 4.2 dB, and our total gain is 7 dB. This is *an approximate 3 dB overall gain*, and this almost *doubles your 150 watts to an approximate 286 watts*. **ANSWER D**

E9H02 What is the effective radiated power of a repeater station with 200 watts transmitter power output, 4-dB feed line loss, 3.2-dB duplexer loss, 0.8-dB circulator loss and 10-dBd antenna gain?

A. 317 watts   C. 126 watts
B. 2000 watts   D. 300 watts

Our total loss is 8 dB, and our total gain is 10 dB gain. This gives us a net gain of 2 dB; therefore, from chart we have a gain of 1.585 times. Therefore, with 200 watts input, *the ERP is 317 watts (200 × 1.585).*

To check your answer, remember

E $dB = 10 \log_{10} \dfrac{P_1}{P_2}$ where: P_1 = Power Output
P_2 = Power Input

Therefore,

$$dB = 10 \log_{10} \frac{317}{200}$$

$$dB = 10 \log_{10} 1.585 \qquad \text{The } \log_{10} \text{ of } 1.585 \text{ is } 0.2$$

$$dB = 10 \times 0.2 = 2$$

Since the output power is 317 watts and the input power is 200 watts, there is a net gain of 2 dB. **ANSWER A**

E9H03 What is the effective radiated power of a repeater station with 200 watts transmitter power output, 2-dB feed line loss, 2.8-dB duplexer loss, 1.2-dB circulator loss and 7-dBd antenna gain?

A. 159 watts   C. 632 watts
B. 252 watts   D. 63.2 watts

Here is our last calculation with dB values. Our total loss adds up to a 6 dB loss, and our total gain is 7 dB, for an actual *gain of 1 dB*. This would be a slight increase to our 200 watts output in effective radiated power, so *ERP is 252 watts.* **ANSWER B**

E0A04 When evaluating a site with multiple transmitters operating at the same time, the operators and licensees of which transmitters are responsible for mitigating over-exposure situations?

A. Only the most powerful transmitter
B. Only commercial transmitters
C. Each transmitter that produces 5% or more of its maximum permissible exposure limit at accessible locations
D. Each transmitter operating with a duty-cycle greater than 50%

If you are setting up a new repeater station on a mountaintop with many other transmitters, and *if your station produces 5 % or more of the maximum permissible* exposure at that location, it will be *your responsibility for mitigating* this 5% over of the maximum permissible exposure. **ANSWER C**

E9D01 How does the gain of a parabolic dish antenna change when the operating frequency is doubled?

A. Gain does not change
B. Gain is multiplied by 0.707
C. Gain increases 6 dB
D. Gain increases 3 dB

From 1270 MHz on up, you may wish to use a *parabolic dish antenna* for microwave work. If you *double the frequency, the gain of the dish increases by 6 dB, a 4 times increase.* **ANSWER C**

Gordo's Parabolic Antenna for 10GHz Tropo

E9D03 How does the beamwidth of an antenna vary as the gain is increased?
A. It increases geometrically
B. It increases arithmetically
C. It is essentially unaffected
D. It decreases

The parabolic dish concentrates that beamwidth as gain increases. The *higher the gain of a dish, the narrower the beamwidth*. Beamwidth decreases as gain increases. **ANSWER D**

E9D04 Why is it desirable for a ground-mounted satellite communications antenna system to be able to move in both azimuth and elevation?
A. In order to track the satellite as it orbits the Earth
B. So the antenna can be pointed away from interfering signals
C. So the antenna can be positioned to cancel the effects of Faraday rotation
D. To rotate antenna polarization to match that of the satellite

You need both an *azimuth* as well as an *elevation* rotor control to *track the satellites* up in orbit. I hope you will also join AMSAT to support amateur satellites – visit www.amsat.org to learn more. **ANSWER A**

E0A11 Which of these items might be a significant hazard when operating a klystron or cavity magnetron transmitter?
A. Hearing loss caused by high voltage corona discharge
B. Blood clotting from the intense magnetic field
C. Injury from radiation leaks that exceed the MPE limits
D. Ingestion of ozone gas from the cooling system

Any time you are working around microwave klystrons or cavity magnetron tubes in a transmitter, be cautious about *RF radiation* leaks that *could exceed the maximum permissible exposure (MPE) limits*. We want you around for a long time as a new Amateur Extra Class ham radio operator. **ANSWER C**

E0A10 What material found in some electronic components such as high-voltage capacitors and transformers is considered toxic?
A. Polychlorinated biphenyls
B. Polyethylene
C. Polytetrafluroethylene
D. Polymorphic silicon

You know the dangers of power pole transformers that contain *PCBs (PolyChlorinated Biphenyls)*. **ANSWER A**

E0A05 What is one of the potential hazards of using microwaves in the amateur radio bands?
A. Microwaves are ionizing radiation
B. The high gain antennas commonly used can result in high exposure levels
C. Microwaves often travel long distances by ionospheric reflection
D. The extremely high frequency energy can damage the joints of antenna structures

I run 10 GHz microwave, and a relatively large 20 dB dish antenna, and I am always cautious to never let anyone stand in *the antenna main lobe when transmitting.* I don't want to *"cook" my neighbors with my microwave transmissions!* **ANSWER B**

E0A03 Which of the following would be a practical way to estimate whether the RF fields produced by an amateur radio station are within permissible MPE limits?
A. Use a calibrated antenna analyzer
B. Use a hand calculator plus Smith-chart equations to calculate the fields
C. Walk around under the antennas with a neon-lamp probe to find the strongest fields
D. Use a computer-based antenna modeling program to calculate field strength at accessible locations

Antenna literature that comes with your new beam may not show calculations for field strength near the station, but if you use a *computer-based antenna modeling software* program showing your new specific antenna system, and where it's located, and where it's aimed, and your power output, you *can accurately calculate field strength from your station.* **ANSWER D**

E0A08 What does SAR measure?
A. Synthetic Aperture Ratio of the human body
B. Signal Amplification Rating
C. The rate at which RF energy is absorbed by the body
D. The rate of RF energy reflected from stationary terrain

SAR stands for *Specific Absorption Rate*, the rate at which RF *energy is absorbed by the human body.* **ANSWER C**

E0A02 When evaluating exposure levels from your station at a neighbor's home, what must you do?
A. Make sure signals from your station are less than the controlled MPE limits
B. Make sure signals from your station are less than the uncontrolled MPE limits
C. Nothing; you need only evaluate exposure levels on your own property
D. Advise your neighbors of the results of your tests

Your *neighbor's house is considered "uncontrolled"* when calculating maximum permissible exposure limits. Always make sure you do the calculations before putting up your new antenna system, and make absolutely sure you are always less than the uncontrolled MPE limit rule. **ANSWER B**

E0A06 Why are there separate electric (E) and magnetic (H) field MPE limits?
A. The body reacts to electromagnetic radiation from both the E and H fields
B. Ground reflections and scattering make the field impedance vary with location
C. E field and H field radiation intensity peaks can occur at different locations
D. All of these answers are correct

Radio transmissions contain both an *electric field* as well as a *magnetic field*. These field radiations *may peak at different distances* from the antenna plus *ground reflections and scattering will vary the field intensity as well*. Also, the *human body reacts differently to E and H fields*, so do your calculations for both magnetic and electric fields. **ANSWER D**

E9C13 When constructing a Beverage antenna, which of the following factors should be included in the design to achieve good performance at the desired frequency?
A. Its overall length must not exceed 1/4 wavelength
B. It must be mounted more than 1 wavelength above ground
C. It should be configured as a four-sided loop
D. It should be one or more wavelengths long

The *Beverage antenna* is a tremendous signal-grabber and radiator, but for best performance, it *really needs to be L O N G!* The longer the better for a Beverage antenna. **ANSWER D**

E9H09 What is a receiving loop antenna?
A. A large circularly-polarized antenna
B. A small coil of wire tightly wound around a toroidal ferrite core
C. One or more turns of wire wound in the shape of a large open coil
D. Any antenna coupled to a feed line through an inductive loop of wire

A receiving loop antenna, for ham radio receive purposes, is usually many turns of wire wound in the shape of a large open coil or square loop. The more turns you add, the greater the gain of the receiving loop antenna. Most modern, high-frequency transceivers offer a separate antenna port for your homebrew *"one or more turns of wire"* large open-coil antenna. **ANSWER C**

E9H10 How can the output voltage of a receiving loop antenna be increased?
A. By reducing the permeability of the loop shield
B. By increasing the number of wire turns in the loop and reducing the area of the loop structure
C. By reducing either the number of wire turns in the loop or the area of the loop structure
D. By increasing either the number of wire turns in the loop or the area of the loop structure

To *make a loop antenna more powerful*, either *increase the number of wire turns* in the loop or *make the loop physically larger*. **ANSWER D**

E9H11 Why is an antenna with a cardioid pattern desirable for a direction-finding system?

- A. The broad-side responses of the cardioid pattern can be aimed at the desired station
- B. The response characteristics of the cardioid pattern can assist in determining the direction of the desired station
- C. The extra side lobes in the cardioid pattern can pinpoint the direction of the desired station
- D. The high-radiation angle of the cardioid pattern is useful for short-distance direction finding

A *cardioid pattern* is shaped like a heart. There is a broad *reception pattern in one direction and a deep null in the other*. When the button is pushed to "sense" the direction of the incoming signal on a direction-finding system that has a cardioid antenna pattern, the deep null in the pattern is normally 180 degrees away from the incoming signal. It's easier to use the null point to sense the signal direction of the incoming signal than it is the broad pattern – look for the minimum signal, not the maximum. **ANSWER B**

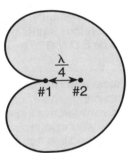

Two 1/4 wave vertical antennas fed 90-degrees out of phase will have a cardioid radiation pattern. The deep null will be 180-degrees from the transmitter, and is very helpful in direction-finding.

E9H12 What is an advantage of using a shielded loop antenna for direction finding?

- A. It automatically cancels ignition noise pickup in mobile installations
- B. It is electro-statically balanced against ground, giving better nulls
- C. It eliminates tracking errors caused by strong out-of-band signals
- D. It allows stations to communicate without giving away their position

Transmitter hunting down on 75 meters is an international sport. Most operators use a shielded loop antenna for T-hunting because the *shielding offers better directivity.* **ANSWER B**

E9H05 What is the main drawback of a wire-loop antenna for direction finding?

- A. It has a bidirectional pattern
- B. It is non-rotatable
- C. It receives equally well in all directions
- D. It is practical for use only on VHF bands

Wire loop direction finding antennas will pick up maximum signal strength when the loop is broadside to the signal source. It is *bi-directional* – it will pick up noise sources on either side of the loop. **ANSWER A** www.lwca.org

E9H07 Why is an RF attenuator desirable in a receiver used for direction finding?

A. It narrows the bandwidth of the received signal
B. It eliminates the effects of isotropic radiation
C. It reduces loss of received signals caused by antenna pattern nulls
D. It prevents receiver overload from extremely strong signals

When using a receiver for direction finding, a step adjustable or variable adjustable attenuator is necessary on the input when you get extremely close to the signal source. You *add additional attenuation* in order *to keep your receiver from overloading* as you maintain maximum sensitivity for signal variations as the antenna direction is changed. **ANSWER D** www.homingin.com

E9H08 What is the function of a sense antenna?

A. It modifies the pattern of a DF antenna array to provide a null in one direction
B. It increases the sensitivity of a DF antenna array
C. It allows DF antennas to receive signals at different vertical angles
D. It provides diversity reception that cancels multipath signals

On high frequency automatic radio direction finder systems, the double loop may employ an additional rigid whip to act as a *sense antenna*. Push the ADF sense button and the fixed double loop DF (direction finding) *antenna will null out* ambiguity as to which way the incoming signal is arriving from at that double loop. The sense antenna must be rigid, and never a flexing whip. **ANSWER A**

E9H06 What is the triangulation method of direction finding?

A. The geometric angle of sky waves from the source are used to determine its position
B. A fixed receiving station plots three headings from the signal source on a map
C. Antenna headings from several different receiving stations are used to locate the signal source
D. A fixed receiving station uses three different antennas to plot the location of the signal source

Amateur radio operators participating in a joint "T-hunt" will swing their beams and record a magnetic bearing to where signal strength is the greatest. *Through triangulation, they can then determine the approximate location of the transmitting station.* All participating stations should agree to use either magnetic north or true north for their heading directions. **ANSWER C**

Gordo and Chip, K7JA, fox-hunting with a 2-meter cubical quad antenna.

Taking the Extra Class Examination

Get set to pass the Element 4 examination and gain additional kilohertz of band privileges as an Extra Class operator! If you are upgrading from General to Extra Class, you will gain a whopping 500 kHz of *additional* frequencies on the 75/80-meter, 40-meter, 20-meter, and 15-meter worldwide service bands. If you are upgrading from a grandfathered Advanced Class license, you will gain an *additional* 250 kHz of operating area on the 75/80-meter, 40-meter, 20-meter, and 15-meter worldwide amateur service bands. Your Extra Class license gives you full privileges and full frequency coverage on every amateur service band assigned by the Federal Communications Commission.

In this chapter, we'll tell you how to prepare yourself for the exam, what to expect when you take the exam, and how you'll get your new, upgraded Extra Class license.

EXAMINATION ADMINISTRATION

Three Extra Class accredited Volunteer Examiners are required to administer your Element 4 exam. Many of you preparing for your Extra Class examination are already part of a Volunteer Examination team. If you are, it's perfectly acceptable to allow your fellow team members to administer a computer-generated, fresh Extra Class written theory examination.

Let's take a moment to review how well the Volunteer Examination program is working. The examination sessions are coordinated by national or regional Volunteer Examiner Coordinators (VECs) who accredit General Class, Advanced Class and Extra Class amateur operators as Volunteer Examiners (VEs). Your Extra Class examination **must** be taken at an official examination session in front of a team of three accredited Extra Class VEs.

The Volunteer Examiners are not compensated for their time and skills, but they are permitted to charge you an examination fee for certain reimbursable expenses incurred in preparing, administering, and processing the examination. The maximum fee is adjusted annually based on inflation by the Federal Communications Commission. It is currently about $14.00.

HOW TO FIND AN EXAM SITE

Exam sessions are held regularly at sites throughout the country to serve their local communities. The exam site could be a public library, a fire house, someone's office, in a warehouse, and maybe even in someone's private home. Each examination team may regularly post their examination locations down at the local ham radio store. They also inform their VEC when and where they regularly hold test sessions. So the easiest way for you to find an exam session that is near you and at a convenient time is to call the VEC.

A complete list of VECs is located on page 273 in the Appendix of this book. The W5YI VEC and the ARRL VEC are the two largest examination groups in the country. They test in all 50 states and in foreign countries, too. Their 3-member, accredited examination teams are just about *everywhere*. So when you call the W5YI-VEC in Texas, or the ARRL-VEC in Connecticut, be assured they probably have an examination team only a few miles from where you are reading this book right now!

Want to find a test site fast?
Visit the W5YI-VEC website at www.w5yi.org, or call them at 800-669-9594.

Any of the VECs listed will provide you with the phone number of a local Volunteer Examiner team leader who can tell you the schedule of upcoming exam sessions near you. Select a session you wish to attend, and make a reservation so the VEs know to expect you. Don't be a "no-show" and don't be a "surprise-show." Make a reservation. And don't hesitate to tell them how much we all appreciate their efforts in supporting ham radio testing.

Ask them ahead of time what you will need to bring to the examination session. And ask them how much the current fee is for your exam session.

WHAT TO BRING TO THE SITE

Here is what you'll need to bring with you to the exam site for your upgrade from General or grandfathered Advanced to Extra Class:

1. The original and 2 copies of your present General or grandfathered Advanced Class license, or any CSCE issued within the last 365 days confirming examination credit. If you show up without your present license or copies of your present license, your examination or examination results could be put on a major hold.
2. A picture ID. Usually your Driver's License will suffice. Kids should bring their school ID, and very young kids should bring an adult to verify that they are who they are!
3. An examination fee of approximately $14.00 in cash, *exact change, please*. Personal checks will not be accepted, and plastic is out of the question. Ask the VE how much the fee will be when call to make your exam reservation.
4. If you have a physical disability that may require additional assistance by your examination team, let them know ahead of time so they may prepare an examination that accommodates your special requirements. This could be special reading equipment, a volunteer examiner reader, access for a wheelchair, or any other special requirements that they may be able to set up for you. But they must know ahead of time what requirements need to be met, so please contact the volunteer examiner team leader in advance.

5. You will definitely want to **bring your calculator**. Calculators are indeed permitted and quite necessary for the Extra Class exam. Since some of the questions are from the old Advanced test, you can be sure you will have at least 8 or 10 formula problems to work on the calculator keys. The Volunteer Examination team leader may ask you to remove the battery from the calculator in order to verify memory dump. Don't be surprised if they ask you to completely clear your calculator in this fashion.

6. Bring plenty of sharp pencils and a fine-tip pen. Have backups. No red ink, please.

Try to arrive at the examination location about an hour before the exam begins. Introduce yourself to the Volunteer Examiners who will be conducting the test, and see if they need a hand in setting up the room. If it is a morning examination, Gordon West Radio School students usually bring donuts, hot coffee, tea, and hot chocolate for the Volunteer Examiners as a way of expressing their appreciation for the time and effort the examiners expend arranging and giving these tests. Start their day off with a smile and go for a dozen donuts! Believe me, they will appreciate the thought.

RUMOR MILL

While standing in line ready to enter the examination room, rumors usually begin to fly. Someone who is ill-informed may say they are still requiring the 20-wpm code test for Extra. Nonsense!

Someone may remark that all of the test questions have been changed, and this "new" 2008 test is different than the book. Nonsense! Again, the questions in this Extra Class book are valid from July 1, 2008, through June 30, 2012.

Someone comes out of the exam room indicating the Extra Class test had numerous questions not found in his book. Again, ridiculous! This book has every single test question, exactly as they will appear on the test. Only the A, B, C, and D order of the possible answers may be scrambled.

TAKING THE EXAMINATION

Get a good night's sleep before the exam day. Continue to study the Extra Class formulas right up to the moment you go into the examination room. Don't believe that old saying that too much study will cause you to forget the subject material. If you purchased my audio CD course, continue to play them up to the last minute.

Listen carefully for the instructions of your Volunteer Examiners. Most examination sessions will conduct all levels of testing, so stay tuned in on the announcements they give on who should come forward to pick up what type of test materials.

Make no marks on the examination sheet. If you don't know an answer, slightly shade in one of the answer sheet boxes, and make yourself a big note to go back and work out the correct answer. Using this technique will keep you from accidentally skipping a hard question, and misaligning your answer boxes with the easier questions. If you finish the exam at question #49, chances are you skipped a question and all of your work will be out of synch with your answer sheet. Double check that all 50 answer boxes indeed have a mark.

When you are taking the written examination, *take your time!* Some answers stand out looking correct, but end up wrong at the end. Don't speed read the exam – getting careless after all this preparation could undo all the hard work you have put in on preparing for the Extra Class exam.

If you don't know an answer, eliminate the obviously wrong answers, and then take your best guess. NEVER LEAVE AN ANSWER BLANK! Leaving a specific answer blank is counted as a wrong answer. We also find that going back and second-guessing an answer will sometimes get you into the wrong answer category. Usually your first impression is the correct one. Another trick is to read your answer first and then see if it agrees with what the question asks. Start this technique at Answer 50, and go backwards.

AND THE RESULTS ARE...

When you are satisfied that you have passed the Extra Class exam, turn in all of your examination papers – including scratch paper and the original test paper. Thank your examiners for their courtesy, and follow their instructions while they prepare to score your paper. *Don't stand over the examiners* as they grade your test.

When you pass the test, the examiners may or may not indicate how many questions you missed. You missed only one? But which one? DON'T ASK – the examiners may tell you it is against the rules to divulge which question you got wrong, although we're not aware of any rule that states they cannot tell you what you got wrong. It's usually just a case of not enough time to spend with any one applicant pouring over their test performance. They usually will tell you your test score, and passing the exam is exactly what you want to hear!

Since we know you are going to be successful in your Extra Class written exam, we know that your examiners will issue you an official CSCE – Certificate of Successful Completion of Examination. This is an important document that is official proof that you have passed the exam. Check to see that it is signed by all three volunteer examiners. Did they get your name and call sign correct on the certificate? Write in your address if all they have is your name on the certificate, and be sure to sign your CSCE. Double-check that the date is correct. If the computer system should gobble up all of your test results, this is LEGAL PROOF that you indeed passed a particular examination element.

COMPLETING NCVEC FORM 605

Your examiners will assist you in filling out the NCVEC Form 605. They also will have copies of the most current version of this form at the examination session. (See sample form on page 276.) *Be aware that this form is **not** FCC form 605*, which is not suitable for use when taking an amateur radio examination or for changing an address, name, routine call sign change, or renewing your license through a VEC. Note that NCVEC Form 605 asks for your Social Security Number. Look at the copy of your current ham radio license and spot the numbers that show your Federal Registration Number (FRN). These numbers go in place of where they ask for your Social Security Number on the application. If this is your FIRST ham radio test, along with Technician and General Class, you will initially need to enter your Social Security number. If you have a current callsign, you most likely have the FRN, and this number and this number goes in place of your SSN

It is very important that you complete the NCVEC Form 605 legibly – preferably in black or blue ball-point pen. If the VEC and VE examiners cannot read the information you have written down, your upgrade could be delayed in the electronic processing phase.

When you are filling-out NCVEC Form 605, it is important to compare the information on your present license with what you are writing on the Form 605. Any difference in your name or address requires that you check the appropriate CHANGE box. For example, if your current license reads "Jack" as your first name and you write down "John" on Form 605, your application will automatically be rejected when it is filed electronically. Same thing for your middle initial – does it appear on your original license? And make certain that your signature matches your name. Be sure to date the application.

Only fill out the top portion (Section 1) of NCVEC Form 605 when taking an examination. Section 2 (certifying section) is completed by the Volunteer Examiners after you complete the examination.

CHANGING CALL SIGNS

After passing the Extra Class exam, you have an opportunity to change your call sign systematically. Most examinees keep the one they have. If you check the box "CHANGE my station call sign systematically," the FCC computer will assign you the next Group "A" call sign from an alphabetized list.

The key word is *systematically.* You will not get to choose a specific call sign at an examination session. If you live in the continental United States, your assigned Group "A" systematic call sign will be in a 2-by-2 format with the first letter being "A." A 2-by-2 format has two letters followed by

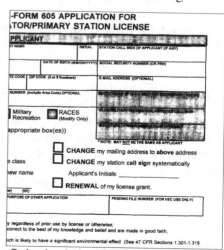

Only check the "CHANGE" my station call sign box if you want the FCC computer to give you a new call sign. If you want to choose a call sign, apply for a vanity call.

a numeral and two more letters, such as AK6CS. Only the AA through AL block is assigned since AM through AZ 2-by-2 letters are not internationally allocated for use in the U.S. Once all 2-by-2 Group "A" call signs are assigned (the last will be AK1ZZ if you are in the first call district), the FCC then assigns call signs from the next lower (Group B) level to Extra Class amateurs. These will be 2-by-2 call signs beginning with K, N and W.

You must initial the request if you decide to systematically change your call sign. Once changed, it cannot easily be changed back to your previous call sign. The only way you can go back to a previously-held call sign is under the Vanity call sign program and this will cost you a small fee. So be thinking about it right now – do you want to stay with your present call sign, or do you want to change over to a new Extra Class 2-by-2 call sign?

VANITY CALL SIGNS

The ability to select a vacant station call sign of your choice began in 1996 and it has been immensely popular, especially with Extra Class amateurs who historically like to have short call signs. While only a little more than 10% of all radio amateurs ever make it to the top Extra Class level, they hold nearly half of all Vanity call signs issued!

Extra Class radio amateurs can choose an available station call sign containing any Group, A, B, C or D Amateur format. Most try to get a 1-by-2 or a 2-by-1 format, which are only available to an Extra Class licensee. A 1-by-2 Group "A" call sign begins with either K, N or W (but not "A") followed by a numeral and two letters. For example: W5YI is a Group "A" call sign.

An example of a 2-by-1 call sign is AA1A. The two letter prefix must be from the AA to AL, KA to KZ, NA to NZ or the WA to WZ prefix block followed by a numeral and a single letter. To make matters more confusing, certain prefixes (AH, AL, KH, KL, KP, NH, NL, NP, WH, WL and WP) are reserved for amateurs who have a mailing address outside of the 48 contiguous U.S. states.

You can find out all the rules (and there are many!) surrounding obtaining a Vanity call sign by visiting the W5YI Group website at www.w5yi.org and clicking on the "Vanity Call Signs" button near the top of the home page.

There is an additional regulatory fee associated with a Vanity call sign of about $12.00. You can complete FCC Form 605 (not NCVEC Form 605) and accompanying Form 159 (Remittance Advice) and file the application yourself either using paper documents or online. Additional information on Vanity call signs is available from the FCC's Amateur Radio website located at:

http://wireless.fcc.gov/services/amateur/licensing/vanity.html

An easier way to get a Vanity call sign is to let the W5YI Group handle everything for you. They charge a small, additional fee and do all the paperwork and filing for you. You can obtain complete details on this service by going to: www.w5yi.org/vanity.htm

As for me, I'm staying with my original-issue WB6NOA call sign. If I changed it, I would be breaking a 40+ year tradition.

GOING FURTHER - GROL

The Extra Class license is the highest level license you can achieve in the Amateur Radio service. Did you know you can also take the commercial general radio operator (GROL) license exams, too? The commercial license allows you to work on marine and aeronautical two-way radio equipment, and the commercial GROL license often is required by two-way radio employers before being hired.

And guess what? The GROL technical element uses almost identical test questions as those you have just studied for your amateur Extra Class license. In fact, except for just a couple of numbers, the commercial radiotelephone examination may use identical math problems that you just studied.

So, why not upgrade to a professional-level FCC license? You can order the *GROL-Plus* book by calling the W5YI Group at 800-669-9594.

BECOMING A VOLUNTEER EXAMINER

When you successfully complete your Extra Class exam, ask your 3-member accredited Volunteer Examination team for a volunteer examiner sign-up application. It only takes a couple of weeks to process, and you'll be joining a cadre of thousands of other Extra Class hams who give something back to ham radio when it comes to testing – just a few hours a month, and some paper and computer processing. It is a rewarding "extra credit" as an Extra Class operator, and you and two other accredited examiners could even give tests abroad all over the world.

Accredited Volunteer Examiners also may help develop new questions when the amateur radio question pools undergo periodic updating. Your comments and suggestions will be filed with the prestigious NCVEC Question Pool Committee, and they will consider your valued contributions when each Element 2, Element 3, and Element 4 question pool is updated. Each pool gets updated once every 4 years with a public notice for radio experts to submit new or improved examination questions along with 4 suggested right and wrong answers. Join in – as an Extra Class, it's fun to see that you have contributed to the new question pool.

> *Here's how to become a volunteer examiner:*
> Write the W5YI-VEC at: P. O. Box 565101, Dallas, TX 75356,
> or call them at 817-860-3800 during regular business hours to obtain a VE application. You also may apply online at: www.w5yi.org.
> Click on the "Become a Volunteer Examiner" button.

SUMMARY

You made it through Extra Class! Congratulations! Allow me to send you a free certificate of achievement. Send a large envelope, self-address, with 12 first class stamps on the inside to me at Gordon West Radio School, 2414 College Drive, Costa Mesa, California 92626. It will take about 15 days to get the certificate back to you, and a hearty congratulations on making it to the top.

I hope to work you soon on the worldwide airwaves, or see you at an upcoming hamfest. Think about getting that commercial radio license, too, based on all of the study you have just completed for amateur Extra Class.

Welcome to the top!

73
Gordon West,
WB6NOA

**I know congratulations will be in order very soon
when you pass your Extra Class exam with flying colors!**

APPENDIX

U.S. VOLUNTEER EXAMINER COORDINATORS IN THE AMATEUR SERVICE

Anchorage Amateur Radio Club
8023 E. 11th Ct.
Anchorage, AK 99504-2003
907/338-0662
e-mail: jwiley@alaska.net

ARRL/VEC
225 Main Street
Newington, CT 06111-1494
860/594-0300
860/594-0339 (fax)
e-mail: vec@arrl.org
Internet: www.arrl.org

Central America VEC, Inc.
1215 Dale Drive SE
Huntsville, AL 35801-2031
256/536-3904
256/534-5557 (fax)
e-mail: dontunstil@comcast.net

Golden Empire Amateur Radio Society
P.O. Box 508
Chico, CA 95927-0508
530/345-3515
wa6zrt@aol.com

Greater Los Angeles Amateur Radio Group
9737 Noble Avenue
North Hills, CA 91343-2403
818/892-2068
818/892-9855 (fax)
e-mail: gla.arg@gte.net

Jefferson Amateur Radio Club
9912 Paula Dr.
River Ridge, LA 70123-1920
e-mail: doug@bellsouth.net

Laurel Amateur Radio Club, Inc.
P.O. Box 1259
Laurel, MD 20725-1259
301/937-0394 (6-9 PM)
e-mail: aa3of@arrl.net

The Milwaukee Radio Amateurs Club, Inc.
P.O. Box 070695
Milwaukee, WI 53207-0695
262/797-6722
e-mail: tfuszard@aero.net

MO-KAN/VEC
228 Tennessee Road
Richmond, KS 66080-9174
785/867-2011
wo0e@pgtv.net

SANDARC-VEC
P.O. Box 2446
La Mesa, CA 91943-2446
619/697-1475
e-mail: n6nyx@arrl.net

Sunnyvale VEC Amateur Radio Club, Inc.
P.O. Box 60307
Sunnyvale, CA 94088-0307
408/255-9000 (exam info 24 hours)
e-mail: vec@amateur-radio.org
Internet: www.amateur-radio.org

W4VEC
Rae Everhart K4SWN
P.O. Box 41
Lexington, NC 27293-0041
e-mail: raef@lexcominc.net
Internet: www.w4vec.com

Western Carolina WCARS
7 Skylyn Ct.
Asheville, NC 28806-3922
e-mail: mail@wcarsvec.org
Internet: www.wcarsvec.org

W5YI-VEC
P.O. Box 565101
Dallas, TX 75356-5101
817/860-3800
800-669-9495
e-mail: w5yi-vec@w5yi.org
Internet: www.w5yi.org

2008-12 ELEMENT 4 Q&A CROSS REFERENCE

The following cross reference presents all 741 question numbers in numerical order included in the 2008-12 Element 4 Extra Class question pool, followed by the page number on which the question begins in this book. This will allow you to located specific questions by question number. Note: 3 questions were deleted from the pool by the Question Pool Committee, resulting in an active pool of 738 questions. The deleted questions do not appear in this book, but their numbers are listed here followed by the word, deleted.

FCC Form 605 is used to process routine license renewals and license changes that are submitted directly to the FCC. The FCC will not accept NCVEC Form 605.

NCVEC Form 605 is used to process test results, license upgrades, call sign changes, and changes of address submitted through a VEC. VECs will not accept FCC Form 605.

SCHEMATIC SYMBOLS

RESISTORS
FIXED
ADJUSTABLE

CAPACITORS
FIXED
VARIABLE

SWITCHES
SPST   SPDT   NORMAL OPEN
TOGGLE   NORMAL CLOSED
MULTPOINT   MOMENTARY

BATTERIES
SINGLE CELL   MULTI CELL

GROUNDS
CHASSIS   EARTH

IC AMPLIFIERS
GENERAL AMPLIFIER
OP AMP

LOGIC (U#)
AND   NAND
OR   NOR
XOR   INVERT

WIRING
CONDUCTORS NOT JOINED
CONDUCTORS JOINED

INDUCTORS
FIXED
VARIABLE

DIODES
LED (DS#)
DIODE/ RECTIFIER
SCHOTTKY

TRANSFORMERS
AIR CORE
WITH CORE

TRANSISTORS
NPN   P-CHANNEL   P-CHANNEL
PNP   N-CHANNEL   N-CHANNEL
BIPOLAR   SINGLE-GATE DEPLETION MODE MOSFET   SINGLE-GATE ENHANCEMENT MODE MOSFET

RELAYS
SPST   SPDT   DPDT

ANTENNA
OR

SPEAKER CRYSTAL
OR

SCIENTIFIC NOTATION

Prefix	Symbol		Multiplication Factor
exa	E	10^{18} =	1,000,000,000,000,000,000
peta	P	10^{15} =	1,000,000,000,000,000
tera	T	10^{12} =	1,000,000,000,000
giga	G	10^{9} =	1,000,000,000
mega	M	10^{6} =	1,000,000
kilo	k	10^{3} =	1,000
hecto	h	10^{2} =	100
deca	da	10^{1} =	10
(unit)		10^{0} =	1

Prefix	Symbol		Multiplication Factor
deci	d	10^{-1} =	0.1
centi	c	10^{-2} =	0.01
milli	m	10^{-3} =	0.001
micro	μ	10^{-6} =	0.000001
nano	n	10^{-9} =	0.000000001
pico	p	10^{-12} =	0.000000000001
femto	f	10^{-15} =	0.000000000000001
atto	a	10^{-18} =	0.000000000000000001

SUMMARY OF QUESTION POOL FORMULAS

Question	Formula	Where:
E5H01-10	**Decibels** $dB = 10 \log_{10} \dfrac{P_1}{P_2}$	P_1 = Power (usually output) in **watts** P_2 = Power (usually input) in **watts**
E4B04-09	**Counter Readout Error** Readout Error = f × a	f = Frequency in **MHz** being measured a = Counter accuracy in **parts per million**
E4C14, 27	**Intermodulation Product** $f_{IMD(2)} = 2f_1 - f_2$ $f_{IMD(4)} = 2f_2 - f_1$	f_{IMD} = Intermodulation product at particular f in **Hz** f_1 = Frequency of transmitted signal in **Hz** f_2 = Possible frequency of interfereing signal in **Hz**
E5A01-09, 18-25	**Resonance** $X_L = X_C$ $2\pi f_r L = \dfrac{1}{2\pi f_r C}$ $f_r = \dfrac{1}{2\pi\sqrt{LC}}$	X_L = Inductive reactance in **ohms** X_C = Capacitive reactance in **ohms** f_r = Resonant frequency in **hertz** L = Inductance in **henrys** C = Capacitance in **farads** π = 3.14
E5A10	**Phase Between V and I** ELI = Voltage (E) leads current (I) in an inductive (L) circuit ICE = Current (I) leads voltage (E) in a capactive (C) circuit	E = Voltage in circuit I = Current in circuit L = Inductance in circuit C = Capacitance in circuit
E5A12-17 E5F02	**Half-Power Bandwidth** $BW_{-3dB} = \dfrac{f_r}{Q}$	BW_{-3dB} = Half-Power bandwidth in **kHz** f_r = Resonant frequency in **kHz** Q = Circuit **quality factor**
E5B01-11	**Time Constants** $\tau = RC$ $\tau = \dfrac{L}{R}$	τ = Time Constant in **seconds** R = Resistance in **ohms** C = Capacitance in **farads** L = Inductance in **henries**

Time Constant Curve

Time Constant τ	% of Change in τ	RC		RL	
		% of Final Q or V on C When Charging	% of Initial Q or V on C When Discharging	% of Final I When Increasing	% of Initial I When Decreasing
1	63.2	63.2	36.8	63.2	36.8
2	23.3	86.5	13.5	86.5	13.5
3	8.5	95.0	5.0	95.0	5.0
4	3.2	98.2	1.8	98.2	1.8
5	1.1	99.3	0.7	99.3	0.7

Appendix

SUMMARY OF QUESTION POOL FORMULAS (continued)

Question	Formula	Where:

E5B06

Capacitors　　　　**Resistors**

Series: $C_T = \dfrac{C_1 \times C_2}{C_1 + C_2}$　　$R_T = R_1 + R_2$

Parallel: $C_T = C_1 + C_2$　　$R_T = \dfrac{R_1 \times R_2}{R_1 + R_2}$

C = Capacitance in **farads**
R = Resistance in **ohms**

E5C10

Inductive Reactance
$$X_L = 2\pi fL$$

X_L = Inductive reactance in **ohms**
L = Inductance in **henries**
f = Frequency in **hertz**
π = 3.14

E5C11

Capacitive Reactance

$$X_C = \dfrac{1}{2\pi fC}$$

X_C = Capacitive reactance in **ohms**
C = Capacitance in **farads**
f = Frequency in **hertz**
π = 3.14

$$X_C = \dfrac{10^6}{2\pi fC}$$

Impedance in Series
$$Z_T = Z_1 + Z_2$$

Impedance in Parallel ⟶ Special Case:

$$Z_T = \dfrac{Z_1 \times Z_2}{Z_1 + Z_2}$$

f = Frequency in **MHz**
C = Capacitance in **picofarads**
Z = Impedance in **ohms**
π = 3.14

When Z_1 = R and Z_2 = ± jX

$$Z_T = \dfrac{RX \;\underline{/\theta = \pm 90^\circ}}{\sqrt{R^2 + X^2}\;\underline{/\text{arctan} \pm X/R}}$$

E5C11-12
E5D08-13

Rectangular Coordinates
$$Z = R \pm jX$$

Polar Coordinates
$$Z = Z\,\underline{/\pm\theta}$$

Conversion:

$Z = R\pm jX$ to $Z\,\underline{/\pm\theta}$　　$Z = \sqrt{R^2 + X^2}\; Z\,\underline{/\text{arctan} \frac{X}{R}}$

$Z\,\underline{/\pm\theta}$ to $Z = R\pm jX$　　$R = Z \cos \theta$

$\pm jX = Z \sin \theta$

Z = Impedance in **ohms**
R = Resistance in **ohms**
$+jX$ = Inductive reactance X_L in **ohms**
$-jX$ = Capacitive reactance X_C in **ohms**
θ = Phase angle in **degrees**
arctan = angle whose tangent is

E5D01-05, 08-11

**Phase Angle
Between V and I**

$$\text{Tan } \phi = \dfrac{X}{R}$$

ϕ = Phase angle in **degrees**
X = $(X_L - X_C)$ = Total reactance in **ohms**
R = Resistance in **ohms**

SUMMARY OF QUESTION POOL FORMULAS (continued)

Question	Formula	Where:
E5E05-08, 16-20	Do Addition and Subtraction in Rectangular Coordinates	Do Multiplication and Division in Polar Coordinates

$$Z_1 = R_1 + jX_1 \quad Z_2 = R_2 - jX_2$$

$$Z_1 = Z_1\,\underline{/\Theta_1} \quad Z_2 = Z_2\,\underline{/\Theta_2}$$

Addition

$$Z_T = (R_1 + jX_1) + (R_2 - jX_2)$$
$$Z_T = (R_1 + R_2) + j(X_1 - X_2)$$

Multiply

$$Z_1\,Z_2 = Z_1 \times Z_2\,\underline{/\Theta_1 + \Theta_2}$$

Subtraction

$$Z_T = (R_1 + jX_1) + (R_2 - jX_2)$$
$$Z_T = (R_1 - R_2) + j(X_1 + X_2)$$

Divide

$$\frac{Z_1}{Z_2} = \frac{Z_1\,\underline{/\Theta_1}}{Z_2\,\underline{/\Theta_1}} = \frac{Z_1}{Z_2}\,\underline{/\Theta_1 - \Theta_2}$$

E5G01-05, 13-16 Circuit Quality Factor

$$Q = \frac{R}{X_L}$$

$$Q = \frac{R}{2\pi f_r L}$$

Q = Circuit **quality factor**
$X_L = 2\pi f_r L$
X_L = Inductive reactance in **ohms**
f_r = Resonant frequency in **Hz**
L = Inductance in **henrys**
R = Resistance in **ohms**
$2\pi = 6.28$

E5G11
E5H13-16

True Power

$$P_T = P_A \times PF$$

$$P_A = E \times I$$

$$PF = \cos\phi$$

P_T = True power in **watts**
P_A = Apparent power in **watts**
ϕ = Phase angle in **degrees**
PF = Power factor
E = Applied voltage in **volts**
I = Circuit current in **amps**

E6B11-16 Inverting IC Op-Amp Gain

$$G = -\frac{R_f}{R_1}$$

G = Gain in **non-dimentional units**
R_f = Feedback resistance in **ohms**
R_1 = Input resistance in **ohms**

E6D13 Turns for L Using Ferrite Toroidal Cores

$$N = 1000\sqrt{\frac{L}{A_L}}$$

N = Number of turns needed
A_L = Inductance index in **mH per 1000 turns**
L = Inductance in **millihenrys**

E6D14 Turns for L Using Powdered-Iron Toroidal Cores

$$N = 100\sqrt{\frac{L}{A_L}}$$

N = Number of turns needed
A_L = Inductance index in **µH per 100 turns**
L = Inductance in **millihenrys**

SUMMARY OF QUESTION POOL FORMULAS (continued)

Question	Formula	Where:
E8A08-12 E8D01, 06	**Peak, Peak-to-Peak and RMS Voltages** $**V_P = \dfrac{V_{PP}}{2}$ $*V_{RMS} = 0.707\ V_P$ $**V_{PP} = 2V_P$ $*V_P = 1.414\ V_{RMS}$	V_P = Peak voltage in **volts** V_{PP} = Peak-to-peak voltage in **volts** V_{RMS} = Root-mean-square voltage in **volts** * Equations for sinewaves ** Equations for symmetrical waves

Question	Formula	Where:
E8A16 E8D05	**Peak Envelope Power** $PEP = P_{DC} \times$ Efficiency	PEP = Peak envelope power in **watts** P_{DC} = Input DC power in **watts**

Amplifier Class	Efficiency
C	80%
B	60%
AB	50%
A	<50%

Question		
E8B11-12	**Modulation Index**	

$$\text{Modulation Index} = \frac{\text{Deviation of FM Signal }(\textbf{in Hz})}{\text{Modulating Frequency }(\textbf{in Hz})}$$

Question		
E8B13	**Deviation Ratio**	

$$\text{Deviation Ratio} = \frac{\text{Maximum Carrier Frequency Deviation }(\textbf{in kHz})}{\text{Maximum Modulation Frequency }(\textbf{in kHz})}$$

SUMMARY OF QUESTION POOL FORMULAS (continued)

Question	Formula	Where:
E8C07	**Bandwidth for CW** $$BW_{CW} = \text{baud rate} \times \text{wpm} \times \text{fading factor}$$	BW_{CW} = Necessary bandwidth in **hertz** wpm = Morse code signal rate in **words per minute** Fading factor = Constant of 5 for **CW**
E8C08-10	**Bandwidth for Digital** $$BW = \text{baud rate} + (1.2 \times f_s)$$	BW = Necessary bandwidth in **hertz** f_s = Frequency shift in **hertz** Baud rate = Digital signal rate in **bauds**
E9D03	**Antenna Beamwidth** $$\text{Beamwidth} = \frac{203}{(\sqrt{10})^X}$$	Beamwidth = Antenna beamwidth in **degrees** A_G = Antenna gain in **dB** $X = \dfrac{A_G}{10}$
E9E10-11	**Physical Length vs. Electrical Length** $$L = \frac{984\lambda V}{f}$$ Feedline Velocity Factor Coax 0.66 Parallel 0.95 Twin-Lead 0.80	L = Physical length in **feet** λ = Electrical length in **wavelengths** V = **Velocity factor** of feedline f = Frequency in **MHz**

AUTHORIZED FREQUENCY BANDS – AMATEUR SERVICE (for U.S. Amateur Stations operating from ITU-Region 2–North and South America)

Current License Class[1]					
Grandfathered[2]	Novice	Technician	General	Advanced	Extra Class
METERS 160			1800-2000 kHz/All	1800-2000 kHz/All	1800-2000 kHz/All
80 / 75	3525-3600 kHz/CW	3525-3600 kHz/CW	3525-3600 kHz/CW 3800-4000 kHz/Ph	3525-3600 kHz/CW 3700-4000 kHz/Ph	3500-4000 kHz/CW 3600-4000 kHz/Ph
40	7025-7125 kHz/CW	7025-7125 kHz/CW	7025-7125 kHz/CW 7175-7300 kHz/Ph	7025-7125 kHz/CW 7125-7300 kHz/Ph	7000-7300 kHz/CW 7125-7300 kHz/Ph
30			10.1-10.15 MHz/CW	10.1-10.15 MHz/CW	10.1-10.15 MHz/CW
20			14.025-14.15 MHz/CW 14.225-14.35 MHz/Ph	14.025-14.15 MHz/CW 14.175-14.35 MHz/Ph	14.0-14.35 MHz/CW 14.15-14.35 MHz/Ph
17			18.068-18.11 MHz/CW 18.11-18.168 MHz/Ph	18.068-18.11 MHz/CW 18.11-18.168 MHz/Ph	18.068-18.11 MHz/CW 18.11-18.168 MHz/Ph
15	21.025-21.2 MHz/CW	21.025-21.2 MHz/CW	21.025-21.2 MHz/CW 21.275-21.45 MHz/Ph	21.025-21.2 MHz/CW 21.225-21.45 MHz/Ph	21.0-21.45 MHz/CW 21.2-21.45 MHz/Ph
12			24.89-24.99 MHz/CW 24.93-24.99 MHz/Ph	24.89-24.99 MHz/CW 24.93-24.99 MHz/Ph	24.89-24.99 MHz/CW 24.93-24.99 MHz/Ph
10	28.0-28.5 MHz/CW 28.3-28.5 MHz/Ph	28.0-28.5 MHz/CW 28.3-28.5 MHz/Ph	28.0-28.3 MHz/CW 28.3-29.7 MHz/Ph	28.0-28.3 MHz/CW 28.3-29.7 MHz/Ph	28.0-29.7 MHz/CW 28.3-29.7 MHz/Ph
6		50-54 MHz/CW 50.1-54 MHz/Ph	50-54 MHz/CW 50.1-54 MHz/Ph	50-54 MHz/CW 50.1-54 MHz/Ph	50-54 MHz/CW 50.1-54 MHz/Ph
2		144-148 MHz/CW 144.1-148 MHz/All	144-148 MHz/CW 144.1-148 MHz/All	144-148 MHz/CW 144.1-148 MHz/All	144-148 MHz/CW 144.1-148 MHz/All
1.25	222-225 MHz/All	222-225 MHz/All [3]	222-225 MHz/All	222-225 MHz/All	222-225 MHz/All
0.70		420-450 MHz/All	420-450 MHz/All	420-450 MHz/All	420-450 MHz/All
0.33		902-928 MHz/All	902-928 MHz/All	902-928 MHz/All	902-928 MHz/All
0.23	1270-1295 MHz/All	1240-1300 MHz/All	1240-1300 MHz/All	1240-1300 MHz/All	1240-1300 MHz/All

[1] Effective 4-15-00 [2] Prior to 4-15-00 [3] Effective 2/1/94 219-220 MHz is authorized for point-to-point fixed digital message forwarding systems.

Note: Morse code (CW, A1A) may be used on any frequency allocated to the amateur service. Telephony emission (abbreviated Ph above) authorized on certain bands as indicated. Higher class licensees may use slow-scan television and facsimile emissions on the Phone bands; radio teletype/digital on the CW bands. All amateur modes and emissions are authorized above 144.1 MHz. In actual practice, the modes/emissions used are somewhat more complicated than shown above due to the existence of various band plans and "gentlemen's agreements" concerning where certain operations should take place.

ELEMENT 4 (EXTRA CLASS) QUESTION POOL SYLLABUS

The syllabus used by the QPC for the development of the question pool is included here as an aid in studying the subelements and topic groups. Review the syllabus before you start your study to gain an understanding of how the question pool is used to develop the Element 4 written examination. Remember, one question will be taken from each topic group within each subelement to create your exam. The QPC topic groups are not the same as those used by Gordon West in this book.

E1 – COMMISSION'S RULES
[6 Exam Questions – 6 Groups]

E1A Operating Standards: frequency privileges for Extra Class amateurs; emission standards; automatic message forwarding; frequency sharing; FCC license actions; stations aboard ships or aircraft

E1B Station restrictions and special operations: restrictions on station location; general operating restrictions, spurious emissions, control operator reimbursement; antenna structure restrictions; RACES operations

E1C Station control: definitions and restrictions pertaining to local, automatic and remote control operation; control operator responsibilities for remote and automatically controlled stations

E1D Amateur Satellite service: definitions and purpose; license requirements for space stations; available frequencies and bands; telecommand and telemetry operations; restrictions, and special provisions; notification requirements

E1E Volunteer examiner program: definitions, qualifications, preparation and administration of exams; accreditation; question pools; documentation requirements

E1F Miscellaneous rules: external RF power amplifiers; Line A; national quiet zone; business communications; compensated communications; spread spectrum; auxiliary stations; reciprocal operating privileges; IARP and CEPT licenses; third party communications with foreign countries; special temporary authority

E2 – OPERATING PRACTICES & PROCEDURES
[5 Exam Questions – 5 Groups]

E2A Amateur radio in space: amateur satellites; orbital mechanics; frequencies and modes; satellite hardware; satellite operations

E2B Television practices: fast scan television standards and techniques; slow scan television standards and techniques

E2C Operating methods, part 1: contest and DX operating; spread-spectrum transmissions; automatic HF forwarding; selecting an operating frequency

E2D Operating methods, part 2: VHF and UHF digital modes; packet clusters; Automatic Position Reporting System (APRS)

E2E Operating methods, part 3: operating HF digital modes; error correction

E3 – RADIO WAVE PROPAGATION
[3 Exam Questions -- 3 Groups]

E3A Propagation and technique, part 1: Earth-Moon-Earth communications; meteor scatter

E3B Propagation and technique, part 2: transequatorial; long path; gray line; multi-path propagation

E3C Propagation and technique, part 3: Auroral propagation; selective fading; radio-path horizon; take-off angle over flat or sloping terrain; earth effects on propagation; less common propagation modes

E4 – AMATEUR RADIO TECHNOLOGY & MEASUREMENTS
[5 Exam Questions – 5 Groups]

E4A Test equipment: analog and digital instruments; spectrum and network analyzers, antenna analyzers; oscilloscopes; testing transistors; RF measurements

E4B Measurement technique and limitations: instrument accuracy and performance limitations; probes; techniques to minimize errors; measurement of "Q"; instrument calibration

E4C Receiver performance characteristics, part 1: phase noise, capture effect, noise floor, image rejection, MDS, signal-to-noise-ratio; selectivity

E4D Receiver performance characteristics, part 2: blocking dynamic range, intermodulation and cross-modulation interference; 3rd order intercept; desensitization; preselection

E4E Noise suppression: system noise; electrical appliance noise; line noise; locating noise sources; DSP noise reduction; noise blankers

E5 – ELECTRICAL PRINCIPLES
[4 Exam Questions – 4 Groups]

E5A Resonance and Q: characteristics of resonant circuits: series and parallel resonance; Q; half-power bandwidth; phase relationships in reactive circuits

E5B Time constants and phase relationships: R/L/C time constants: definition; time constants in RL and RC circuits; phase angle between voltage and current; phase angles of series and parallel circuits

E5C Impedance plots and coordinate systems: plotting impedances in polar coordinates; rectangular coordinates

E5D AC and RF energy in real circuits: skin effect; electrostatic and electromagnetic fields; reactive power; power factor; coordinate systems

E6 – CIRCUIT COMPONENTS
[6 Exam Questions – 6 Groups]
E6A Semiconductor materials and devices: semiconductor materials (germanium, silicon, P-type, N-type); transistor types: NPN, PNP, junction, power; field-effect transistors: enhancement mode; depletion mode; MOS; CMOS; N-channel; P-channel
E6B Semiconductor diodes
E6C Integrated circuits: TTL digital integrated circuits; CMOS digital integrated circuits; gates
E6D Optical devices and toroids: vidicon and cathode-ray tube devices; charge-coupled devices (CCDs); liquid crystal displays (LCDs); toroids: permeability, core material, selecting, winding
E6E Piezoelectric crystals and MMICS: quartz crystals (as used in oscillators and filters); monolithic amplifiers (MMICs)
E6F Optical components and power systems: photoconductive principles and effects, photovoltaic systems, optical couplers, optical sensors, and optoisolators

E7 – PRACTICAL CIRCUITS
[8 Exam Questions -- 8 Groups]
E7 Digital circuits: digital circuit principles and logic circuits: classes of logic elements; positive and negative logic; frequency dividers; truth tables
E7B Amplifiers: Class of operation; vacuum tube and solid-state circuits; distortion and intermodulation; spurious and parasitic suppression; microwave amplifiers
E7C Filters and matching networks: filters and impedance matching networks: types of networks; types of filters; filter applications; filter characteristics; impedance matching; DSP filtering
E7D Power supplies and voltage regulators
E7E Modulation and demodulation: reactance, phase and balanced modulators; detectors; mixer stages; DSP modulation and demodulation; software defined radio systems
E7F Frequency markers and counters: frequency divider circuits; frequency marker generators; frequency counters
E7G Active filters and op-amps: active audio filters; characteristics; basic circuit design; operational amplifiers
E7H Oscillators and signal sources: types of oscillators; synthesizers and phase-locked loops; direct digital synthesizers

E8 – SIGNALS & EMISSIONS
[4 Exam Questions -- 4 Groups]
E8A AC waveforms: sine, square, sawtooth and irregular waveforms; AC measurements; average and PEP of RF signals; pulse and digital signal waveforms
E8B Modulation and demodulation: modulation methods; modulation index and deviation ratio; pulse modulation; frequency and time division multiplexing
E8C Digital signals: digital communications modes; CW; information rate vs. bandwidth; spread-spectrum communications; modulation methods
E8D Waves, measurements, and RF grounding: peak-to-peak values, polarization; RF grounding

E9 – ANTENNAS & TRANSMISSION LINES
[8 Exam Questions -- 8 Groups]
E9A Isotropic and gain antennas: definition; used as a standard for comparison; radiation pattern; basic antenna parameters: radiation resistance and reactance, gain, beamwidth, efficiency
E9B Antenna patterns: E and H plane patterns; gain as a function of pattern; antenna design (computer modeling of antennas); Yagi antennas
E9C Wire and phased vertical antennas: beverage antennas; terminated and resonant rhombic antennas; elevation above real ground; ground effects as related to polarization; take-off angles
E9D Directional antennas: gain; satellite antennas; antenna beamwidth; losses; SWR bandwidth; antenna efficiency; shortened and mobile antennas; grounding
E9E Matching: matching antennas to feed lines; power dividers
E9F Transmission lines: characteristics of open and shorted feed lines: 1/8 wavelength; 1/4 wavelength; 1/2 wavelength; feed lines: coax versus open-wire; velocity factor; electrical length; transformation characteristics of line terminated in impedance not equal to characteristic impedance
E9G The Smith chart
E9H Effective radiated power; system gains and losses; radio direction finding antennas

E0 – SAFETY
[1 exam question — 1 group]
E0A Safety: amateur radio safety practices; RF radiation hazards; hazardous material

GRID-SQUARE MAP FOR UNITED STATES

This Grid Square Map was created using the "Maidenhead" system that is used around the world.

Each 20° x 10° square is designated with a two-letter field. Each field is then divided into 100 – 2° x 1° squares, designated with a two-digit number.

For detailed Grid Square locations within each state, refer to the U.S. Repeater Mapbook 1996/97 edition.

http://home.earthlink.net/~artsci

© 1996 Artsci Inc

Reprinted by Permission of Artsci Inc. P.O. Box 1428, Burbank, CA 91507

Appendix

ITU Regions

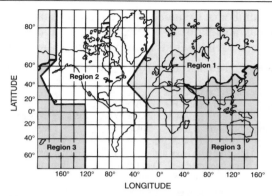

List of Countries Permitting Third-Party Traffic

Country	Call Sign Prefix	Country	Call Sign Prefix	Country	Call Sign Prefix
Antigua and Barbuda	V2	El Salvador	YS	Paraguay	ZP
Argentina	LU	The Gambia	C5	Peru	OA
Australia	VK	Ghana	9G	Philippines	DU
Austria, Vienna	4U1VIC	Grenada	J3	St. Christopher & Nevis	V4
Belize	V3	Guatemala	TG	St. Lucia	J6
Bolivia	CP	Guyana	8R	St. Vincent & Grenadines	J8
Bosnia-Herzegovina	T9	Haiti	HH	Sierra Leone	9L
Brazil	PY	Honduras	HR	South Africa	ZS
Canada	VE, VO, VY	Israel	4X	Swaziland	3D6
Chile	CE	Jamaica	6Y	Trinidad and Tobago	9Y
Colombia	HK	Jordan	JY	Turkey	TA
Comoros	D6	Liberia	EL	United Kingdom	GB*
Costa Rica	TI	Marshall Is	V6	Uruguay	CX
Cuba	CO	Mexico	XE	Venezuela	YV
Dominica	J7	Micronesia	V6	ITU-Geneva	4U1ITU
Dominican Republic	HI	Nicaragua	YN	VIC-Vienna	4U1VIC
Ecuador	HC	Panama	HP		

Countries Holding U.S. Reciprocal Agreements

Antigua, Barbuda	Chile	Greece	Liberia	Seychelles
Argentina	Colombia	Greenland	Luxembourg	Sierra Leone
Australia	Costa Rica	Grenada	Macedonia	Solomon Islands
Austria	Croatia	Guatemala	Marshall Is.	South Africa
Bahamas	Cyprus	Guyana	Mexico	Spain
Barbados	Denmark	Haiti	Micronesia	St. Lucia
Belgium	Dominica	Honduras	Monaco	St. Vincent and
Belize	Dominican Rep.	Iceland	Netherlands	Grenadines
Bolivia	Ecuador	India	Netherlands Ant.	Surinam
Bosnia-	El Salvador	Indonesia	New Zealand	Sweden
Herzegovina	Fiji	Ireland	Nicaragua	Switzerland
Botswana	Finland	Israel	Norway	Thailand
Brazil	France[2]	Italy	Panama	Trinidad, Tobago
Canada[1]	Germany	Jamaica	Paraguay	Turkey
		Japan	Papua New Guinea	Tuvalu
1. Do not need reciprocal permit		Jordan	Peru	United Kingdom[3]
2. Includes all French Territories		Kiribati	Philippines	Uruguay
3. Includes all British Territories		Kuwait	Portugal	Venezuela

POPULAR Q SIGNALS

Given below are a number of Q signals whose meanings most often need to be expressed with brevity and clarity in amateur work. (Q abbreviations take the form of questions only when each is sent followed by a question mark.)

QRG   Will you tell me my exact frequency (or that of _____)? Your exact frequency (or that of _____) is _____ kHz.

QRH   Does my frequency vary? Your frequency varies.

QRI   How is the tone of my transmission? The tone of your transmission is _____ (1. Good; 2. Variable; 3. Bad)

QRJ   Are you receiving me badly? I cannot receive you. Your signals are too weak.

QRK   What is the intelligibility of my signals (or those of _____)? The intelligibility of your signals (or those of _____) is _____ (1. Bad; 2. Poor; 3. Fair; 4. Good; 5. Excellent).

QRL   Are you busy? I am busy (or I am busy with _____). Please do not interfere.

QRM   Is my transmission being interfered with? Your transmission is being interfered with _____ (1. Nil; 2. Slightly; 3. Moderately; 4. Severely; 5. Extremely).

QRN   Are you troubled by static? I am troubled by static _____ (1-5 as under QRM).

QRO   Shall I increase power? Increase power.

QRP   Shall I decrease power? Decrease power.

QRQ   Shall I send faster? Send faster (_____ WPM).

QRS   Shall I send more slowly? Send more slowly (_____ WPM).

QRT   Shall I stop sending? Stop sending.

QRU   Have you anything for me? I have nothing for you.

QRV   Are you ready? I am ready.

QRW   Shall I inform _____ that you are calling on _____ kHz? Please inform _____ that I am calling on _____ kHz.

QRX   When will you call me again? I will call you again at _____ hours (on _____ kHz).

QRY   What is my turn? Your turn is numbered _____ .

QRZ   Who is calling me? You are being called by _____ (on _____ kHz).

QSA   What is the strength of my signals (or those of _____)? The strength of your signals (or those of _____) is _____ (1. Scarcely perceptible; 2. Weak; 3. Fairly good; 4. Good; 5. Very good).

QSB   Are my signals fading? Your signals are fading.

QSD   Is my keying defective? Your keying is defective.

QSG   Shall I send _____ messages at a time? Send _____ messages at a time.

QSK   Can you hear me between your signals and if so can I break in on your transmission? I can hear you between my signals; break in on my transmission.

QSL   Can you acknowledge receipt? I am acknowledging receipt.

QSM   Shall I repeat the last message which I sent you, or some previous message? Repeat the last message which you sent me [or message(s) number(s) _____].

QSN   Did you hear me (or _____) on _____ kHz? I heard you (or _____) on _____ kHz.

QSO   Can you communicate with _____ direct or by relay? I can communicate with _____ direct (or by relay through _____).

QSP   Will you relay to _____ ? I will relay to _____ .

QST   General call preceding a message addressed to all amateurs and ARRL members. This is in effect "CQ ARRL."

QSU   Shall I send or reply on this frequency (or on _____ kHz)?

QSW   Will you send on this frequency (or on _____ kHz)? I am going to send on this frequency (or on _____ kHz).

QSX   Will you listen to _____ on _____ kHz? I am listening to _____ on _____ kHz.

QSY   Shall I change to transmission on another frequency? Change to transmission on another frequency (or on _____ kHz).

QSZ   Shall I send each word or group more than once? Send each word or group twice (or _____ times).

QTA   Shall I cancel message number _____ ? Cancel message number _____ .

QTB   Do you agree with my counting of words? I do not agree with your counting of words. I will repeat the first letter or digit of each word or group.

QTC   How many messages have you to send? I have messages for you (or for _____).

QTH   What is your location? My location is _____ .

QTR   What is the correct time? The time is _____ .

Source: ARRL

Appendix

ITU Emission Designators

First Symbol – Modulation system

A – Double sideband AM
C – Vestigial sideband AM
D – Amplitude/angle modulated
F – Frequency modulation
G – Phase modulation
H – Single sideband/full carrier
J – Single sideband/suppressed carrier
K – AM pulse
L – Pulse modulated in width/duration

M – Pulse modulated in position/phase
N – Unmodulated carrier
P – Unmodulated pulses
Q – Angle modulated during pulse
R – Single sideband/reduced or variable level carrier
V – Combination of pulse emissions
W – Other types of pulses

Second Symbol – Nature of signal modulating carrier

0 – No modulation
1 – Digital data without modulated subcarrier
2 – Digital data on modulated subcarrier
3 – Analog modulated
7 – Two or more channels of digital data

8 – Two or more channels of analog data
9 – Combination of analog and digital information
X – Other

Third Symbol – Information to be conveyed

A – Manually received telegraphy
B – Automatically received telegraphy
C – Facsimile (FAX)
D – Digital information
E – Voice telephony

F – Video/television
N – No information
W – Combination of these
X – Other

The signal may be "assembled" from the different elements of the emission designators. For example, an amplitude-modulated voice single sideband signal is J3E: J = single sideband; 3 = analog, single channel; E = telephony.

1. **CW** - International Morse code telegraphy emissions having designators with A, C, H, J or R as the first symbol, 1 as the second symbol, A or B as the third symbol.
2. **DATA** - Telemetry, telecommand and computer communications emissions having designators with A, C, D, F, G, H, J or R as the first symbol: 1 as the second symbol; D as the third symbol; and also emission J2D. Only a digital code of a type specifically authorized in the §Part 97.3 rules may be transmitted.
3. **IMAGE** - Facsimile and television emissions having designators with A, C, D, F, G, H, J or R as the first symbol; 1, 2 or 3 as the second symbol; C or F as the third symbol; and also emissions having B as the first symbol; 7, 8 or 9 as the second symbol; W as the third symbol.
4. **MCW (Modulated carrier wave)** - Tone-modulated international Morse code telegraphy emissions having designators with A, C, D, F, G, H or R as the first symbol; 2 as the second symbol; A or B as the third symbol.
5. **PHONE** - Speech and other sound emissions having designators with A, C, D, F, G, H, J or R as the first symbol; 1, 2 or 3 as the second symbol; E as the third symbol. Also speech emissions having B as the first symbol; 7, 8 or 9 as the second symbol; E as the third symbol. MCW for the purpose of

performing the station identification procedure, or for providing telegraphy practice interspersed with speech, or incidental tones for the purpose of selective calling, or alerting or to control the level of a demodulated signal may also be considered phone.

6. **PULSE** - Emissions having designators with K, L, M, P, Q, V or W as the first symbol; , 1, 2, 3, 7, 8, 9 or X as the second symbol; A, B, C, D, E, F, N, W or X as the third symbol.
7. **RTTY (Radioteletype)** - Narrow-band, direct-printing telegraphy emissions having designators with A, C, D, F, G, H, J or R as the first symbol; 1 as the second symbol; B as the third symbol; and also emission J2B. Only a digital code of a type specifically authorized in the §Part 97.3 rules may be transmitted.
8. **SS (Spread Spectrum)** - Emissions using bandwidth-expansion modulation emissions having designators with A, C, D, F, G, H, J or R as the first symbol; X as the second symbol; X as the third symbol. Only a SS emission of a type specifically authorized in §Part 97.3 rules may be transmitted.
9. **TEST** - Emissions containing no information having the designators with N as the third symbol. Test does not include pulse emissions with no information or modulation unless pulse emissions are also authorized in the frequency band.

Glossary

Advanced: An amateur operator who has passed Element 2, 3A, 3B, and 4A written theory examinations and Element 1A and 1B code tests to demonstrate Morse code proficiency to 13 wpm.

Amateur communication: Non-commercial radio communication by or among amateur stations solely with a personal aim and without personal or business interest.

Amateur operator/primary station license: An instrument of authorization issued by the Federal Communications Commission comprised of a station license, and also incorporating an operator license indicating the class of privileges.

Amateur operator: A person holding a valid license to operate an amateur station issued by the FCC. Amateur operators are frequently referred to as ham operators.

Amateur Radio services: The amateur service, the amateur-satellite service and the radio amateur civil emergency service.

Amateur-satellite service: A radiocommunication service using stations on Earth satellites for the same purpose as those of the amateur service.

Amateur service: A radiocommunication service for the purpose of self-training, intercommunication and technical investigations carried out by amateurs; that is, duly authorized persons interested in radio technique solely with a personal aim and without pecuniary interest.

Amateur station: A station licensed in the amateur service embracing necessary apparatus at a particular location used for amateur communication.

AMSAT: Radio Amateur Satellite Corporation, a non-profit scientific organization.
(850 Sligo Avenue, Silver Spring, MD 20910-4703)

Antenna gain: The increase as a result of the physical construction of the antenna which confines the radiation to desired or useful directions. Usually specified in dB, referenced to the gain of a dipole.

ARES: The emergency division of the American Radio Relay League. See RACES

ARRL: American Radio Relay League, national organization of U.S. Amateur Radio operators. (225 Main Street, Newington, CT 06111)

ATV: Amateur fast-scan television.

Audio Frequency (AF): The range of frequencies that can be heard by the human ear, generally 20 hertz to 20 kilohertz.

Authorized bandwidth: The allowed frequency band, specified in kilohertz, and centered on the carrier frequency.

Automatic control: The use of devices and procedures for station control without the control operator being present at the control point when the station is transmitting.

Automatic Position Reporting System (APRS): Links a remote GPS unit to a ham transceiver which transmits the location to a base station.

Automatic Volume Control (AVC): A circuit that continually maintains a constant audio output volume in spite of deviations in input signal strength.

Beam or Yagi antenna: An antenna array that receives or transmits RF energy in a particular direction. Usually rotatable.

Block diagram: A simplified outline of an electronic system where circuits or components are shown as boxes.

Broadcasting: Information or programming transmitted by means of radio intended for the general public.

Business communications: Any transmission or communication the purpose of which is to facilitate the regular business or commercial affairs of any party. Business communications are prohibited in the amateur service.

Call Book: A published list of all licensed amateur operators available in North American and Foreign editions.

Call sign assignment: The FCC systematically assigns each amateur station their primary call sign.

Carrier frequency: The frequency of an unmodulated electromagnetic wave, usually specified in kilohertz or megahertz.

Certificate of Successful Completion of Examination (CSCE): A certificate verifying successful completion of a written and/or Morse code examination Element. Credit for passing is valid for 365 days.

Coaxial cable, Coax: A concentric, two-conductor cable in which one conductor surrounds the other, separated by an insulator.

Control point: Any place from which a transmitter's function may be controlled.

Control station: A station directly associated with the control point of a radio system, commonly used to control repeaters.

Control operator: An amateur operator designated by the licensee of an amateur station to be responsible for the station transmissions.

Coordinated repeater station: An amateur repeater station for which the transmitting and receiving frequencies have been recommended by the recognized repeater coordinator.

Coordinated Universal Time (UTC): Some-times referred to as Greenwich Mean Time, UCT or Zulu time. The time at the zero-degree (0∞) Meridian which passes through Greenwich, England. A universal time among all amateur operators.

Crystal: A quartz or similar material which has been ground to produce natural vibrations of a specific frequency. Quartz crystals produce a high-degree of frequency stability in radio transmitters.

CW: Continuous wave, another term for the International Morse code.

Dipole antenna: The most common wire antenna. Length is equal to one-half of the wavelength.

Direct Digital Frequency Synthesizer: Modern frequency synthesizer employing technology to reduce phase noise to an insignificant level.

Dummy antenna: A device or resistor which serves as a transmitter's antenna without radiating radio waves. Generally used to tune up a radio transmitter.

Duplex: Transmitting on one frequency, and receiving on another, commonly used in mobile telephone use, as well as mobile business radio on UHF frequencies.

Duplexer: A device that allows a single antenna to be simultaneously used for both reception and transmission.

Effective Radiated Power (ERP): The product of the transmitter (peak envelope) power, expressed in watts, delivered to the antenna, and the relative gain of an antenna over that of a half-wave dipole antenna.

Emergency communication: Any amateur communication directly relating to the immediate safety of life of individuals or the immediate protection of property.

Examination Element: The written theory exams and Morse code test required to obtain amateur radio licenses. Technicians are required to pass written Element 2 theory; Generals are required to pass written Element 3 theory plus Element 1 Morse code test at five (5) words-per-minute; and Extras are required to pass written Element 4 theory.

FCC Form 605: The universal application form used to renew or modify an existing license. (See NCVEC Form 605)

Federal Communications Commission (FCC): A board of five Commissioners, appointed by the President, having the power to regulate wire and radio telecommunications in the United States.

Feedline transmission line: A system of conductors that connects an antenna to a receiver or transmitter.

Field Day: Annual activity sponsored by the ARRL to demonstrate emergency preparedness of amateur operators.

Filter: A device used to block or reduce alternating currents or signals at certain frequencies while allowing others to pass unimpeded.

Frequency: The number of cycles of alternating current in one second.

Frequency coordinator: An individual or organization recognized by amateur operators eligible to engage in repeater operation that recommends frequencies and other operating and/or technical parameters for amateur repeater operation in order to avoid or minimize potential interferences.

Frequency Modulation (FM): A method of varying a radio carrier wave by causing its frequency to vary in accordance with the information to be conveyed.

Frequency privileges: The transmitting frequency bands available to the various classes of amateur operators. The privileges are listed in Part 97.7(a) of the FCC rules.

General: An amateur operator who has passed the Element 3 written theory examination and Element 1 code test to demonstrate Morse code proficiency to 5-wpm.

Ground: A connection, accidental or intentional, between a device or circuit and the earth or some common body and the earth or some common body serving as the earth.

Ground wave: A radio wave that is propagated near or at the earth's surface.

Half-Duplex: A method of operation on a duplex (separate transmit, separate receive) frequency pair where the operator only receives when the microphone button is released. Half-duplex does not permit simultaneous talk and listen.

Handi-Ham system: Amateur organization dedicated to assisting handicapped amateur operators. (3915 Golden Valley Road, Golden Valley, MN 55422)

Harmful interference: Interference which seriously degrades, obstructs or repeatedly interrupts the operation of a radio communication service.

Harmonic: A radio wave that is a multiple of the fundamental frequency. The second harmonic is twice the fundamental frequency, the third harmonic, three times, etc.

Hertz: One complete alternating cycle per second, abbreviated Hz. Named after Heinrich R. Hertz, a German physicist. The number of hertz is the frequency of the audio or radio wave.

High Frequency (HF): The band of frequencies that lie between 3 and 30 megahertz. It is from these frequencies that radio waves are returned to earth from the ionosphere.

High-Pass filter: A device that allows passage of high frequency signals but attenuates the lower frequencies.

Interference: The effect that occurs when two or more radio stations are transmitting at the same time. This includes undesired noise or other radio signals on the same frequency.

International Telecommunication Union (ITU): World organization composed of delegates from member countries, which allocates frequency spectrum for various purposes, including amateur radio.

Ionosphere: Outer limits of atmosphere from which HF amateur communications signals are returned to earth.

Jamming: The intentional, malicious interference with another radio signal.

Key clicks, Chirps: Defective keying of a telegraphy signal sounding like tapping or high varying pitches.

Lid: Amateur slang term for poor radio operator.

Linear amplifier: A device that accurately reproduces a radio wave in magnified form.

Long wire: A horizontal wire antenna that is one wavelength or longer in length.

Low-Pass filter: A device that allows passage of low frequency signals but attenuates the higher frequencies.

Machine: A ham slang word for an automatic repeater station.

Malicious interference: Willful, intentional jamming of radio transmissions.

MARS: The Military Affiliate Radio System. An organization that coordinates the activities of amateur communications with military radio communications.

Maximum authorized transmitting power: Amateur stations must use no more than the maximum transmitter power necessary to carry out the desired communications.

Maximum usable frequency (MUF): The highest frequency that will be returned to earth from the ionosphere.

Medium frequency (MF): The band of frequencies that lies between 300 and 3,000 kHz (3 MHz).

Mobile operation: Radio communications conducted while in motion or during halts at unspecified locations.

Mode: Type of transmission such as voice, teletype, code, television, facsimile.

Modulate: To vary the amplitude, frequency or phase of a radio frequency wave in accordance with the information to be conveyed.

Monolithic Microwave Integrated Circuit (MMIC): A four-legged device designed for RF amplification. Well-suited for VHF, UHF and microwave applications.

Morse code (see CW): The International Morse code, A1A emission. Interrupted continuous wave communications conducted using a dot-dash code for letters, numbers and operating procedure signs.

NCVEC Form 605: The form provided by VECs that is used to apply for an amateur radio license or license upgrade.

Noise level: The strengths of extraneous audible sounds in a given location, usually measured in decibels.

Novice operator: An FCC licensed, entry-level operator in the amateur service. Novices may operate a transmitter in the following meter wavelength bands: 80, 40, 15, 10, 1.25 and 0.23.

Ohm's law: The basic electrical law explaining the relationship between voltage, current and resistance. The current I in a circuit is equal to the voltage E divided by the resistance R, or $I = E/R$.

OSCAR: Acronym for "Orbiting Satellite Carrying Amateur Radio," the name given to a series of satellites designed and built by amateur operators of several nations.

Oscillator: A device for generating oscillations or vibrations of an audio or radio frequency signal.

Output power: The radio-frequency output power of a transmitter's final radio-frequency stage as measured at the output terminal while connected to a load of the impedance recommended by the manufacturer.

Packet radio: A digital method of communicating computer-to-computer. A terminal-node controller makes up the packet of data and directs it to another packet station.

Peak Envelope Power (PEP): 1. The power during one radio frequency cycle at the crest of the modulation envelope, measured under normal operating conditions. 2. The maximum power that can be obtained from a transmitter.

Phone patch: Interconnection of amateur service to the public switched telephone network, and operated by the control operator of the station.

Power supply: A device or circuit that provides the appropriate voltage and current to another device or circuit.

Propagation: The travel of electromagnetic waves or sound waves through a medium.

Q-signals: International three-letter abbreviations beginning with the letter Q used primarily to convey information using the Morse code.

QSL Bureau: An office that bulk processes QSL (radio confirmation) cards for (or from) foreign amateur operators as a postage saving mechanism.

RACES (radio amateur civil emergency service): A radio service using amateur stations for civil defense communications during periods of local, regional, or national civil emergencies.

Radiation: Electromagnetic energy, such as radio waves, traveling forth into space from a transmitter.

Radio Frequency (RF): The range of frequencies over 20 kilohertz that can be propagated through space.

Radio wave: A combination of electric and magnetic fields varying at a radio frequency and traveling through space at the speed of light.

Repeater operation: Automatic amateur stations that retransmit the signals of other amateur stations.

Repeater station: An intermediate station in a system which is arranged to receive a signal from a station, amplify and retransmit the signal to another station. Usually performs this function in both directions, simultaneously.

RST Report: A telegraphy signal report system of Readability, Strength and Tone.

S-meter: A voltmeter calibrated from 0 to 9 that indicates the relative signal strength of an incoming signal at a radio receiver.

Selectivity: The ability of a circuit (or radio receiver) to separate the desired signal from those not wanted.

Sensitivity: The ability of a circuit (or radio receiver) to detect a specified input signal.

Short circuit: An unintended, low-resistance connection across a voltage source resulting in high current and possible damage.

Shortwave: The high frequencies that lie between 3 and 30 megahertz that are propagated long distances.

Simplex: A method of operation of a communication circuit which can receive or transmit, but not both simultaneously. Thus, system stations are operating on the same transmit and receive frequency.

Single-Sideband (SSB): A method of radio transmission in which the RF carrier and one of the sidebands is suppressed and all of the information is carried in the one remaining sideband.

Skip wave, Skip zone: A radio wave reflected back to earth. The distance between the radio transmitter and the site of a radio wave's return to earth.

Sky wave: A radio wave that is refracted back to earth in much the same way that a stone thrown across water skips out. Sometimes called an ionospheric wave.

Spectrum: A series of radiated energies arranged in order of wavelength. The radio spectrum extends from 20 kilohertz upward.

Sporadic-E: Radio propagation caused by refraction of signals by dense ionization at the E-layer of the ionosphere.

Spread spectrum: Modulation method which employs lightning-fast frequency "hopping" to allow multiple users to share a band.

Spurious Emissions: Unwanted radio frequency signals emitted from a transmitter that sometimes causes interference.

Station license, location: No transmitting station shall be operated in the amateur service without being licensed by the FCC. Each amateur station shall have one land location, the address of which appears on the station license.

Sunspot Cycle: An 11-year cycle of solar disturbances which greatly affects radio wave propagation.

TAPR: Tucson Amateur Packet Radio Corporation, a non-profit research and development organization. (8987-309 E. Tangue Verde Rd. #337, Tucson, AZ 85749-9399)

Technician operator: An amateur radio operator who has successfully passed Element 2. This operator has not passed Element 1, the 5-wpm code test.

Technician with Code Credit: An amateur operator who has passed a 5-wpm code test in addition to Technician Class requirements.

Telecommunications: The electrical conversion, switching, transmission and control of audio signals by wire or radio. Also includes video and data communications.

Telegraphy: Telegraphy is communications transmission and reception using CW International Morse Code.

Telephony: Telephony is communications transmission and reception in the voice mode.

Temporary operating authority: Authority to operate your amateur station while awaiting arrival of an upgraded license.

Terrestrial station location: Any location within the major portion of the Earth's atmosphere, including air, sea and land locations.

Third-party traffic: Amateur communication by or under the supervision of the control operator at an amateur station to another amateur station on behalf of others.

Transceiver: A combination radio transmitter and receiver.

Transmatch: An antenna tuner used to match the impedance of the transmitter output to the transmission line of an antenna.

Transmitter: Equipment used to generate radio waves. Most commonly, this radio carrier signal is amplitude or frequency modulated with information and radiated into space.

Transmitter power: The average peak envelope power (output) present at the antenna terminals of the transmitter. The term "transmitted" includes any external radio frequency power amplifier which may be used.

Ultra High Frequency (UHF): Ultra high frequency radio waves that are in the range of 300 to 3,000 MHz.

Upper Sideband (USB): The operating mode for sideband transmissions where the carrier and lower sideband are suppressed.

Vanity call sign: Custom-chosen call sign instead of "next-in-sequence" assignment from the FCC.

Very High Frequency (VHF): Very high frequency radio waves that are in the range of 30 to 300 MHz.

Volunteer Examiner: An amateur operator of at least a General Class level who administers or prepares amateur operator license examinations. A VE must be at least 18 years old and not related to the applicant.

Volunteer Examiner Coordinator (VEC): A member of an organization which has entered into an agreement with the FCC to coordinate the efforts of volunteer examiners in preparing and administering examinations for amateur operator licenses.

Index

FREE
CQ Mini-Sub!

We'd like to introduce you to a Ham Radio magazine that's fun to read, interesting from cover to cover and written so that you can understand it—FREE! The magazine is **CQ Amateur Radio**—read by thousands of people every month in 116 countries around the world. Get your FREE 3 issue mini-sub, courtesy **CQ** and **Master Publishing**!

CQ is aimed squarely at the **active** ham. You'll find features and columns covering the broad and varied landscape of the amateur radio hobby from contesting and DXing to satellites and the latest digital modes. Equipment reviews, projects and articles on the science as well as the art of radio communications—all in the pages of **CQ Amateur Radio.**

Reserve your FREE 3-month mini-sub today!

Remove this page, fill in your information below, fold, tape closed with the postage-paid **CQ** address showing and mail today!

Send my FREE 3-Issue CQ Mini Sub to:

Name _____

Address _____

City _____ State _____ Zip _____

Make a great deal even better!

Add a one-year CQ subscription to your FREE mini-sub at a
**Special Introductory Rate - 15 issues for only $29.95
a 60% savings off the newsstand price!**

Yes! I want to take advantage of this special 15-issue offer.

☐ Check/Money Order enclosed.
Bill my: ☐ Visa ☐ MasterCard ☐ AMEX ☐ Discover
Insert your credit card number below:

Credit Card Expiration Date: _____

**Fax your order to: 516-681-2926
Visit our web site: www-cq-amateur-radio.com**

FREE
CQ Amateur Radio
Mini-Sub!

Fill in your address information
on the reverse side of this page, fold in half,
tape closed and mail today!

The Radio
Amateur's Journal

25 Newbridge Road
Hicksville, NY 11801-9962